QUAKERS, BUSINESS, AND INDUSTRY

Quakers and the Disciplines:
Volume 4

Edited by:
Stephen W. Angell and Pink Dandelion

Quakers
and the
Disciplines

Full Media Services
http://www.fullmediaservices.com

Friends Association for Higher Education
http://www.quakerfahe.org

Volume 1.
Quaker Perspectives in Higher Education
May 2014

Volume 2.
Befriending Truth: Quaker Perspectives
June 2015

Volume 3.
Quakers and Literature
June 2016

Volume 4.
Quakers, Business, and Industry
June 2017

Longmeadow, MA | Philadelphia, PA | Windsor, CT

ISBN: 0-9983374-4-7
ISBN-13: 978-0-9983374-4-9

Quakers and the Disciplines Editorial Committee:

Paul Anderson
(Series Editor, 2014-2017)

Donn Weinholtz
Abigail E. Adams
Ben Pink Dandelion
Barbara Addison
Don Smith
Jean Mulhern
Stephen W. Angell

As a venture of the Friends Association for Higher Education, the Quakers and the Disciplines series gathers collections of essays featuring the contributions of Quakers to one or more of the academic disciplines. Noting historic values embraced within the Religious Society of Friends regarding particular fields of inquiry, each volume includes essays highlighting contributions by Quakers as means of addressing the needs of contemporary society. Each volume is designed to be serviceable within classroom and other discussion settings, fostering explorations of how pressing issues of the day might be addressed with creativity and passionate concern, informed by a rich heritage of faith, discovery, and action.

For Arthur O. Roberts and John Punshon, In Memoriam

CONTENTS

LIST OF CONTRIBUTORS

Stephen W. Angell is Leatherock Professor of Quaker Studies at the Earlham School of Religion. His books include (with Pink Dandelion) *The Oxford Handbook of Quaker Studies* (OUP, 2013) and *Black Fire: African American Quakers on Spirituality and Human Rights* (with Harold D. Weaver, Jr., and Paul Kriese) (Quaker Press of FGC, 2011). He is Associate Editor of Quaker Studies, and of Quaker Theology, and he has published extensively in the areas of Quaker Studies and African American Religious Studies.

Nicholas Burton is a Senior Lecturer in strategic management and corporate responsibility at Newcastle Business School. He convenes the Spirituality in Management and Law research group at Newcastle Business School, and the Academic Research Working Group at Quakers & Business. He publishes in the area of management and Quakers in business, recently presenting papers on Quakers and decision-making and Quakers and commerce at leading international management conferences in the UK and US, bringing Quaker values and ethics in business to a wider scholarly audience. Nicholas is also an Associate Editor for the Management, Spirituality and Religion group of the Academy of Management.

Paul Chrystal is an author, broadcaster and historical advisor. He has a BA and an MPhil in Classics and has advised on the creation of 'York's Chocolate Story' and on the establishment of the National Trust's Goddard's House – former home of the Terry family in York. He is the author of eighty or so books, including *The Rowntree Family of York* (2013); *York Industries* (2013); *Old Haxby & New Earswick* (2015); *Old Bournville* (2015); *Cadbury & Fry* (2014); *A History of Chocolate in York (2011)* and *In Bed with the Ancient Greeks* (2016). He writes regularly for history magazines and national newspapers and has appeared on the BBC PM programme, the World Service and BBC local radio in Manchester, York and Teesside.

Pink Dandelion directs the work of the Centre for Research in Quaker Studies, Woodbrooke and is Professor of Quaker Studies at the University of Birmingham and a Research Fellow at Lancaster University. He edits *Quaker Studies* and convenes the Quaker Studies Research Association. His books include (with Stephen Angell) *Early Quakers and their Theological Thought* (CUP 2015), (with Stephen Angell) *The Oxford Handbook of Quaker Studies* (OUP, 2013), (with Peter Collins) *The Quaker Condition* (Cambridge Scholars Publishing, 2009), *The Quakers: a very short introduction* (OUP, 2008), (with Jackie Leach Scully) *Good and Evil: Quaker perspectives* (Ashgate, 2007), *Introduction to Quakerism* (CUP, 2007), *The Liturgies of Quakerism* (Ashgate, 2005), *The Creation of Quaker Theory* (Ashgate, 2004), the multi-authored *Towards Tragedy/Reclaiming Hope* (Ashgate, 2004) and *The Sociological Analysis of the Theology of Quakers: the silent revolution* (Edwin Mellen Press, 1996).

Andrew Fincham is a doctoral candidate in Theology and Religion at the University of Birmingham, UK. He holds a Masters in Politics, Philosophy and Economics from Oxford University. His current work seeks to explain the links between Quaker values and commercial success during the long eighteenth century. A member of Britain Yearly Meeting, he edited *'Cadbury's Angels'*, a profile of the business practices of George Cadbury (IBiS, 2011). With over thirty year's experience as an international management consultant, he is also the author of *'Service Excellence Strategies'* (Haymarket, 1999). His collection *'Centre of Gravity'* (IBiS, 2004) received the *Poezja dzisiaj/UNESCO* World Poetry Day Award.

Colin Mckenzie was born into a Scottish family whose roots lie in the Outer Hebrides. His father worked all his adult life on railways, retiring as a Regional Manager in the immediate post-Beeching era. Colin's passion for railways, especially steam, originated in his family roots and he is a life member of a preserved steam railway in West Yorkshire and one in North Yorkshire. As a Quaker, Colin is particularly interested in the work started by George Bradshaw, in Manchester, who was also a Quaker and whose family are buried in the Quaker Burial Ground at Sale Quaker Meeting House where Colin worships every Sunday. Railway timetables and other works by Bradshaw form a large section of Colin's library. He is particularly interested in the contribution towards railway development made by Quakers - Bradshaw, Wordsell, Wilkinson, Ransome and May, Edmondson and not least Bradshaw.

Tim Marshall lives in rural North Bucks where he has been a dealer in English antique clocks since 1988, specialising in the distinctive work of the North Oxfordshire Quaker clockmakers. He is the author of *The Quaker Clockmakers of North Oxfordshire* (Mayfield 2013). His new book *Buckinghamshire Clock and Watchmakers* is due for publication in 2017.

Jean Mulhern recently retired from the S. Arthur Watson Library, Wilmington College (Ohio), where she was the director after previously serving for 23 years as the library director at Wilberforce University. At Wilmington she worked with Dr. T. Canby Jones to organize and preserve his papers and with Dr. D. Neil Snarr to digitally preserve Quaker historical documents held in private collections. She earned her Ph.D. in leadership in Higher Education from the University of Dayton with previous degrees from Kent State University and Heidelberg University (Ohio). She continues to be active in historical and genealogical research and as a library consultant.

Cathy Pitzer recently retired from Wilmington College (Ohio) where she taught sociology. During her eighteen years of teaching she designed many innovative projects to encourage students to engage with their local communities in courses such as Society and Business and Rural Sociology. She holds degrees from the University of Pennsylvania and Emory University and is on the Executive Board of the Friends Association for Higher Education. She is currently an agricultural researcher for the U.S Department of Agriculture in southern Ohio. She is an avid golfer and reader of mystery novels.

Nicola Sleapwood is a PhD candidate in Theology & Religion at the University of Birmingham, UK. Her doctoral project is supported by the Quakers and Business Group. It seeks to establish the reasons behind Quaker business decline over the course of the late nineteenth and twentieth centuries, through one principal business case study. As part of this she is also looking at the complexity of defining a 'Quaker business', and working on a model for this. Her other publications include a short section on Quaker businesses during the First World War in a pamphlet aimed at the general reader. Nicola loves studying the history of religion more broadly, and holds an MA from the University of York in Medieval Studies.

Karen Tibbals received an MA in Quaker Studies from Earlham School of Religion in 2014. Her thesis topic was the Theological Basis behind Quaker Businesses. She also holds an MBA in Marketing from Rutgers University and consults for the pharmaceutical industry.

Introduction

By Stephen W. Angell and Pink Dandelion

The intimate relationship between Quakers and the world of commerce is a prime signifier of Quaker identity in the public eye. Mention 'Quakers' and other than porridge oats or pacifism or a perception of puritanism, the association that comes to mind may well be one of the many businesses that Quakers have started. The list is not insubstantial and the Quaker reputation for business is perhaps the most public legacy of members of the Religious Society of Friends. The fruits of that association continues to this day, even whilst the number of Quakers in industry has diminished, with much of the work of Britain Yearly Meeting, for example, subsisting on 'chocolate money'.

The received wisdom has been that British Quakers, denied access to the professions and the universities went into business, and, as it turns out, thrived. Seminal work, focusing mostly on the eighteenth century, by Arthur Raistrick (1950) and Frederick Tolles (1948) has charted this relationship between Meeting House and counting house. More recent work by James Walvin (1997), and a plethora of histories of individual businesses, have confirmed the positive inter-relationship between Quakers and industrial innovation (and wealth creation). We know of the strategic marriage alliances that cemented business partnerships (Walvin 1997) and of industrial espionage between competing chocolate companies (Cadbury 2010). We know too of how bankruptcy was seen as a sign of apostasy and would result in disownment (Marietta 2007). The essay by Mark Freeman in the 2013 *Oxford Handbook of Quaker Studies* provides an excellent entry point to recent research in the area (Freeman 2013).

Even Quakers on the margins have made great contributions, as we have been finding out. There is incidental mention in essays in this volume by Jean Mulhern and Cathy Pitzer, and Stephen Angell, of time management expert Frederick Winslow Taylor (1856-1915), who had Quaker parentage in Pennsylvania (the son of a Hicksite father and Orthodox mother, his family hence not really welcome in either sectarian setting), and who is regularly

1

accounted by business historians to be "the most influential person in management and business history" (Wren 2011, 12; Kanigel 1997).

We know also how twentieth century Quakers, mostly converts replacing dynastic and endogamous Quakerism, chose different professions from their forbears. In Britain, Quakers and other non-conformists could attend the Universities after 1871 and teaching became the preferred profession for twentieth century British Friends. Quaker businesses disbanded under new state business legislation on how businesses were structured and through the dissembling of the dynastic pattern: now Friends could marry whom they wished, their children no longer necessarily became or remained Quakers. As access to education seems to coincide with the dramatic twentieth century decline in the number of British Quakers involved in business, so the idea that denial of education caused Quakers to enter business seems further supported.

However, as with any academic knowledge, paradigm shifts in our understanding occur. The things we thought we knew are turned on their head. The chapter by Andrew Fincham begins that process for Quaker industrial history. In his chapter, the opening one of the volume, he outlines an overview of his doctoral work into the origins of the Quaker propensity for business. Rather than seeing this in terms of a consequence of the constraint bestowed upon non-conformists in terms of the professions and the universities, Fincham argues that a) Those converting to Quakerism were often already in commerce, b) that elements of Quaker faith made commerce an attractive and convenient way to earn an income. As the joke runs, Quakers went to America to do good, and did very well.

Thus, it is not simply a reaction to the constraints of being cast as non-conformists within a nation, England, beset with an established church and acts of uniformity, that promoted business success. They prospered even whilst in control of colonies such as Pennsylvania. Endogamy and close intra-faith networks gave access to a Quaker market as well as Quaker creditors. Quaker education nurtured a steady stream of entrepreneurial spirit and ability. Quaker faith itself, expressed through the books of extracts in the eighteenth century affirmed business as a godly endeavour. Philanthropy and the disavowal of worldly fashion further affirmed the pursuit if wealth. In other words, those who became Quakers had freely chosen industry and to choose to remain in industry post-conversion, managing their business interests through internal allegiances and a Quaker pro-business theological ethic. In a similar way to how Max Weber argued about Calvinists in his most notable work *The Protestant Ethic and the Spirit of Capitalism*, Fincham suggests here that Quaker religiosity fitted and formed and affirmed a business ethic that allowed the combination of faith and financial surplus. To extrapolate, even had the Universities and professions been available to them (and in some places and instances they were), Fincham is arguing that Quakers would have chosen, and did choose, business as their primary activity in' the world'.

This book is rich in other areas as well. It charts in more detail some of the Quaker pioneers of industry.

The prevalence of Quaker clockmakers from the seventeenth to the nineteenth centuries is given its most in-depth treatment to date in this volume, thanks to Tim Marshall. Marshall's appendix lists about 220 Quaker clockmakers in both the British Isles and North America. Marshall also includes a helpful glossary for those who are unfamiliar with the clock makers' vocabulary. Marshall's article points to many interesting features of the labours of Quaker clock makers, from their technological and design innovations, to their interaction with the culture of the times, including the ways in which they exemplified such Quaker testimonies as integrity and equality. For example, one American clock maker, Joseph Hollinshead, Jnr., trained the first African American clock maker in the United States, Peter Hill. Quakers remained involved with clockmaking until the tradition of manufacturing clocks from scratch died out, around 1870.

Marshall points out that the 220 clockmakers he profiles are only "some Quaker clockmakers;" he does not claim completeness in this regard. As an example, we might add that one of Marshall's subjects, clockmaker and surveyor Andrew Ellicott, was a close associate of African-American Quaker scientist and clockmaker Benjamin Banneker (1731-1806), whose astronomical calculations were the basis of annual almanacs sold widely in the 1790s through Philadelphia Quaker business networks. Banneker is one Quaker clockmaker not included in Marshall's account (Angell 2011, 1-5; Bedini 2000). This appendix will soon be online as part of the Woodbrooke Quaker Study Centre Resource Centre so that we can all add to and amend this valuable resource produced by Tim Marshall.

The under-researched life of the pioneer of railway timetables, George Bradshaw, is charted by Colin Mackenzie. Mackenzie points out that it was Bradshaw's genius to realise that, since the wary railway companies were not willing to share their data with competitors, that there was the need for an impartial outside party to compile timetables for the travelers' use. Bradshaw very practically became a shareholder in as many railway companies as possible in order to obtain the necessary data. Bradshaw died suddenly of cholera in Oslo, Norway, in 1853, but his work was so helpful to so many that it was revised faithfully for decades after his untimely death, well into the twentieth century.

The life of Hicksite Quaker Joseph Wharton (1826-1909), steel magnate and founder of the Wharton Business School, is explored by Jean Mulhern and Cathy Pitzer. Mulhern and Pitzer's work explores "to what extent Wharton's grounding in the Quaker faith and heritage informed his life choices, his business and career decisions, and the ways in which he spent his time and wealth to solidify his rank among the American captains of industry." American industrialists of Wharton's era have often been castigated as "robber barons," however, and the authors argue that Wharton was not one of those, in large part because of the ways that he lived out his Quaker heritage. He was a significant philanthropist supporting Quaker causes like Swarthmore College. In his work at Bethlehem Steel, "he embodied the Quaker equalitarian ethos, putting in countless hours daily on the shop floor and in the laboratory, solving problems, improving processes, and creating jobs." Before the American Civil War, however, he was a gradualist on the slavery issue, and at no time in his life was he a pacifist, as his firms manufactured munitions for both the Civil War and the Spanish-American War of 1898. In the area of theology, he made known his strong anti-Trinitarian convictions. The whole essay is fascinating in terms of its sensitive and nuanced portrayal of the many ways this businessman sought to negotiate the various facets of his Quaker identity.

This volume also looks at Quakers and social responsibility.

Karen Tibbals looks at the Quaker theology of debt. After reviewing Catholic and Calvinist precedents, she reviews in depth the evolution of Quaker faith and practice in relation to debt, from the founders' generation, up to and including the crisis surrounding the collapse of the South Sea Company bubble in 1720, and its immediate aftermath. George Fox and other seventeenth-century Quakers had been attracted to the Apostle Paul's admonition (Romans 13:8) to owe no one anything, except love. She describes how this was found to be impractical and subsequently how Quaker advices as to ways to handle debt developed. Not only scholars, but also Quaker business people of today, will undoubtedly find her exposition to be enlightening and thought provoking.

Paul Chrystal describes the ways that the Rowntree family, famous for their contributions to the chocolate industry, were also mostly "enlightened pioneers in industrial relations, workers' rights, housing reform and poverty relief," although some of them were also engaged in some less admirable activities such as industrial espionage. Chrystal gives a vivid and succinct account of Rowntree family members' responses to many momentous events from the mid-nineteenth to the mid-twentieth century, including the Irish Potato Famine, the Boer War, and both World Wars. He concludes, "The Rowntrees are a complex family and they, to varying extents, have touched, championed and are responsible for not a few of the good things we see today in our society."

Stephen Angell compares the entrepreneurial social vision of William Penn and Herbert Hoover. His chapter does not seek to chart the business success of these two very public Quakers but rather to examine these two men "whose humanitarian and political activities were greatly affected by and, to some extent, presupposed broad business interests, oriented toward more personal, even selfish, goals." Angell's work is highly engaging, looking at the way both Penn and Hoover were committed to Quakerism, business and politics. Sometimes their actions exhibited multiple commitments, sometimes these commitments were in conflict. Both had maximum governmental responsibility in their own spheres for a time. Both were idealists but also both fell short. Both however, can be seen to put social justice ahead of a motive to profit or pride.

Finally, this volume also looks at shifting expressions of Quaker commerce.

Nicola Sleapwood shows how the geographical dispersal of Birmingham Quaker businesses in the latter half of the nineteenth century led to the formation of different Quaker meetings and the changing nature of business networks predicated on shared worship in what had been the single Birmingham Quaker meeting. Sleapwood's account abounds in interesting nuggets of information. Here, as in Mulhern and Pitzer's profile of William Wharton, the question arose as to whether Quaker business people should manufacture munitions, but with a different result: when the Bull Street Meeting in 1795 admonished that Quakers must not engage in such manufacturing, Samuel Galton senior submitted to the Meeting's guidance, while Samuel junior persisted in manufacturing warmaking materials and suffered disownment as a result. Unlike Wharton, Birmingham businessmen ran for public office in the nineteenth century; Wharton lobbied on behalf of his firms, but apparently had Quaker scruples against office holding. This book fortuitously is rich in revealing transatlantic comparisons like these; see how many you can find.

Sleapwood highlights Emma Gibbins' attendance in 1897 of a management meeting for the Birmingham Metal and Battery Company, commenting, "she must have been an engaged, respected woman, as it was very rare for women" to have undertaken such roles at that time.

Nicholas Burton considers how Quaker discernment practice within the Meeting House has and could be used in Quaker and non-Quaker businesses. He comments that typical "hierarchical, Board-based forms of corporate governance are 'individualising', whereas the governance structures of the Society are, in contrast, 'socialising' and non-hierarchal, providing the framework for a powerful form of collectivised decision-making." Despite its powerful advantages and preserving and strengthening the unity of the larger group, Quaker business process also requires time and patience, and thus is challenging to translate into the culture of non-Quaker businesses. Despite this and other challenges, Burton ultimately argues that Quaker business process might well profitably be utilized in non-Quaker settings: "With many contemporary businesses striving to find new ways to improve engagement and participation throughout the organisation, and ultimately to make better decisions, such a collaborative and unitive decision-making process should be of interest to practitioners."

Bibliography

Angell, Stephen W. 2011. "The early period." In Harold D. Weaver, Jr., Paul Kriese, and Stephen W. Angell, *Black fire: African-American Quakers on spirituality and human rights*. Philadelphia, PA: Quaker Press of FGC. pp. 1-43.

Bedini, Silvio. 2000. "Benjamin Banneker." *American National Biography Online*. Oxford: Oxford University Press. http://proxy.earlham.edu:2249/articles/13/13-00081.html. Accessed Jan. 8, 2017.

Cadbury, Deborah. 2010. *The chocolate wars: from Cadbury to Kraft – 200 years of sweet success and bitter rivalry*. London: Harper Press.

Freeman, Mark. 2013. "Quakers, Business and Philanthropy." In Stephen W. Angell and Pink Dandelion, *The Oxford Handbook of Quaker Studies*. Oxford: Oxford University Press. pp. 420-433.

Kanigel, Robert. 1997. *The one best way: Frederick Winslow Taylor and the enigma of efficiency*. New York: Viking.

Marietta, Jack D. 2007 [1984]. *The reformation of American Quakerism, 1748-1783*. Philadelphia, PA: University of Pennsylvania Press.

Raistrick, Arthur. 1950. *Quakers in science and industry: being an account of the Quaker contributions to science and industry during the 17th and 18th centuries*. London: Bannisdale Press. New York, NY: Philosophical Library. Subsequent editions, 1968, 1993.

Tolles, Frederick Barnes. 1948. *Meeting house and counting house: The Quaker merchants of colonial Philadelphia, 1682-1763*. Chapel Hill, NC: University of North Carolina Press. Subsequent editions, 1963, 2012.

Walvin, James. 1997. *The Quakers: money and morals*. London: John Murray.

Wren, Daniel A. 2011. "The centennial of Frederick W. Taylor's *The Principles of Scientific Management*: A retrospective commentary." *Journal of Business and Management* 17: 11-22.

PART I
Theorising Quaker Commerce

1| Factors Supporting the Rise of Quaker Commerce

By Andrew Fincham

Quakers began to be associated with worldly success almost from their inception, and the unsympathetic Commonwealth took delight in drawing unflattering parallels between Friends' financial prosperity and their piety. Claims that Quakers had bought up 'all the best horses the country could afford' were relayed to Cromwell (ESP 1911, 146), while ballad-sheets mocked the Quaker crossing to the Americas 'in need of wealth and large possessions' with primitive verses:

> "Yet be it what it will
> So we get our fill
> Of Riches, and good possessions;
> When occasion shall be,
> We can change, you shall see,
> Both our Habits, and our Professions"
> (Anon. 1675)

Contemporaries attacked the exclusive nature of trading between Quakers, implying commercial benefit was a well-recognized reason for membership: 'for that if a man hath been very meanly bred, and was never worth much beyond a groat in all his life, do but turn Quaker, he is presently set up in one shopkeeping trade or other, and then many of them will compass sea and land to get this new Quaking shopkeeper a trade, their custom being to sell to all the world, but they will buy only of their own tribe' (Thirsk & Cooper 1972, 98). Quaker convert Thomas Story recounts how his father's hostility to his turning Quaker was ameliorated by hope that his son would prosper amongst those 'opulent people', joking that he might 'soon learn to preach among them, get Money, and become rich too' (Storey 1747, 46-48). By 1700 specific accusations were levelled at the

Society for using the prospect of better living standards as a means to attract new members. An anonymous pamphlet at the start of the new century specifically makes the accusation that Quakers used improved commercial prospects to target the impecunious: those identified for converts are 'small game, mean and needy persons…who are presently put in hopes of a better trade or livelihood by turning Quakers' (Anon. 1700, 3). Such strong contemporary approbation would seem to indicate that many detractors felt the Society was vulnerable on account of commercial success - if not for the typical accusations of hypocritical excessive personal wealth or luxury, then for the employment of money to promote the Society's ends. That such criticism was considered at least partially valid is perhaps indicated by contemporaneous efforts to avoid those who, in George Keith's words, 'are crept into the form and profession of Friends' way… [from] some worldly interest or advantage &c.' (JFHS 1913, 70-75).[1]

Notwithstanding the veracity of the accusations, both the extent and endurance of such criticism point towards the reality of Friends' success in commerce. These achievements over the period have been chronicled in detail across both science and industry, (Raistrick 1950) and extended far beyond the Iron Masters into banking, through groceries into pharmaceuticals, and ultimately chocolate (Cadbury 2010, Raistrick 1953, Corley 1972). Edward Milligan identified almost three thousand Quakers in his commercial biographical dictionary, believing as many were in London alone or even Yorkshire (Milligan 2007). The traditional explanation for such success has largely rested on Quaker principles, stating that "…probably the most important [factors] are the high qualities of mind and spirit that were characteristic of many Friends" (Raistrick 1950, 42). Yet the historian Fredrick Tolles found Raistrick's account disappointing: admitting the *facts* of Quaker success, he found the material 'as unwrought iron, awaiting the refining fire of analysis and interpretation'. This chapter therefore seeks to offer a more systematic analysis to give a comprehensive explanation to account for British Quaker commercial achievements during the first half of the 'long eighteenth century'.

The starting point is the social composition of Quakers at the beginning of the period, to identify who it was that embodied the 'qualities of mind and spirit' within the Religious Society of Friends, and who '*by telling the truth and diligently refraining from putting sand in their sugar… rose to positions of wealth and importance*' (Carter 1950, 817).

---

[1] Keith's concerns arose during a visit to Philadelphia in the early 1690's. Keith would subsequently leave the Quaker movement, as he had the Presbyterian, to propagate the gospel as an Anglican missionary.

From this beginning, the chapter will examine how four factors contributed to encourage success in commerce during the period. First, the Quaker emphasis on Education and Apprenticeships which produced the 'raw material' which developed into shopkeepers, merchants, and manufacturers; Second, the communal financial infrastructure, which supplied the capital to trade; thirdly, the network of Quakers in the Atlantic world, which facilitated interaction at all stages of the wealth creation process; and finally the Discipline of the Society of Friends, which acted in the wider context to promote values which were compatible with commercial success.

Together, these provided a unique environment in the first half of the eighteenth century which practically promoted wealth creation.

Social Origins

It seems clear that most Friends did not have to be drawn into trade - almost all made their living either by selling, or buying, or both. Subsequent detailed studies of the social origins of Quakers all tend to support Braithwaite's original conclusion - that early Friends were drawn "principally from the trading and yeoman classes, though there were also some artisans and labourers, a fair number of merchants, and a few gentry" (Braithwaite 1912, 512). The proportions, and the presence of other social groups are disputed, largely as a result of geographical and methodological debate, with research suggesting in turn a preponderance of economically-pressed yeomen (Cole 1957), trader-yeoman (Vann 1969a), and general 'petite bourgeoisie' suggested by Judith Hurwich (Vann 1970, 162). Earnest Taylor produced a detailed comparison of the 'known occupations' of the Valiant Sixty (active from around 1654) and the larger number of Friends noted as First Publishers of Truth (211 names, active mostly before 1680) shows most (68% and 59% respectively) 'engaged in agriculture', with 13% and 22% 'commercial', and 12% and 18% 'professional' (Taylor 1922, 66-81). Significantly, these proportions are higher than those for the population as a whole taken from Gregory King's famous Study of 1688, but that comparison is indicative at best: neither the classifications of Yeoman' nor 'Husbandman' appear in King, and have caused considerable confusion in that they appear to indicate status rather than wealth, including small gentry down to smaller farmer, whose annual income would overlap with the wealthier Husbandmen making more than poorer Yeoman.[2] An examination of the occupations in London meetings (Beck & Ball 1869, 90) shows that in 1680 around one quarter were commercial dealers, a tenth professional and the

---

[2] Income range is in the region of £40 to over £200 per annum for this period. The Taylor analysis lacks data for 40% of the later sample.

remainder craftsmen, artisans or farmers. This aligns with Vann's conclusion that 'the stronghold of early Quakerism was among the substantial yeomen and traders; that there were some gentlemen and professional men among the first converts; and that poor husbandmen and artisans were numerically insignificant' (Vann 1969a, 68).[3] The importance of the preponderance of traders is magnified when one considers those that moved to populate the colonies. Gary Nash has noted that simply by moving, a substantial number could move from artisan to trader status, and cites Samuel Richardson, the Jamaica bricklayer, who had amassed one of the largest fortunes in the colony by the beginning of the eighteenth century. The future ranks of the Philadelphia merchants were made up less by the descendents of the first successful traders, only 20% of whom had sons who survived to continue with business, but by the sons of other settlers who had 'prospered sufficiently to give their sons a secure base from which to launch a mercantile career'. Interestingly, rising property values in the city may have actually dissuaded some craftsmen from the more risky world of commerce: several artisan fathers passed on wealth gained from multiplying land values (Nash 1996, 390). That such investment opportunities were scarce in the English speaking world was further motivation for the pursuit of trade: in a world where the 'professions' were in their infancy, and civil and state posts to serve King and country both few and rarely remunerative, and occasionally expensive (as Admiral Penn found), wealth was not easy to manage. In Pennsylvania, where Quakers could and would occupy positions of civil authority, the remuneration of the post has not been considered an incentive by scholars.[4] In the seventeen century, wealth as largely held in land, or invested in mortgages or personal bonds. For the nascent Quaker merchant, it will be argued below, one of the major reasons why commerce held such an appeal was freedom from the burdens associated with landed estates or financial instruments (Price 1996).

Education and Apprenticeship

The purpose of Quaker education was to raise children who would both accept, and continue to spread, the Quaker message (Extracts 1802, 121-129). Because of the emphasis on 'inner light', the sect was freed from the orthodox dependence on traditional education for preaching, teaching, and theologizing which formed the basis for most of the established schools, and the Universities. The focus for Friends was both vocational and utilitarian, with a view to earning

---

[3] There is also some evidence from the use of Quaker trade tokens in place of small coins of the realm during the interregnum as indicators of Friends status in trade.
[4] The subject is not considered by, for example: Tolles, Landes, or Marietta.

a practical living; as such the place of education for most remained the home for much of the period.

Perhaps because of this need for self-sufficiency, Friends saw a value in learning: the 'Seventy' were recognised by William Penn as containing *"many of them of good capacity, substance, and account amongst men…some of them not wanting in parts, learning or estate"*, which suggests a level of literacy unusual for the time. A call went out for 'faithful friends' to act as schoolmasters from 1695, but affluent Friends followed the generally adopted practice of tutoring at home (Advice #14 & #15) (Extracts 1802, 169). A Printed Epistle of 1690 warned against the use of schools which were not led by 'faithful friends', for fear of 'corrupt ways, manners, fashions and language of the world; and of the heathen in their authors'. Quaker advices made clear that suitable education for those within the sect should ensure that children were not exposed to doctrines or ideas which were contrary to Quaker beliefs, and which bred the children up to 'some useful and necessary employments, that they may not spend their precious time in idleness' – Advice #2, #4 1703 (Extracts 1802, 122). Friends who did not employ a tutor were tasked to impart suitable instruction to their offspring, noting that mothers 'have frequently the best opportunities'. Friends were encouraged to 'stir up' families deficient in such care. Education would remain a major concern within the Society of Friends for the first half of the eighteenth century (Jones 1921, II:667): in twenty-seven of the first forty years additional minutes restate its importance (Tuke 1843). The focus of attention for much of the advice was, perhaps naturally, spiritual, and over the course of the century the repeated admonitions become somewhat repetitious as the epistles seek to reinforce the duties of parents while giving additional detail as the snares into which children might fall: by 1767 the Quaker educationalist is urged to guard their charges against 'the reading of plays, romances, and other licentious publications' and 'likewise against the public pastimes', which included games. In their place, the curriculum was encouraged to include 'some modern tongues, as French, High and Low Dutch, Danish etc' to encourage truth spreading and so be of service to the church – Advice #8 1737 (Extracts 1802, 124).

Given this emphasis on home tuition, it is not surprising that the earliest steps towards Quaker schools were motivated by the need to provide opportunities for children of poorer Friends. Such efforts should be viewed in the context of the general debate on the reform of poor relief in the last quarter of the seventeenth century. Both would appear to be motivated by a combination of economic necessity and the obligations of 'Christian duty'. A prime example of such reformism can be found in the ideas of former Lord Chief Justice Matthew Hale, who proposed the aggregating of parish spending to fund supervised institutions where the poor might learn a trade. His vision is comprehensive, and goes as far as to provide a mechanism to ensure a 'living wage' during slack times (Hale 1683, 18)[5], concluding that 'The want of a due Provision for Education and Relief of the Poor in a way of Industry, is that which fills the Gaols with Malefactors' (Hale 1683, 25). Later that decade the merchant Sir Josiah Child addressed the same issue as part of his 'Discourse on Trade', making the liberal suggestion that no oaths be required for the positions of 'Fathers of the Poor' as it would bar non-conformists 'amongst whom there will be found some excellent instruments for this work'. He also recommends that that the 'workhouse' be allowed to produce whatever is fit, without consideration of patents or privileges, and makes specific reference to the children at Clerkenwell workhouse who had been prevented from making 'Hangings' (Child & Hale 1699, 11). This publication predates the known start of the Quaker institution by two years, but is suggestive of a close knowledge of both the institution and the issues Quakers would attempt to address in that parish.[6]

Outside the home, the earliest established Quaker tutor was probably Thomas Lawson of Newby Stones, who took pupils from 1657. Another early schoolmaster was Ambrose Rigge, whose later 'warning' was to prove an integral part of financial management. An informal school was conducted for a time during 1662 at the Friary gaol at Ilchester. Fox put in hand the formation of schools at Waltham Abbey and Shacklewell from 1668, where the tuition was to include Lawyers Latin, Court Hand, and Quaker schoolmaster Charles Taylor's *Compendium Trium Linguarum* (Braithwaite 1912, 370, Braithwaite 1919, 102; f254; 525-529). At the Sidcot school in Somerset, run by William Jenkins from 1699 until 1728, a pupil in 1714 writes of learning grammar, the Latin testaments, arithmetic, and 'merchants accounts' (Braithwaite 1919, 531). Such practical choices of subject are significant. In the eighteenth-century England was not unusual in having neither a state policy nor a system of education, with the Grammar Schools and both Universities monopolised by the Church of England as nurseries for the Anglican clergy (Hans 1951,15-20). The gentlemen commoners attending the 'great nine' English public schools followed a antiquated curriculum of dictation, translation and grammar which had hardly changed in centuries, while those who continued to University often found a less than intellectual menu which has been characterised as one of 'extravagance,

---

[5] "It is not unknown how that some covetous Masters in hard times, if they are will stocked and of Abilities, will set on work many Poor, but they must take such Wages as they are not able to live upon"

[6] The first record of a non-Quaker workhouse in Clerkenwell is that set up in 1727. No local institution is recorded in *An Account of Several Work-houses for Employing and Maintaining the Poor* (1725, SPCK);

debt, drunkenness, gambling, and an absurd attention to dress.' (Hans 1951, 42) Neither the prospects arising from such experience or such companionship were attractive to the Quaker, for whom the purpose of education was honest activity combined with a continuity of discipline to secure the good of succeeding generations - Advice #3 Poor (Extracts 1802, 137).

Across the Atlantic, a chartered Quaker school was created in Philadelphia in 1698. It is tempting to draw conclusions regarding the intent of Penn's tolerance from the fact that this accepted both Quaker and non-Quaker children (the poor at no cost) who were to be 'fit to be put out apprentices, or Capable to be masters or ushers in the said school'. While practical considerations concerning numbers of pupils may have played a part, local minutes confirm that segregation was not considered necessary at that time. (James 1962, 93)

At the turn of the eighteenth century Friends had taken forward their economic-obligation 'philanthropy' with a detailed national report from a dedicated education committee (Tuke 1843, 24). It recommended that education be augmented with 'some profitable labour' in addition to 'languages, sciences and the way of Truth'; it identified needs, sought recommendations for suitable teachers, and asked that costs be met by Local Meetings.[7] Monthly Meeting contributions to the Yearly Meeting report of 1701 reveal substantial regional variations in both Quaker education provision and need: Bristol 'has schools in our workhouse settled for the benefit of our youth'; Devonshire reports 'a want of Friends schools in many places; Durham 'have schools'; London 'have schools in many parts of the city'; Northamptonshire 'No Public Schools, but greatly wanted; Somersetshire 'have a school in good order'; Westmoreland 'have three schools'; Wilshire 'have one school'; Worcestershire 'have two schools' (Tuke 1843, 23). The reports quantify the Society's poor, with the total need for assistance given as 184 aged and 47 children. This number, constituting a tiny fraction of a Society numbering between thirty and forty thousand, is both illustrative of the emphasis on home tutoring and the relative prosperity of the membership, as well as the effectiveness of existing provisions to address 'need'. This link between poverty, economic self-sufficiency, and education was clearly made in the printed Epistles of 1709 and 1718. Both sought to use the wealth of the Society to fund 'instruction and necessary learning' to replace idleness, looseness and vice of rich and poor alike with self-denying truth. The epistles followed the attempt by the Society to create at Clerkenwell what would become a typical hybrid 'labour-school' environment, such as became widespread after the Knatchbull Act of 1723 in providing employment for the (aged) poor, and

---

[7] One Richard Scoryer of Wandsworth is named as a teacher trainer; the need to train teachers reoccurs in a minute of YM 1715; and later in the Fothergill report of 1758

with an educational element added to address the needs of (poor) children. Begun in 1702 to provide work for 32 'poor', it took boys from 1706 (Tuke 1843, 24).[8] The Society's concern was to create an environment, which supported Quaker beliefs, and there was always a provision for education as well as useful labour (Tuke 1843, 23). Clerkenwell has been represented as an attempt to implement some of the philanthropic proposals of John Bellers' 1695 *'College of Industry'*, and was projected to return a profit by selling the produce of the inmates, old and young. The boys' day began at dawn, continuing until five or six, mostly spent spinning and weaving; and included two hours for reading and writing daily (Tuke 1843, 25) Perhaps unsurprisingly, and largely owing to infirmity, the scheme generated under a half-penny per inmate per daily, thus failing to generate the financial returns anticipated by Bellers. In 1712 a committee of Friends put an end to any attempt at making the institution pay. Tuke concludes that 'man cannot be put into a lathe', yet the experiment did form part of an evolving solution, and (of equal importance) demonstrated a practical approach to a problem within the society which was not being addressed in the wider society (Tuke 1843, 112). The continued importance of education may be inferred from the number of advices issued to Friends: between 1700 and 1740, 28 further advices were issued (Tuke 1843, 37-41). The need to increase further the effectiveness of cross-generational acculturation was writ large in the move towards boarding schools, which occurred in the second half of the century.

With twenty board schools by 1780, serving almost 650 children (Tuke 1843, 72-72) organised Quaker education predated Raikes' 1781 Sunday Schools movement by more than a century (Power 1863) and strived to instil a level of literacy and numeracy not made compulsory in England and Wales until the Elementary Education Act of 1870.[9]

The often cited effect on commerce of the legal barriers to Quaker entry into both the Universities and the Professions, caused by Friends refusal to take the required oath of allegiance, remains difficult to answer, largely because of the impossibility of counterfactuals. The primary role of the Universities was to prepare Anglican Clergy, and this, with the absence of 'simplicity' discussed above would suggest that such a road was always unlikely to appeal. This is supported by Geoffrey Cantor, who notes that even after the removal of the Test

---

[8] Saffron Walden School traces its origins back to this institution.
[9] One Hanna Ball has been credited with the first individual Sunday School in 1769, inspired by John Wesley's teaching. For England and Wales, the Education Act of 1880 made schooling compulsory until the age of 10. By 1891, it was also free. Scotland had created a similar provision by Acts in 1633 and 1646

Acts in the 1870s, 'contemporary Quakers saw little value in the education offered by Oxford and Cambridge' (Cantor 2005, 91). A study of England's intellectual elite educated during the Eighteenth century finds that only one third attended the two Universities; the majority either were schooled abroad (in Scotland, Holland, or other foreign universities) or went directly to study under a 'professional'. This would suggest that a University education was not a pre-requisite for entry into that elite. Perhaps of significance within the 3500 intellectual men collated from the Oxford Dictionary of National Biography are the 125 Catholics, of whom 104 went directly into the professions and 21 of which qualified abroad (Hans 1951, 17). During this period, English Catholics numbered around 80,000, or 1.3% of the population. This suggests that they became over-represented in the intellectual elite despite similar barriers to University and civil progress. It further suggests that the number of Quakers (at most half the number of Catholics, and quite possibly closer to a quarter) that might have expected to attend the Universities would have been very small indeed (Field 2012).

For the century, mathematician John Venn calculated total University admissions of 25,000 for Oxford and 15,000 at Cambridge. Thus around 1% of the male population of England perhaps attended, of whom just over three quarters finally took degrees: applying a similar factor to Quakers would suggest one or at most two attending each year. Reducing the numbers to take account of social origins might reduce this number further, to a level where even the most sensitive merchant would find it hard to detect a dip on the scale of Quaker commerce (Hans 1951, 42-45). Intriguingly, Cantor has some evidence that even the most devoutly educated Quaker would take an oath on occasion: Dr John Fothergill, the celebrated physician and founder of Ackworth school, was amongst eight Quakers listed as signing their names to the standard oath on graduation from Edinburgh, where the first Quaker recorded as using the alternative 'sponsio' affirmation was not until 1772 (Cantor 2005, f71).

The impact of Quaker education on successful wealth creation was undoubtedly enhanced far more directly by the systematic approach taken towards apprenticeships - which thrived on a cadre of youth already encouraged towards a commercial life (Raistrick 1950, 48-49). It has been suggested that this was a highly relevant issue for the 'Valliant Sixty', whose median age was just twenty-three - compared with thirty-three for converts (Huntington 1982). A letter from Fox of 1660 suggests the allocation of legacies, with those to Quarterly Meetings used for fees, and those to local meetings to set up businesses for those 'freed' (Grubb 1930, 76-77). A further epistle of 1669 recommends a quarterly basis for assigning apprentices, principally as a means to ensure a family could support the aged. Appropriate trades are given by Fox as *"bricklayers, masons, carpenters, wheelwrights, ploughwrights, tailors, tanners, curriers, blacksmiths, shoemakers, nailers, butchers, weavers of linen and woollen, stuffs and serges, &c."* (Fox 1669, 76).[10] The advice on apprentices was extended to the Society at large in 1697 - advice #3 (Extracts 1802, 122). Examples of those who had completed apprenticeships who took up as shopkeepers, traders or proprietors include William Stout, John Lawson (Raistrick 1950, 61-65), or John Atkinson (Grubb 1930, 74). Thus were both Quaker apprentices and intellects were channelled into fuelling the rapid growth of ever more complex eighteenth century industrialisation and mechanisation (Raistrick 1950, 122-132).

Though Quaker schools remained relatively few in number on both sides of the Atlantic during the first half of the century, they formed part of an educational policy that worked with the support of both home and meeting discipline to ensure the transmission of the sect's beliefs. Since some of these beliefs had a positive impact on wealth creation (as will be considered below) the schools had a double effect of both practical education and inculcation of the positive commercial values within the Disciplines. While Tuke, a keen observer from the nineteenth century, could state that the schools were 'far from generally favourable to the formation of true religious character' (Tuke 1843, 84), and Dr. Fothergill could later declare in 1778 'too few of the youth educated therein have turned out to be useful or respectable members of Society' (Tuke 1843, 74), considered as a basis for nascent commercial entrepreneurs, it would seem that such a comprehensive education as was provided: in language, numeracy, foreign tongues - or simply work - proved as valuable as it was unusual.

Networks

As noted above, the apprentice system provided trusted hands for both the new products and new markets, and played their part in creating the unusually dense set of networks that supported Quaker wealth creation from the start of the Long eighteenth century. These networks benefited those involved through integrating Quaker efforts at all stages of production, sales and distribution; they extended across a wide geographical area; supported the sharing of superior technical and market information; helped to mitigate shared risk; and leveraged substantial Quaker capital. The general importance of the networks within the Quaker movement is widely accepted, as their effectiveness allowed the movement first to expand, and later to maintain the tight internal organisation which controlled the evolution of membership values to enable survival as an

---

[10] Possibly marriage to Margaret Fell two months earlier had brought children to the fore.

independent sect (Landes 2015; Tolles 1948; Walvin 1997). Most historians have focused on the role of networks in helping the Quaker community achieve this necessary level of cohesion and order. Jordan Landes notes three main networks: organisation; theology (and the distribution of books); and transatlantic commerce (Landes 2015, 7-8). Robynne Rogers Healey cites the importance of networks created by the travelling ministry, and while noting that 'ministry and commerce were to be kept strictly separate', suggests many Quakers successfully blended the two - not least out of necessity arising from the duration of their journeys (Healey 2013, 52-57). Frederick Tolles places more emphasis on the importance of trade, noting the Philadelphia Quakers' 'single-minded devotion to mercantile pursuits' (Tolles 1948, 85) while acknowledging that the community sought a balance between the creation of personal riches ('which in their due place are not to be neglected') and the erection of 'temples of holiness and righteousness, which God may delight in...' (Tryon 1684).[11] The importance of the inter-connected nature of Quaker networks is developed by Angus Winchester (1991), who links the strength of the Pardshaw meeting in the eighteenth century with the level of trade between Whitehaven and the American colonies, and finds sufficient links to propose a triple-thread of interwoven causes: religious, kinship, and mercantile. Clearly shared values supported shared outcomes, which had both a commercial and spiritual dimension. In distinguishing between networks which had a direct influence on wealth creation from those intended to promote institutional unity, it should also be noted that the latter had positive effect by increasing the overall density, which in turn re-enforced the pro-commerce impact of Discipline (Rowley 1997).

Amongst other motivations for associating with a religious movement, Robert Currie identifies 'organisational utility' (Currie 1977). Positing the existence of a secular 'utility' in the Religious Society Friends does not imply that this acted as the primary criteria for all or even many adherents, even if, as noted earlier, it was perceived as an attraction for some. Contemporary Friends would not appear to have objected to members trading with one another; there is a notable absence of Advices on the subject, in contrast with frequent diktats on norms of commerce, including what could be traded, the extent, and in what manner (Extracts 1802, 195-200). Vann argues that extended networks would have existed amongst the earliest Friends, who 'as wholesalers or substantial producers of grain, would bulk large at the very earliest stage in Quaker history'. In this he follows both Max Weber, who identified early Christians as 'itinerant artisans', (Vann 1970, 162-166) and Braithwaite, who believed these

---

[11] Thomas Tryon (d1703) – a vegetarian abstainer, pacifist and early advocate of animal rights was a former Anabaptist who does not appear to have become a Quaker.

characteristics applied to the majority of First and Second period, and the search for material prosperity 'played a chief part' in emigrations of Quakers (Braithwaite 1912, 408): William Penn issued a special invitation to 'Laborious Handicrafts' to settle (Penn 1681, 209), while a much quoted letter to Fox ascribes a desire to 'leave fullness to their posterity' as the reason for accepting the Lord's colonial open door.

Trading was a way of life - even during imprisonment, and there is evidence that it was occasionally conducted with the gaoler! (Taylor 1922, 79).[12] Over the period, occupations can be shown to move towards merchandising and away from poorer artisans. Those who produced usually sold to fellow Quakers, who acted both as middlemen and distributors (Raistrick 1950, 31). Across the oceans, Quaker individuals who traded with each other often invested together, and shared risk. Adrian Davies instances a vessel owned by one John Abraham from Colchester which was under the command of the Wivenhoe mariner Edward Feedum, to carry the goods of Josiah Taylor, John Furly, Abraham Case, and Stephen Crisp (Davies 2000, 86): all were Friends. Business benefits included integrated supply chains, shared resources, and expanded market access. Within the Quaker commercial network, their dependability in repaying debts removed risks associated with success since investors would get their money in time, but the willingness of Quakers to 'jointly hazard' total loss is often recorded. William Stout can be regarded as suitable representative of the reasonably successful middleman during the first fifty years of the period. A useful illustration of his attitude to risk in commercial ventures is shown by his 1698 investments: he was invited by five other Friends to share the cost of fitting out a ship of 80 tons for a voyage for Virginia, there to purchase a cargo for sale in the colonies, which in turn would fund the purchase of a cargo of tobacco to be sold on return. For his share of this substantial investment, Stout was required to visit London - a trip put in jeopardy when his brother's horse died. Undeterred, the ever-thrifty Quaker returned a borrowed horse for a neighbour, which additionally saved the stabling costs in London. He 'duly attended the general yearly meeting which was large, unanimous, peaceful, and edifying' and afterwards bought 'sails, rigging, anchors cables etc', and sailed home via Liverpool. In the same year he sent £110 of 'woollen, linen, and other goods' to Philadelphia wholly in the care of one George Godsalve, 'a young man brought up in a drapers shop' and keen to try a career as a merchant - one of twenty Lancaster Quakers who sold up and shipped out from Liverpool to extend the network (Stout 1851, 48-51). In neither of these transactions did Stout or his partners have any guarantee of any profit, or indeed

---

[12] Citing Swarthmore Mss, iv., 264 for the Caton-Derrix correspondence on the price of fish.

of any return at all. They shared investment costs, and risked complete losses, to make a commercial return. In this latter they were no different from other international traders. However, the importance of a network of trust - without contract or the possibility of legal redress - illustrates the power of the shared values within the commercial network of Quakers. Networks could also increase solvency, as with Henry Taylor, a shipbroker who used Friends to 'assist in dispatching' coal in a hurry - if at a loss (Grubb 1930, 148). While these connections existed in multiple forms all served to intensify the contribution to commercial success by increasing the overall density. Networks were enhanced by travel, in which Friends engaged on behalf of the Society, and where business often followed worship. This enabled Quakers to integrate the value chain from raw material to wholesale distribution. As in textile production, (Raistrick 1950, 338) so Bristol's Quaker brass makers used Cornish Quaker tin, and Quaker coal from Wales powered the engines to mine and refine Quaker silver and lead; and large numbers of Quakers were employed by concerns such as those of Sharp, Gurney, or Derby (Grubb 1930, 145-150).

The commercial connection was to provide a lucrative network for many Quakers across the Atlantic. The number and extent of non-spiritual connections is strongly indicative of a high level of 'organisational utility' which helped a significant proportion of Friends at many nodes across many business networks: whether as makers or sellers, as aggregators or dealers, or proto-bankers. This multi-faceted nature of Quaker networks is essential to their early success, and distinguishes them from other dissenting sects and churches in the period.

Finance

The key role played by financial interrelationships between members in the shaping of the Society has perhaps been somewhat neglected. In the early eighteenth century, as in the previous, inequality was the accepted norm. This acceptance originated in a rationalisation (dating from the middle ages) which used a functional theory to reveal a moral purpose in society; by the end of the century, a theory of economic harmonies had been developed which attempted to show that 'to the curious mechanism of human society a moral purpose was superfluous or disturbing' (Tawney 1953, 28). The Society of Friends thus echoed the wider society of which it formed a disparate part in holding views on wealth, which were shaped by social obligations, rather than by social equality. For Friends, spiritual equality was of far more significance than differences in station and the inequalities of wealth that implied: Friends were united in the belief of equality before God, for men, women, and children (Braithwaite 1919, 720). This belief was codified in a temporal equality under the regulations of the

21

Society on issues of discipline: the Book of Extracts, XV states that the provisions applied equally to both sexes, although 'not particularly expressed'; this clause was uniquely re-affirmed no less than seven times between 1737 and 1801 (Extracts 1802, 167). Partly as a result of the social obligations of wealth, money played a highly significant role in the Society of Friends from the start: if the teachings of Fox and his followers supplied the bones on which the Society was built, and the strength of will of the membership the muscle, then finance acted as the blood in having an impact on almost all aspects of the Society by transmitting the sustaining force. This was first institutionalised in the collections for relief of Sufferings, and later by a further centralised fund known as the National Stock which was used to run the Society from the last quarter of the seventeenth century (Extracts 1802, 117), and for which meticulous records were kept of all transactions and approvals. Mutual financial support, originating at Balby and deployed against the repression of non-conformity, can therefore be seen to play a key role from the very beginnings of Quakerism. The central funding of the Society's activities is important when considering how the Society developed, for while the role of wealth changed it did not diminish as the Society evolved during the Second and subsequent periods. Broadly speaking, as the need for funds to relieve Sufferings declined, so funds for the implementation of policy and administration increased in importance (Braithwaite 1919, 7). Initially, the Society had used finance as a way to mitigate the consequences of conflicts with authority, raising money locally through the Monthly Meetings to be administered through an increasingly centralised hierarchy, first through the Six Monthly Meetings, and ultimately under the control of Yearly Meeting. Such assistance was required for many reasons, the best known being payment of fines levied by Secular and Ecclesiastical courts - although never in payment of the dues which gave rise to the prosecutions. Shared financial contributions were solicited in order to defray costs incurred when suffering in 'witness' to demonstrate Quaker beliefs, recorded and subsequently later collated and published by Besse in the mid-eighteenth century as a reminder to a new generation of Friends how precisely an earlier had suffered. [13] Persecution thus provided a catalyst that helped establish Friends financial inter-dependence, as well as a shared bond of suffering. In this way finance played an important role not only as one of the means by which the Society achieved its aims, but which subsequently, through the preponderance of financial interactions which continued after Sufferings had declined, left a legacy of commercial transactions which would come to be, for many, a mark of Quaker identity.

---

[13] 'Precisely' may not be the correct term: the many errors found by Friends in early drafts of the sufferings required Besse to undertake much revision.

As discussed earlier, the network effect of the initially humble domestic markets would over time provide capital for the early Quaker lending, which in turn would create the merchant banking houses of the Gurneys, Peases, Lloyds and Barclays (Vann 1969b). The importance of mutual financial cooperation had appeared as early as 1656 with the Epistle from the Elders at Balby (Moore 2001). Within the twenty advices were several which held the essence of mutual cooperation, including: timely collections for the poor, and relief of prisoners (v); care to be taken for families of those in ministry, or imprisoned (vi); that those in need be helped to work (xii); and that (without being 'busy bodies'), each to bear another's burdens (xvii). The earlier sufferings of imprisoned friends could be and were alleviated by finance, for gaols were run on commercial lines, with gaolers charging inmates for board and lodging (Braithwaite 1912, 239). This provided an opportunity for Friends to ameliorate their conditions through payments, which were often met by Quarterly Meetings. Regular items of expenditure included 'chamber rent' and 'deputation money', and when inmates were not close-confined, fees for leave of absence from the gaol. William Crouch records that when imprisoned for tithes owing, he was taken into the 'Poultry Compter under which confinement I continued about one year and three quarters: but through Favour of the Gaoler, I had I some Liberty to be at home to look after my business, after two months', by paying the chamber rent of 3^d per night (Crouch 1712, 30). Crouch had learned the hard way: prior to this he found himself 'shut up in the Hole, amongst the Common Poor Prisoners' for not paying his prison fees. Outside the prisons, the Society's financial interdependence was exemplified by collections such as the Quaker cloth fund of 1677 (JFHS 1915 XII, 122). Communal-sourced loans were offered and were distanced from usury, as monies were lent 'for a time freely' (Atkins 1660, XVII). Financial success brought approbation: by 1700 perceptions had reached a point where accusations were levelled at the Society for using the carrot of better living standards as a means to attract new members. The anonymous pamphlet that identified 'needy persons' specifically makes the accusation that Quakers used their commercial network and financial 'muscle' to target the impecunious (Anon 1700, 3). Of significance is the Quakers were aversion from joining the landed gentry: Vann believes that persecution made Quakerism much less attractive to those in the male line of descent of landed property, noting Margaret Fell and all her daughters would be converted but neither husband or son (Vann 1969a). However, as discussed below tithes must also have played a major role: notwithstanding, by not investing in landed estates Quakers avoided the vast majority of state taxation which was then based on such ownership. Their accumulated capital was lent to other Friends, (Grubb, 16) who would borrow but not issue paper credit (Extracts 1802, 197). Debt was acceptable even when risky (witness Sarah Fell's borrowing £75 to fit out a ship in 1674), (Penney 1920) provided the borrower could sustain the loss personally. Bankruptcy was never permitted, with Friends morally burdened with the debt until repaid in full, as indicated by advices on Trade (Extracts 1802, 195, 199). What always mattered to Friends was that they should find useful employment for all talents - echoing the Balby advice that 'none be idle in the Lord's vineyard'. Money was no exception, and it was put to work with the typical Quaker requiring a return on financial assets, even if that return did not benefit them personally. A detailed illustration of this is the example of Giles Fettiplace, a wealthy Gloucester Friend, who made money available to the local meeting for poor relief. Rather than simply donate to a collection, Giles instructed that he would supply capital of £100 (somewhere between £10,000 and £20,000 in today's terms) if five Friends each agreed to take up £20 at an annual interest of five percent. The five pounds raised would then provide his annual contribution to poor relief. Thus can the Quaker attitude to wealth be neatly defined: following Max Weber's distinction in the Protestant Ethic they were less those who *pursued* wealth than those who *obtained it* (Chalcraft 2001, 71).[14]

Discipline

It is core to this argument that the Society's 'advices' which guided religious practice were not only compatible with, but also actively promoted, business success and wealth creation. As mentioned earlier, the first documented attempt to describe the general principles by which Quakerism would govern itself is the 'Epistle from the meeting of Elders at Balby', from November 1656, which was both quickly and widely emulated (Braithwaite 1912, 314). At this formative stage the advices were not even to be considered as binding on future Friends: Braithwaite notes a 'fine warning against the invasion of tradition' in an letter from Durham Friends to the General Meeting in Kendal (Braithwaite 1912, 329f). A collection entitled 'Canons and institutions' of 1669 (Anon. 1669) avoids articles of faith, concentrating on rules of behaviour to manage both individual and group reputation. Reputation of the Society was ever the prime concern, starting with financial probity as embedded in the Men's Query V which asks: Are friends just in their dealings, and punctual in fulfilling all their engagements; and are they annually advised carefully to inspect the state of their affairs once in the year?' (Extracts 1802, 143), and schoolmaster Ambrose Rigge's 'warning'

---

[14] Weber's wording is translated as *acquired*. This does not seem to sufficiently emphasis the incidental nature of the wealth, and also fits uncomfortably with his dissatisfaction at the phrase 'acquisitive drive' [*Erwerbstrieb*].

24

advice of 1678 for an annual review of Friends' finances (Grubb 1930, 67). Friends could take on no more business than a man can '*manage honourably and with reputation*' (Extracts 1802, 195-200). Insolvent persons could not change meetings, and bankrupts were disowned (Extracts 1802, 166), although Friends did on occasion rescue those who failed in financial obligations - for example Amos Strettell in 1720 and Edward Browne in 1729 (Grubb 1930, 90). The prohibition on 'marrying out' (Extracts 1802, 69) directly created many consolidated Quaker business empires: Raistrick charts the linking of family trees, including those of Backhouse, Barclay, Fox, Gurney, Lloyd, Pease, and more (Raistrick 1950, 75;77;79;121;287). In between major revisions, key themes were emphasised by the Yearly Advices, as in 1791: 'to be read at least once in the year, in each of the Men's and Women's Quarterly and Monthly Meetings'. Collections of Extracts circulated in manuscript form from the beginning of the eighteenth century, until the first centralised selection made by Yearly Meeting in 1738 entitled Christian and brotherly advices given forth from time to time by the Yearly Meetings in London, alphabetically digested under proper heads (Braithwaite 1919, 377-8; f378). Some important advices were selectively published (Removals in 1729, and Marriage in 1754) before the whole was finally set in print as the ' Extracts from the minutes and advices of the Yearly Meeting of Friends held in London from its first institution' as late as 1783 (Jones 1921,143). The printed Extracts would be subsequently revised three times in the next century (in 1801 and 1822 and 1833 - this last being published under the title 'Rules of Discipline').[15]

When considering how the Quaker disciplines had an impact on commerce, it is perhaps significant that advice on Removals represents the first published set of extracts, for it indicates how the Society was driven to enhance its management of what became primarily a financial and administrational issue rather than a spiritual one. The importance of the 'Rem. & Sett.' Extract may be demonstrated not only by the length (being the longest of all Extracts: number 7 runs for six pages in fifteen subsections), but also by the revisions of seven further Yearly Meetings between 1737 and 1801. In terms of content, the advice requires Friends wishing to relocate to first obtain certification from the current meeting. Initially, this required confirmation of good conduct, but over time the focus became (first equally, then more) on financial independence. Advices on who, and how, Friends should be supported financially multiplied, with specific rules for widows, servants, discharged debtors and those who had previously required relief (Extracts 1802, 160-168) - all of which were handled differently.

---

[15] There was also an extra-Societal version produced by John Fry in 1762

This emphasised the need for all Friends to regard solvency as a priority, and ultimately prevented any Friend's acceptance into a new meeting until four years of financial self-sufficiency had been demonstrated: (Extracts 1822, 284).[16] To confirm its continued importance, the revised edition of 1822 contains a new section on Removals running to fifteen pages, which completely supersede the earlier advices 1-7: by contrast, 'Slavery' gains two pages, and 'Tithes' no more than a modest paragraph.

Following this emphasis on financial self-sufficiency - at least in chronological publication - were the advices on Marriage. Administratively, these were handled under the Men's Query XIII, reported each Autumn Quarterly meeting, and tended to echo the standard requirements of marriage in the established church, in that names of intendeds were promulgated in advance of the union being recorded inform of witnesses. Of more importance to the promotion of commerce amongst Quakers were specific advices concerning the primacy of agreement on the disposition of 'outward estates' (Extracts 1802, Advice 1-1690), the unsuitability of 'mixed' marriages (Extracts 1802, Advice 3-1722), and in particular the inadmissibility of marriage outside the Society (Extracts 1802, Advices 11-1719 and13-1752). Combined with a ban on kinship marriage, and additional difficulties for marriage across Monthly Meetings, these strictures ensured that most matches were made within the immediate circle of associations. Notwithstanding, Quakers showed a greater propensity than the (low) norm to travel to marry, and marriages could often be unequal socially, if not precisely 'mixed' (Davies 2000, 91-94). For those engaged in a trade, this provided an opportunity for expansion of business, consolidation of market share, and extension of trade networks. Families in similar or related trades were a common source of inter-marriage, which consolidated costs and spread technical innovation (Raistrick 1950, 45). The advantages are well illustrated by the Beck & Ball survey, as reviewed by Raistrick (Raistrick 1950, 30-32), which compares the occupations from two hundred and fifty Quaker marriages around 1680 with a similar number from about 1780 (Raistrick 1950, 90). Consolidated into three categories, the latter date clearly shows a major decline in 'craftsmen-artisans' (from 147 to 30) and an increase in 'merchants-dealers' (from 58 to 141); the 'professional etc' group also increases (from 27 to 46).

Beyond marriage, other commercial benefits arose from more 'administrative' advice. As the Society replicated those functions denied to Friends as a consequence of the ban on oaths, which persisted before the

---

[16] Friends were rejected in the event of their '*Being, in the regular course of the exercise of the discipline, recorded, within four years immediately subsequent to the acceptance, as insolvent, either by Othe accepting or any other monthly meeting of which the party may be at the time a member*'

Affirmation Act (Statutes 1820, v7: 152) legal redress, including suing for debts (Braithwaite 1912, 182) was not possible. As a consequence, much Quaker wholesale trading remained within the society, as inter-Quaker trading was preferred to reduce risk. This had been the case since the start of the Society, and engendered much criticism. As one 1691 pamphlet put it: 'their custom being to sell to the whole world, but buy only from their own tribe'.[17] From 1684, a process for arbitration was established under a separate advice (Extracts 1802, 5), which not only saved expense and kept trade flowing (Grubb 1930, 83) but helped preserve the all-important Quaker reputation (Davies 2000, 98-99).

However, perhaps the most underestimated influence on Quaker commercial success arose from the advice condemning the payment of tithes. Sufferings on account of tithes had been collected from the earliest times, and Friends guilty of payment were disbarred from ministry (Extracts 1802, 92). Yet the real consequence was more often financial than religious. The great significance of the tithe is that it pushed conforming Quakers who wished to avoid confrontation towards activities which did not attract 'God's Bounty': there was never an ecclesiastical argument for the taxation of the minerals and ores of the earth, nor their fruits of ingots and 'pigs'. Mining, smelting and associated foundry work became popular simply because it did not require a refusal to pay tithes. The major centres of manufacturing grew up in areas where there were no incumbent ministers to support, did not have established tithe rolls, (Evans 1970, 36) nor charters. nor corporations: these were places where non-conformists could reside without swearing the oath of allegiance (Braithwaite 1919, 52). This is far from suggesting that centres such as Birmingham were 'Dissenters towns' - there was always an establishment majority. Rather, in the absence of guilds and corporation to demand membership on oath, or protest at Quaker intrusion in the market, and with only one parish church to support in 1700 from a population of 15,000, incumbents found the Quakers easier to tolerate, and Quakers found it easier to mind their own business. As a result, it was often the Quakers who moved first into both the industries and the areas where manufactures could flourish, and it was the Quakers' Society that drove, sustained and developed early competitive advantage through intermarriage, which delivered commercial benefits in terms of consolidation, shared technology, innovation, costs and supply chain.

---

[17] [s.n.]*The trade of England Revised* 1681 in Joan Thirsk & P.J. Cooper (eds) *Seventeenth-Century Economic Documents* (Oxford 1972) p394

Conclusion

The long eighteenth century was characterised in part by a general increase in prosperity, to which many things contributed: security of property, (following the lawless periods of c.17th interregnum and 'revolution'); better transport; mobility; more flexible exchange and credit; relative price stability; and most of all the associated expansion of trade (Clark 2014,45-52). Within this context were the Quakers, many of whom were already manufacturing or marketing to a greater or lesser extent. But the world in which the eighteenth century Quaker began to prosper was not one in which a choice was necessary between spiritual and secular success. It was not characterised by the divided mind which would later separate wealth and worship: and the eighteenth century Quaker would have found no practical benefit from deriding Mammon in the cause of serving God. Their efforts at a universal, practical education, linked to apprenticeships helped to secure the financial future of the next generation while increasing Friends' ability to support the present. Their willingness to grant financial assistance, established by usage through the period of non-conformist repression, evolved into material assistance providing working capital for trade, and later into bills of exchange and banking. Their Atlantic network – arising from shared values and trust – both facilitated links between makers, traders and buyers and (as importantly) intensified the importance of those shared values though being almost exclusively Quaker in nature. Finally, those values themselves, collected as extracts of 'Advices' and published in the books of Discipline, were grounded in the need to preserve the Quaker reputation. As a result, the advices insisted on a rule of behaviours in business which promoted sound commercial values: fair dealing; regular reviews of financial commitments; no defaulting on debts; honouring verbal contracts. The disciplines drove other pro-commerce behaviours: inter-marriage, which gave birth to several commercial dynasties; arbitration, which incentivised trade with fellow Friends; and most essentially an aversion to tithes, which encouraged Quakers to mine, refine, develop and manufacture – all activities which grew rapidly during the period, as innovation started the process that would become known as the industrial revolution.

Bibliography

Advice of the Yearly Meeting. 1791. London Yearly Meeting. Haverford Collection.

Anon. 1675 [J.G]] *"The Quakers farewel to England, or Their voyage to New Jersey, scituate on the continent of Virginia, and bordering upon New England.* London: Printed for J.G.; Bod765/Roud V3890.

Anon. 1669. *Canons and institutions drawn up and agreed upon by the General Assembly or Meeting of the heads of the Quakers from all parts of the kingdom at their New-Theatre in Grace-church-street in or about January 1668/9; George Fox being their president.* Society of Friends London. [attributed to George Fox].

Anon. 1700. *Remarks upon the Quakers wherein the plain-dealers are plainly dealt with.* London: Printed for Walter Kettilby.

Anon. 1717. *Collection of the Epistles,* #66; Minutes of New England Yearly Meeting [Quoted in James, Sydney V].

Anon. 1725. *An Account of Several Work-houses for Employing and Maintaining the Poor.* S.P.C.K.

Archer, R. 1921. *Secondary Education in the Nineteenth Century.* Cambridge [Quoted in Hans 42].

Atkins, S Thomas. 1660. *Some reasons why the people called Quakers ought to enjoy their meetings peaceably.* London: Robert Wilson, at the Sign of the Black-Spread-Eagle and Windmill, Martins Le Grand.

Beck, Wm. & Ball, T.F. 1869. *London Friends Meetings.* London.

Bellers, John. 1695. *Proposals for Raising a College of Industry.* London.

Braithwaite, William C. 1912. *The beginnings of Quakerism.* Cambridge: University Press.

Braithwaite, William C. 1919. *Second Period of Quakerism.* London: MacMillan.

Cadbury, Deborah. 2010. *The Chocolate Wars.* Public Affairs.

Cantor, Geoffrey. 2005. *Quakers, Jews, and Science.* Oxford: Oxford University Press.

Carter, C.F. 1950. Review of "Quaker Social History: 1669-1738" by Arnold Lloyd, *The Economic Journal,* Vol. 60, No. 240 (Dec., 1950), 817-819.

Chalcraft, David J. & Harrington, Austin (Editors). 2001. *The Protestant Ethic Debate: Max Weber's Replies to his Critics, 1907-1910.* Liverpool: Liverpool University Press.

Child, Josiah. 1690. *A new discourse of trade, wherein is recommended several weighty points relating to companies of merchants. the act of navigation. Naturalization of strangers. And our woollen manufactures. The ballance of trade. And the nature of plantations, and their consequences, in relation to the kingdom, are seriously discussed. Methods for the employment and maintenance of the poor are proposed. The reduction of interest of money to 4l. per centum, is recommended. And some proposals, for erecting a Court of Merchants, for determining controversies, relating to maritime affairs, and for a law for transferrance of bills of debts, are humbly offer'd .* London: Printed by A. Sowle, at the Crooked Billet in Holloway Lane; Approved in 1689, and originally printed anonymously.

Child, J. & Hale, M. 1699. *A method concerning the relief and employment of the poor humbly offer'd to the consideration of the king and both Houses of Parliament.* London: Printed by the advice of some in authority.

Clark, Jonathan. 2014. *From Restoration to Reform The British Isles 1660-1832.* Vintage.

Cole, W.A. 1957. The Social Origins of the Early Friends." *Journal of the Friends' Historical Society,* Vol. 48.

Corley, T.A.B. 1972. *Quaker Enterprise in Biscuits: Huntley and Palmers of Reading, 1822-1972.* Hutchinson Radius.

Crouch, William. 1712. *Posthuma Christiana; or, a collection of some papers of William Crouch : being a brief historical account, under his own hand, of his convincement of, and early sufferings for the truth, with remarks on sundry memorable transactions, relating to the people call'd Quaker,* J Sowle, London.

Currie, Robert, Gilbert, Alan & Horsley, Lee. 1977. *Churches and Church-Goers: Patterns of Church Growth in the British Isles since 1700.* Oxford: Clarendon Press.

Davies, Adrian. 2000. *The Quakers in English Society, 1655-1725.* Oxford: Clarendon Press.

Evans, Eric J. 1970. *'A History of the Tithe System in England, 1690-1850, with special reference to Staffordshire.'* (Univ. of Warwick Ph.D. thesis, Unpublished).

Extracts from State Papers (ESP). 1911. "Relating to Friends.1658-1664. *Second Series" Supplement 9* to *Journal of Friends Historical Society* (J.F.H.S); London: Headley Brothers.

Extracts. 1802. *Extracts from the Minutes and Advices of the Yearly Meeting of Friends, held in London from it's first institution.* London: W. Phillips George Yard, Lombard Street.

Extracts. 1822. *Supplement to the Second Edition printed in 1802.* London: W. Phillips George Yard, Lombard Street.

Fox, George. 1852. *Journal of George Fox.* ed. Armistead W. Glasgow: W.G. Blackie & Co. II vols.

Field, Clive D. 2012. "Counting Religion in England and Wales: The Long Eighteenth Century, c. 1680–c. 1840.*" The Journal of Ecclesiastical History* 63/4 (October): 693-720.

Fry, John. 1762(?) *An alphabetical extract of all the annual printed epistles which have been sent to the several quarterly-meetings of the people call'd Quakers, in England and elsewhere, from their yearly-meeting ... from the year 1682 to 1762 inclusive.* London: printed for, and sold by the author at Sutton Benger, and by his sons

Joseph Fry, Bristol, and John Fry, London; Second edition (1766) Printed and sold by Luke Hinde.

Grubb, Isabel. 1930. *Quakers in Industry before 1800*. Williams & Norgate.

Hans, Nicholas Hans. 1951 [2001]. *New Trends in Education in the Eighteenth Century*. London: Routledge, and K. Paul.

Higginbotham, Peter. 2012. *The Workhouse Encyclopedia*. Stroud: The History Press.

Hale, Mathew. 1683. *A discourse touching provision for the poor*. London: Printed for William Shrewsbery, at the Bible, Duke Lane.

Healey, Robynne Rogers. 2013. "Quietist Quakerism 1692-c.1805" in *Oxford Handbook of Quaker Studies* ed. Angell and Dandelion. Oxford: Oxford University Press.

Huntington, Frank C. Jr. 1982 "Quakerism during the Commonwealth: The Experience of the Light." *Quaker History*, Vol. 71, No. 2 (Fall 1982), 69-88.

James, Sydney V. 1962. "Quaker Meetings and Education in the Eighteenth Century." *Quaker History*, Vol. 51, No. 2 (Autumn) 87-102.

Jones, Rufus M. 1921. *The Later Periods of Quakerism*. London, 2 vols.

Journal of Friends Historical Society (JFHS). 1913. *"Gospel order and Discipline."* JFHS X Knatchbull Act. 1723. (9 Geo. I c.7).

King, Gregory King. 1688 [1936]. *Scheme of the Income & Expence of the several families of England Calculated for the Year 1688-Two Tracts.* ed. G. E. Barnett. Baltimore: The Johns Hopkins Press

Landes, Jordan. 2015. *London Quakers in the Trans-Atlantic World, The Creation of an Early Modern Community*. Palgrave Macmillan.

Langford, Paul. 1991. *Public Life and the Propertied Englishman, 1689-1798*. Oxford: Clarendon Press.

Milligan, Edward. 2007. *British Quakers in Commerce and Industry 1775 -1920*. Sessions of York.

Minute of Six Week's Meeting, 13th First Month 1676/7. 1915. JFHS. XII.

Moore, Rosemary. 2001. *Epistle from the Elders at Balby 1656*. (Transcript). Quaker Heritage Press, 16 Nov 2001.

Nash, Gary B. 1996. "The Early Merchants of Philadelphia" in *The World of William Penn*, ed Richard S. Dunn & Mary Maples Dunn, University of Pennsylvania Press.

Penn, William. 1681. *Some Account of the Province of Pennsylvania.* ed. Mayers, 209. [Quoted in Tolles, 42].

Penney, Norman. 1920. *Household Accounts book of Sarah Fell.* ed. Cambridge: Cambridge University Press [quoted in Raistrick 57].

Power, John Carroll. 1863. <u>*The Rise and Progress of Sunday Schools: A Biography of Robert Raikes and William Fox.*</u> New York: Sheldon & Company.

Price, Jacob M. 1996 "The Great Quaker Business Families of Eighteenth-Century London: The Rise and Fall of a Sectarian Patriciate" in *The World of William Penn.* eds Richard S. Dunn & Mary Maples Dunn, University of Pennsylvania Press.

Raistrick, Arthur. 1950. *Quakers in Science and Industry.* The Bannidale Press.

Raistrick, Arthur. 1953. *Dynasty of Iron Founders: the Darbys and Coalbrookdale.* The Bannidale Press.

Rowley, Timothy J. 1997. *"Moving beyond Dyadic Ties: A Network Theory of Stakeholder Influences."* The Academy of Management Review, Vol. 22, No. 4 (Oct.) 887-910.

Statutes of the Realm. 1820. *William III, 1695-6: An Act that the Solemne Affirmation & Declaration of the People called Quakers shall be accepted instead of an Oath in the usual Forme.* [Chapter XXXIV. Rot. Parl. 7 & 8 Gul. III. p.9. n.3.] volume 7: 1695-1701.

Story, Thomas. 1747. *A Journal of the Life of Thomas Storey.* Newcastle Upon Tyne: Isaac Thompson & Co.

Stout, William. 1851. *Autobiography of William Stout of Lancaster.* ed Harland, J. London: Simkin, Marshall & Co.

Tawney, R.H. 1953. *Religion and the Rise of Capitalism.* London: Mentor.

Taylor, Ernest E. 1922. "The First Publishers of Truth - A Study." *Journal Friends' Historical Society,* XIX 1922, 66-81.

Thirsk, Joan & Cooper, J. P. 1972. *Seventeenth-Century Economic Documents.* Oxford 394.

Tryon, Thomas. 1684. *The Planter's SPEECH TO HIS Neighbours & Country-Men OF Pennsylvania, East & West-Jersey, And to all such as have Transported themselves into New-Colonies for the sake of a quiet retired Life .* London: Andrew Sowle in Shoreditch.

Tolles, Frederick B. 1963 [1948]. *Meeting House and Counting House: the Quaker merchants of colonial Philadelphia, 1682-1763.* Pub. for the Institute of Early American History and Culture at Williamsburg, Va..; Univ. of North Carolina Press.

Tuke, Samuel. 1843. *Five Papers on the Past Proceedings of the Society of Friends in Connection with the Education of Youth read at the meetings of the Friends' Educational Society, at Ackworth, read in years 1838, 1839, 1840, 1841, 1842.* York: John L Linney.

Vann, Richard. 1969a. "Quakerism and the Social Structure in the Interregnum," *Past and Present* No. 43, May 1969.

Vann, Richard . 1969b. *Social Development of English Quakerism 1655-1750.* Cambridge.

Vann, Richard. 1970. "Rejoinder: The Social Origins of the Early Quakers", *Past & Present*, No. 48 Aug.

Walvin, James. 1997. *The Quakers: Money and Morals.* London: John Murray.

Winchester, Angus J.L. 1991. "Ministers, merchants and migrants: Cumberland Friends and North America in the Eighteenth Century." *Quaker History* 80: 85-99.

PART II
Quaker Pioneers

2| Quaker Clockmakers

By Tim Marshall

Background

For those living in early 17th Century England the rhythm of life for most people was still governed by the rising of and setting of the sun, the apparent motion of the sun regulated society; and the sundial was the only means of accurately measuring what is known as "local apparent time" or "apparent solar time", by which the country ran. ("Apparent solar time" can be simply explained as the sun appearing to move across the sky to complete one circuit of 360 degrees every 24 hours, passing at a rate of one degree of longitude every four minutes, each place sharing the same longitude shares the same time).

Due to the slow means of communication it made no practical difference to the lives people led, that the time would be different further to the east or west. Horological technology had barely advanced from the invention (by an unknown scholar/craftsman) of the first mechanical timekeepers in the late 13th Century – weight driven turret clocks, controlled by a verge and foliot (or balance) escapement, which required frequent adjustment from a sundial to make the uneven hours of solar time audible by the chimes. Then in 15th Century Flanders or possibly Italy another unknown craftsman (probably inspired by Locksmiths work) had the idea of replacing the weight drive with a mainspring to provide the driving power, which resulted in the introductions of small portable drum clocks, the precursors of the watchmaking craft, which became established in France or Nuremburg by the early 16th Century – albeit that accurate mechanical timekeeping remained elusive.

However it was not until the mid-16th Century that the shortcomings of accurate timekeeping became a more serious matter for the scientific community, when in 1543 Copernicus published his revelation that the earth was not stationary at the centre of the universe, but rather it was the sun which stood motionless with the planets revolving around it; to be followed in 1609 with

Kepler's first two rules of planetary motion explaining the planets did not revolve around the sun in a circle but an ellipse, speeding up when they were nearer the sun. These discoveries led to an outpouring of new dialling literature and hence more sophisticated scientific sundials that were far in advance of the best contemporary mechanical timekeepers.

By the time George Fox was born in 1624, English domestic clockmaking was more in its first generation of native born and trained clockmakers, producing what was the first wholly English conceived mechanical timekeeper – the weight driven lantern clock, controlled by a verge and balance escapement. Hitherto clockmaking had been dominated by foreign craftsmen, either exporting their work from the continent or London based of often Huguenot descent (as refugees from intolerance). This output of clocks and watches was regarded as costly novelties or status symbols rather than reliable timekeepers.

Accurate timekeeping would have to wait until the 1650's for one of sciences monumental discoveries – the publication of Christiaan Huygens 'Horologium' in 1658 (from 1656) describing harnessing a pendulum as an independent oscillator, via a crutch to the escapement to control the motive power, (it is the pairing of a pendulum to a crutch which is the important point that is often overlooked) which exponentially increased accuracy. The new precision pendulum clocks could perform with such accuracy over a longer duration providing science and commerce with the accurate meantime they so desperately needed, in addition the equation of time became visible.

The idea was immediately taken up in England by one of the greatest clockmakers of all – Ahasuerus Fromanteel of London, the Anabaptist son of a Norwich wood turner that led to the pre-eminence of English clockmaking for the next 200 years. As clockmaking was making that giant leap forward, George Fox was building a Quaker organisational structure which would ensure it not only survived the early years of persecution, but thrived, especially suited to the tradesman/craftsman class – men of independent thought who had been drawn to the new Religious Society of Friends, by its common approach to religious and everyday life. Among them were clockmakers, who were implicitly literate and numerate, practical men who could contribute much to the new movement, but also take full advantage of any opportunities that might arise in an organisation that placed honesty and trust foremost.

The administrative structure George Fox conceived was to implement a network of meetings, based on a concentric model, with the yearly London meeting at the heart of the organisation to both instruct and offer guidance, radiating out via quarterly regional meetings to the monthly division of circuit meetings (dealing with fundamental issues of births, deaths and marriages) and then to the regular preparative meetings at the local scale. Each one designed to ensure the core Quaker values entered all walks of their lives; and of relevance to clockmaking are these four elements of Education, Apprenticeship, Travel and Trade, each one having a direct impact on the future success of Quaker clockmakers.

Being both literate and numerate and in no small measure trustworthy, clockmakers were often the obvious candidates to represent monthly meetings at both the quarterly and London Yearly Meeting, in terms of travel, this provided the clockmakers not only with the opportunity to form spiritual and personal bonds as they travelled between the meetings, but had the effect of developing trade and business networks that, as we shall see later, spread across the country and then overseas to the American colonies.

As for trade, guidance was issued setting out an ethical code, which imbued their business activities with the core belief of honesty and truth in all matters, that both enhanced the reputation of the individual and the Religious Society of Friends. Quaker tradesmen should not financially overstretch themselves and take an unserviceable debt or enter a business they knew nothing of. Being denied access to the universities and hence a profession, it is not surprising that Quakers were drawn to the natural sciences and metal based technologies, among them clockmaking – producing consistently good quality products at a fair and fixed price (to bargain proved that a price demanded was untrue and hence at odds with the Quaker ethos of truth). As a result, their clocks were in demand, to the financial benefit of both the clockmaker himself and the general stock of the Religious Society of Friends.

Fox saw education as being crucial for the wellbeing and future of the Society, shunning the need for classical learning (what was the point of it if Quakers were barred from universities), instead concentrating on more practical subjects that trade and business required, in the case of clockmaking a sound knowledge of mathematics and applied mechanics was a natural choice for many. This manifested itself in craft apprenticeship within the compass of the Religious Society of Friends, which also had the effect of ensuring the youngsters attended meetings and were brought up in the Quaker way of life. The apprenticeships were sometimes paid for from Quaker funds or more often, especially in country districts it was an arrangement within and between groups of Friends – nowhere more successful than among the North Oxfordshire Quaker clockmakers of the 18th Century.

Although it was not until after the 1689 Act of Toleration for the full benefits of the application of core Quaker Beliefs through education, apprenticeships and travel and business, via the meeting structure to be fulfilled, this context enabled Quaker clockmakers and tradesmen to enjoy economic power way above their numbers, lasted throughout the era of English clockmaking from 17th Century to the 19th Century.

First Generation Quaker Clockmakers

For those first Quaker clockmakers the years leading up to the 1689 Act of Toleration were difficult and often dangerous, not only did they have to contend with an intolerant established Church (and therefore country), at first the Presbyterians of the Interregnum followed by the Episcopalians of the restoration, but also the effects of the plague and great fire of London devastating most of the city's clockmaking districts (just how many were Quakers is unknown). At the same time the Dutch sea wars and the profligate royal family coupled with the uncertainty of a protestant succession all contributed to an unsettled economic climate for trade still recovering from the effects of the civil war.

During the early years of the 1650's and the 1660's those established clockmakers that joined the new religious society were spread over a wide area from Bristol in the west, the midlands and of course London. Their main output, regardless of whether they were town or country clockmakers was the lantern clock (at first balance and then pendulum controlled).

Two of the most interesting Quaker clockmakers from this first generation worthy of comment for very different reasons are the relatively obscure John Roe of Epperstone in Nottinghamshire and the well-known London maker Hilkiah Bedford.

Image 1: A rare wooden framed turret clock by Richard Roe of Epperstone dated 1683 missing it's anchor escapement and part of the striking train. Image courtesy of D.J. and P.H. Whatmore.

John Roe was born c.1637 and spent his long working life at Epperstone, a village four miles north east of Nottingham, a maker of lantern clocks and more interesting – turret clocks of a rare timber framed form found mostly in the midland counties, the earliest at Shelford was installed in 1680. The presence of this clock at this early date (pre- Toleration Act) is interesting, suggesting that in this part of Nottinghamshire, discrimination by the clergy had softened, to the extent that any prejudice against a Quaker clockmaker was outweighed by the quality and value of his work. John Roe was a leading member of his local meeting, becoming a trustee for the Oxton Meeting House in 1699; he died in 1720 and was buried in the Oxton Quaker burial ground.

Hilkiah Bedford of London is a rare example of a mathematical instrument maker and clockmaker, combining both aspects of time measurement. More well known today for his instruments and dials, his output included universal ring dials, quadrants and sundials. Born in 1632 at Sibsey, Lincolnshire, he was the son of Thomas Bedford an early Quaker convert, and was apprenticed through the Stationers Company to John Thompson a mathematical instrument maker in 1646, freed in 1654 and in 1667 became a free brother in the Clockmakers Company despite refusing to take the oath. His clocks date from after his admission into the Clockmakers Company: they included lantern clocks, spring (or bracket) clocks and one early longcase is known – an anchor escapement long pendulum example dating from the early 1670's made just after the invention of the anchor escapement (attributed to Joseph Knibb of Oxford c1670). Its introduction was an important milestone towards precision timekeeping, more accurate and simpler to make than the verge and crownwheel, which it replaced as the standard of pendulum control in longcase clocks thereafter. Whether any of Bedford's clocks were made by his own hand or a journeyman is unclear, certainly a division of labour at a craft level already existed at that time among members of the London trade and was widely used – brass foundries supplied the lantern clock frames, wheel blanks, dials and decorative castings, and of course the specialist engravers, bell founders and cabinet makers and joiners for the cases. It seems likely that Bedford's membership of the Religious Society of Friends was confined to his early years, certainly before his son Hilkiah Bedford was admitted to St. John's College Cambridge in 1679. Hilkiah Bedford died in 1689, the year of the Act of Toleration and was buried in St. Dunstan's Fleet Street.

London

After the accession of William and Mary in 1688, continental influence or furnishing design began to make an impact upon London taste, resulting in some clock cases becoming very grand, albeit in a more elegant manner, greatly influenced by the French designer Daniel Marot. These clocks were for the very wealthy only and among the most eminent of London Clockmakers operating in this exclusive market was the Quaker Daniel Quare.

Born in Somerset in 1647 Quare was admitted into the Clockmakers Company as a great (turret) clockmaker, albeit he did not swear an oath. Initially he worked in St Martins Le Grand, moving to Allhallows, Lombard Street by 1681 and then finally at the sign of the Kings Arms in Exchange Alley by the mid 1680's. From each of these premises he produced watches, spring (bracket) and longcase clocks and barometers of the highest quality for the most affluent customers, including royalty and foreign dignitaries; his Quaker lifestyle presented no handicap.

Images 2, 3 and 4: Three images of an early 18th Century 8 day ebony table clock by Daniel Quare of London numbered 160, with calendar in the arch, rise/fall regulation and strike/silent subsidiary dials, and quarter repeating on a single bell. Images courtesy of Howard Walwyn.

During his illustrious career he took a total of 15 apprentices including his eventual business partner and successor Stephen Horseman. Among his technical achievements was to develop one of the first repeating watches; he patented a "night engine" (presumably some type of early burglar alarm driven by clockwork) and patented his invention for a portable barometer in 1695.

Quare's patent was for a barometer that could be inverted without spilling mercury, probably achieved by simply pinching the top of the tube and shrouding the cistern containing the reservoir of mercury in a leather bag. These barometers were generally of the highest quality, much sought after by the wealthy of those days as they are now, just as popular in France and Germany where the scales (often silver) were engraved in English on one side and French or German on the reverse.

However, it is Quare's long duration clocks which place him among the best of English clockmakers, including a year duration equation of time longcase. So highly was he regarded that despite not taking an oath he became the Master of Clockmakers Company in 1708, and when George 1st ascended the throne he was offered the position of clockmaker to the King; once again the question of not swearing an oath was overcome and he was allowed access to the Sovereign by a back entry. Quare is quoted as saying "The Yeoman of the Guard, lets me frequently go up without calling anybody for leave, as otherwise he would tho persons of quality".

Over a long career, he made a prolific number of clocks; He died on 21 March 1724 and was buried in the Quaker burial ground at Bunhill Fields. The Daily Post of 26 March 1724 reported "Last week dy'd Mr. Daniel Quare, watchmaker in Exchange Alley, who was famous both here and at foreign courts for the great improvements he made in that art, and we hear he is succeeded in his shop and trade by his partner Mr. Horseman. His daughter, Ann, married in 1705, when many European nobles attended".

Towards the end of this "golden" period of London elegance another eminent clockmaker with Quaker origins rose to prominence – George Graham. No account of Quaker clockmakers would be complete without reference to a maker brought up as a Quaker by his family in Cumberland who went on to become one of the greatest clock and watch makers of the 18th Century. George Graham was born in 1673 in Kirklinton parish, Cumberland, the son of a farmer who became a Quaker after his son's birth. He was bound apprentice to Henry Aske of London in 1688, then worked for the most famous clock maker of all – Thomas Tompion, whose niece he married in 1704, then entering into partnership with Tompion in 1711 before taking over the business (at the Dial and Three Crowns) upon his former master's death in 1713.

George Graham became a Warden and then Master of Clockmakers Company in 1722. He was a fellow of the Royal Society and is credited with several important inventions – the deadbeat escapement in 1715 and the mercury compensated pendulum, the combination of both was essential to precision clockmaking, remaining in use until the late 19th century. He perfected the cylinder escapement, a type of deadbeat escapement not subject to change in driving power, which became widely used by French and Swiss watchmakers until into the 20th century, although never as popular with English watchmakers. His workshop produced a prodigious number of high quality watches (said to be around 3,000), spring and longcase clocks and a few humble travelling alarums and most important – precision regulator clocks.

George Graham was also an important scientific instrument maker. His output included an eight-foot quadrant for the Astronomer Royal Edmund Halley in 1725, planetary models, a twenty-two-and-a-half-foot zenith sector and transit instruments; including instruments for the Maupertuis expedition to Lapland in 1736 to prove Newton and Huygens theories that the earth flattened at the poles. It was to the trustworthy 'Honest' George Graham that John Harrison turned to on arrival in London to pursue his quest to build a precision marine timekeeper for finding longitude at sea, providing Harrison with an unsecured interest-free loan.

George Graham died in 1751, one of horology's greatest inventors and is buried in Westminster Abbey. Although in terms of his active participation in Quaker life, there is no evidence that he was a member of the Royal Society of Friends after moving to London to take up his apprenticeship.

1689 to the beginning of the 18th Century

Following the 1688 departure of James the second (a Roman Catholic sympathetic to the Quaker cause in terms of religious toleration), William and Mary quickly granted full liberty of conscience to all religious dissenters, enshrined in the 1689 Act of Toleration – pragmatists, William realised this was necessary for stable government and for an economy to thrive. The Yearly Meeting of 1689 responded by issuing a note of advice which was to set the tone for the next 150 years or so, encouraging Friends to give "no offence nor occasions to those in outward government no way to any controversies, heats or distractions of the world" – sound advice for business and Quaker clockmakers, although with certain drawbacks for a religious movement which hitherto had been at the forefront of challenging the religious establishment; Quakerism never again had the evangelical zeal to reach out to new members (including clockmakers) on the same scale. However, the more inward looking organisation appeared to suit the Quaker clockmakers who could settle down to their work confident that the disturbances of the past 40 years were behind them. The Act of Toleration enabled the Quakers to make the most of the growth and spread of domestic clockmaking from what had until then, been mostly centred in London and a few regional cities Bristol, Oxford, Salisbury, Norwich, Newcastle and York being among the most prominent, was now moving into the market towns and beyond. Quaker clockmakers were setting up in business over a wider geographical area.

In the west country, Abel Cottey of Crediton and Arthur Davis of Westleigh were both in business during the 1680's making lantern clocks (Davies also made much rarer posted movement musical clocks). Cottey is famous for becoming Philadelphia's first clockmaker, after sailing with William Penn aboard the 'Welcome' in 1682. (He returned to Devon in 1695 before finally emigrating again in 1700, leaving behind some uncharacteristic debts). In the south of England, the Howe family of Dorchester in Dorset were producing quite distinctive thirty-hour longcase clocks, with substantial brass plate movements behind simple embellished dials for a country market far removed from the refinements of London fashion. In contrast, Jeremy Spurgin, Colchester's early Quaker clockmaker was understandably more influenced by London styles, as well as lantern clocks he is known for some very elegant marquetry cased eight day clocks at the height of London fashion. Spurgin is also an interesting example of a late 17th century Quaker clockmaker who was permitted to trade in the town upon payment of a fine (£10) in 1697, and was sufficiently established in Colchester to attend vestry meetings to fix the parish rate. He died in 1699 aged just 33 and was buried in the local Quaker burial ground.

In Staffordshire, an important Quaker clockmaking dynasty was being established by three brothers – Samuel, John and Peter Stretch, a name that would resonate in clockmaking circles halfway across the world; from Leek via Wolverhampton, Birmingham and Bristol to Philadelphia, celebrated today as America's first family of clockmakers after Peter Stretch emigrated in 1703. They came from Harpers Gate just outside Leek, Samuel the eldest brother had established his clockmaking business in Leek by 1681, taking younger brother Peter as his apprentice c.1684, eventually handing over the workshop to Peter when he moved away to Wolverhampton c.1697; John, the least well known established his business in Bristol, where he was eventually joined by Samuel c.1714. All three are known today for their lantern and longcase clocks, one such lantern clock made by Samuel c.1685 still retains its original balance control, highlighting the continued demand in some country areas for a basic short duration clock (about 12 hours) some 30 years after the introduction of the pendulum.

Image 5 and 6: A 17th century Lantern Clock by Samuel Stretch of Leek dating c.1685 retaining its original Balance. Images courtesy of John Robey.

The North West of England Quaker Clockmaking Tradition

One of English clockmaking's unique regional styles exclusive to a network of Quaker clockmakers working in some of the remotest parts of the north west of England can be traced back to John Ogden of Bowbridge Hall near Askrigg in Wensleydale during the 1680's. Ogden, a prominent member of the local Meeting and trustees of the Meeting House, pioneered a distinctive form of thirty hour duration clock comprising a large brass posted lantern style movement, the dial engraved with religious or morbid verses, a particular favourite being "Behold this hand, Observe the motion's tip, Man's previous hours, Away like these do slip", or a more simple "Momento Mori" – In this remote place. John Ogden is thought to have trained his two sons John Jnr and Bernard (after they moved to Newcastle then Alnwick and finally Sunderland while Bernard remained at home) as well as five other apprentices – John Ismay, Isaac Hadwen, Robert Brownless, John Sanderson and Mark Metcalfe. The first four of his apprentices continued Ogdens style into the first half of the 18th century, though oddly neither John Ogden himself or either of his sons did, after her moved off to Darlington in 1711, preferring instead to conform to the styles favoured there (although there remains the possibility that Ogden had moved beyond the compass of an unknown engraver responsible for the verse dials). They certainly remained popular with Ismay and Sanderson at Wigton, Brownless at Staindrop and Isaac Hadwen during his time at Sedbergh. Of the four John Sanderson was the most prolific and idiosyncratic in the nature of his work, each clock different from the next, within the distinctive regional style.

Image 7: An early 18th Century lantern posted movement in the Quaker tradition of the far North West of England, unusual in that the striking train is located on the right-hand side by Sanderson of Wigton.

Unlike Sanderson who may well have left Quakerism, Isaac Hadwen remained within the Society of Friends throughout his life, embodying those key principles of education, apprenticeship, travel and trade, which encompassed a wide network. He was born at Burton in Kendal, Westmorland in 1687, (his stepsister was married to the Clifton clockmaker – Thomas Savage) and apprentice to John Ogden c.1701 before beginning work at Sedbergh c.1710. He married Sarah, the daughter of a prosperous local Quaker Dr John Moore of Eldroth Hall, enabling him to quickly establish a thriving business, moving to Kendal in 1722 and then Tunstall in Lancashire. His success as a clockmaker allowed him to travel widely on Quaker business, including two trips to America, the first in 1718 and then again in 1737 where he died of fever at Chester, Delaware. The family business now removed to Liverpool under the stewardship of his widow Sarah until Joseph Jnr. was able to take over, continued to produce good quality longcases, and more importantly sold clocks wholesale to other clockmakers as far away as John Fry the famous Quaker in Wiltshire, who in turn traded with the Gilkes family from North Oxfordshire, thus forming a common link between the two quite distinctive Quaker clockmaking traditions of the 18th century.

Image 8 and 9: An early 18th Century verse dial by Isaac Hadwen of Sedbergh, the corners engraved – "Behold this Hand / Observe ye motions Tipp / Mans pretious Hours / Away like thefe do slip".

The North Oxfordshire Quaker Clockmaking Tradition

The early years of the 18th century saw the emergence of a group of Quaker blacksmiths cum clockmakers in rural North Oxfordshire, namely the Gilkes and Fardon families, who, along with their descendants, relatives and apprentices built a network of Quaker clockmakers who dominated the craft in this area throughout the 18th century and into the 19th century, virtually to the end of English clockmaking. The network diagram (figure one) illustrates the relationship between master and apprentice together with the interaction between Monthly Meetings, which proved so successful for so long.

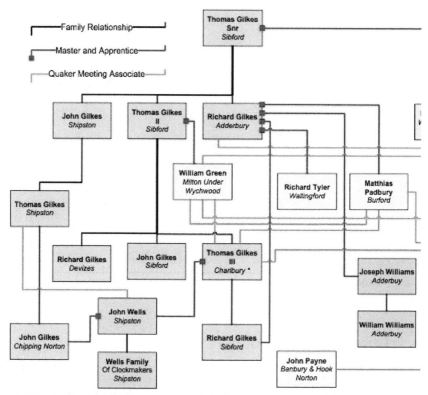

* **Thomas Gilkes III of Charlbury was married to Sarah Fardon, sister of Mary Fardon.**
** **Thomas Harris of Deddington & Bloxham, was married to Mary Fardon, sister of Sarah Fardon.**

Figure 1: Master and apprentice network diagram,
Courtesy of "The Quaker Clockmakers of North Oxfordshire" (Marshall, T.)

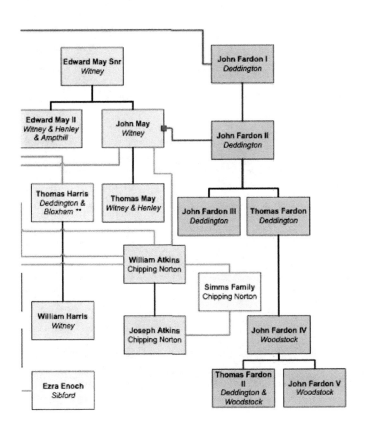

Image 10: A typical North Oxfordshire Quaker Hoop & Spike Clock by Richard Gilkes of Adderbury c.1750, illustrating the ring and zig-zag pattern engraving unique to this group of Quaker Clockmakers.

Founded by Thomas Gilkes Snr. of Sibford Gower, they produced one of the most instantly recognisable styles of English country clockmaking – the 30 hour duration iron posted hoop and spike clock with distinctive ring & zig-zag engraved dials, either for hanging directly on the wall or off a hook located on the backboard of a longcase. Inexpensive – costing somewhere between £2-10s to £4 depending upon whether they were single or two handed, had a calendar or were cased, they found a ready market in a local rural population gradually becoming more prosperous, albeit still beyond the pocket of the labouring and servant classes. The clocks themselves are unique to the North Oxfordshire Quaker tradition, made for the most part in the village clockmakers workshops, forging the iron frames and movement ironwork, engraving the ring & zig-zag pattern dials themselves with only the basic of tools – a graver and compass, casting their own brass spandrels often from a poorly defined mould and repeated many times over. In short they reduced their production costs by making what they could themselves, rather than buying in components; using much cheaper iron instead of the more expensive brass where possible.

First produced by Thomas Gilkes snr. of Sibford in the early years of the 18th century, their production extended through three generations of Quaker clockmakers, some being signed by the Quaker clockmaker and others left unsigned (probably for the wholesale market) ending with the late 18th century examples of John Wells of Shipston or William Green of Milton under Wychwood – they hardly changed at all. During this time, the North Oxfordshire Quaker clockmakers played important roles in each of the Meetings in Banbury and Witney divisions, attending the local and travelling to the Regional and Yearly Meeting, thus extending their business networks even further.

Image 11: An iron posted North Oxfordshire Hoop & Spike Clock c.1730's hanging from a hook on the wall.

The English Midlands

Elsewhere in the country, Quaker clockmakers were producing work more in line with general styles of the period. In Nottinghamshire one notable maker was Joseph Kirk of Skegby and then Nottingham, he was born at Hardstoft in neighbouring Derbyshire, where his earliest clocks are signed. A maker of good quality 30 hour and 8 day longcases he was succeeded in the clockmaking business by his daughter Ann who upon her marriage to a non-Quaker in 1738 was disowned by Nottingham Monthly Meeting – a not unfamiliar story as the century progressed.

In Derbyshire during the late 17th century and early 18th century the Tantum family - Francis, Jonathon and Daniel (all brought up as Quakers) were highly regarded for their longcase clocks, Francis Tantum of Loscoe made some interesting 8-day clocks incorporating a passing strike. They are also notable for two of their apprentices – James Wooley from Codnor (bound to Francis) and William Barnard of Newark (bound to Daniel) who both went on to become well known regional clockmakers. However, it seems unlikely that any of the Tantums remained within the Society of Friends after marrying out.

Further South at Kettering in Northamptonshire we come across a most ingenious man working during the first half of the 18th century – Thomas Eayre who combined clockmaking with bell founding, casting a ring of bells for St Botolphs, Boston (the famous 'stump') he was also a chimes maker and a surveyor & cartographer who made his own waywiser. His son Joseph Eayre was brought up as a Quaker, and trained by Thomas to become a notable provincial clockmaker at St. Neots,is well known for his equation of time clocks and his friendship with the antiquary William Stukeley.

The Industrial Revolution

While several families of Quaker Clockmakers were established in the North of England during the 18th Century – some like the Greaves family on the Quayside at Newcastle from the 1730's (perhaps more notable for buying their engraved dials from Beilby and Bewick during the 1770's) and at York the Storr's and Terry's (a name more associated later with the city's confectionary manufacturing) - they all continued to supply their traditional client base. Others, and it is not clear just who and how many, became involved in the mechanisation process for the new manufacturing mills being established in Yorkshire and Lancashire; bear in mind that clockmakers (Quaker and otherwise) were just about the only people with an understanding of practical applied mechanics, capable of cutting wheels and making running gear for the new manufacturers, during the early pioneering days. What we do know is that the Hargreaves family of Settle certainly provided timekeepers for the new mills – Langcliffe Cotton Mill in 1785 is one example.

However, it is the son of German immigrants living in Epworth in Lincolnshire who made one of the most significant technological discoveries of the 18th century. Benjamin Huntsman, a Quaker clockmaker working in Doncaster during the 1740's, invented the crucible steel manufacturing process that made Sheffield steel world famous. After moving to Sheffield he left the clockmaking craft to capitalise on his new invention, setting up in business as a Sheffield steelmaker in 1751 - that company name survives to this day.

Image 12: A fine quality longcase arch dial dating from c.1730 by Benjamin Huntsman of Doncaster, made during his earlier years at Doncaster. Image courtesy of Sworders Auctioneers.

Another example of a Quaker clockmaker with an entrepreneurial spirit taking to manufacturing, albeit in the wrong place was Joseph Oxley of

Fakenham, another Lincolnshire born clockmaker, who set up in business manufacturing worsted in Norwich during the 1750's, some distance from the more centralised urban industrialisation about to take place in the West Riding of Yorkshire. Two Manchester Quaker clockmakers with interests in the latest scientific ideas of the day, more often associated with the Lunar Society were father and son – Peter Clare Snr. and Jnr. Peter Clare Snr. came from Hatton, Cheshire where he was a member of the Local Meeting before moving to Deansgate in Manchester, was a clockmaker, inventor and lecturer. He made high quality longcase clocks, turret clocks and smoke jacks, for which he obtained the King's Royal Patent, and gave public lectures about: electricity and lightening, pneumatics and mechanics. He was remembered in a poem published in the Palatine Notebook of 1884, almost 100 years after his death –

> "There is the cottage of Peter
> That cunning old fox
> who kept the sun right
> by the time of his clocks"

He died in 1799, the local Manchester press reported, "…one of the Society of Quakers, a man of intrinsic merit as a mechanic and philosopher."

His son Peter Jnr. was equally famous; as well as producing high quality longcases including musical clocks and regulators, he was a wholesaler of movements to other clockmakers and made watchman's clocks for use in the mills around Manchester and house bell systems for his wealthier clients. Peter was a close friend and executor of Dr. John Dalton - an eye witness describes them out walking.

> "at a slow pace owing to the Doctor's feebleness…Peter Clare was always remarkably neat and well dressed in a suit of black, wearing knee breeches with silver buckles, which showed his fine, well shaped legs, and a broad brimmed hat. His linen was of the purest white, and he presented a clean, happy and cheerful looking face."

Peter was an eminent member of Manchester's scientific community, becoming the secretary of the Literary and Philosophical Society in 1821, Fellow of the Astronomical Society and honorary member of Manchester's Portico Library. He died in 1851 and is buried in the Quaker burial ground at the Mount Street Quaker Meeting House.

Precision Clockmaking

While the majority of Quaker clockmakers were concerned with producing reliable timekeepers for their local domestic customers, in terms of precision timekeeping, two London clock/watchmakers stand out. Both were brought up as Quakers in rural England – the first of course was George Graham, whose deadbeat escapement and mercury compensated pendulum set the standard in precision clocks for the next 100 years or so. The second was the man who spent his early years as a watchmaker employed by Graham making escapements, before setting up in business on his own account – Larcum Kendall, the Charlbury born watchmaker, whose workmanship and skill was unsurpassed in his day. Kendall was apprenticed to John Jeffreys in 1735, a highly regarded London watchmaker who produced work for John Harrison of longitude fame - from the outset Kendall was associated with the best precision clock and watchmakers of the day, so much so that in 1765 he was among those named by the Board of Longitude to whom John Harrison was obliged to reveal this method of construction of his fourth marine timekeeper (H4) - it was Kendall who was entrusted to make an exact copy of H4 in 1766 to accompany Captain James Cook on his voyage to the South Seas in 1772. Kendall's timekeeper known as K1 cost £450 and performed impeccably, enabling Cook to chart New Zealand and the east coast of Australia with such accuracy and detail was far more efficient than the alternative lunar observation method. Kendall went on to make two other marine chronometers (as they became known) of historical importance - K2 costing £200 (which accompanied Captain Bly on the Bounty in 1772) and K3 in 1774 costing £100 (crucially due to Kendall omitting the remontoire to reduce cost) which sailed on Cook's fateful 1776 expedition to the North Pacific. While both timekeepers performed exceedingly well during their service, neither could match K1, they were cheaper simplified versions of his great masterpiece (the copy of Harrison's H4) but no improvement – Kendall was a great watchmaker craftsman but not an innovator.

When he died in 1790 his obituary in "The Gentleman's Magazine" tells us that although Kendall left the Quakers and never dressed in their manner, "they received his body into the bosom of their church, at his death". It also includes this tribute to K1 – "that as a piece of workmanship, whether we consider the truth of handling or exquisite finishing of it, it has never been equalled, and perhaps never may". Today K1 can be seen at the National Maritime Museum at Greenwich where it is exhibited alongside Harrison's H4 timekeeper as one of nation's great treasures.

America

With the arrival of Abel Cottey in Philadelphia, initially in 1682 and then permanently in 1700, followed closely by Peter Stretch from Leek in Staffordshire in 1703, Quaker clockmaking in America became established. Both men were from country clockmaking backgrounds in England and quickly settled down to produce thirty hour and eight-day duration longcase clocks in their familiar English regional styles. Cottey, the older of the two men died in 1711, while Peter Stretch went on to found one of America's most famous (and first) family of clockmakers, gradually evolving a style for the new colonial market quite distinct from English clocks of the period, suggesting that he began sourcing his materials (certainly engraved dials) from local suppliers from quite an early stage – brass foundries had already been established in the colony. Having said that, there was still a strong tendency for some clockmakers to continue importing their materials from England (much to the chagrin of the Clockmakers Company who opposed the export of component parts, as opposed to finished clocks). Although the biggest difference between the early colonial longcase clocks and their English counterparts were the cases, Stretch's principal casemaker was a fellow Quaker emigre from England – John Head from Mildenhall in Suffolk, who supplied him with 42 tall cases between 1722 and 1742, typically costing between three of four pounds.

There was certainly a strong demand for Peter Stretch's clocks. Philadelphia by the beginning of the 18th century was rapidly developing into a great centre of regional trade with a well-established civic community. This community aspired to a prosperous colonial life, and were eager to furnish their new elegant town houses with the latest luxury goods of the day, which Peter Stretch could provide, selling his clocks to the merchant classes, politicians and prominent citizens. He became a member of the Common Council of Philadelphia in 1708, and was entrusted to make the precious metal weights and scales for the town's tradesmen, so essential in a city of immigrants using all manner of silver coinage in their daily transactions. He trained his three sons William, Thomas and Daniel and his grandson Isaac as clockmakers, and their output ranged from the early 30 hour and 8 day clocks of Peter to the later more complicated musical clocks of William.

Peter Stretch died in 1746, having become a wealthy man, investing his profits in property and land in Philadelphia. His address on the south-west corner of Second and Chestnut Streets became known as Stretch's corner. He was buried in the Friend's burial ground at 4th and Arch Streets.

While the Stretch family were prospering in Philadelphia, another Quaker family of clockmakers, the Chandlee's were thriving in Maryland. Benjamin

Chandlee Snr., born in 1685, came from County Kildare in Ireland and was apprentice to Abel Cottey in Philadelphia, marrying his master's daughter Sarah in 1710. He trained his son Benjamin Jnr, before moving to Wilmington in 1741. Benjamin Jnr. set up his clockmaking business in Nottingham, Maryland, then each of his three sons – Ellis, Isaac and Goldsmith continued the family tradition into the 19th century.

At Burlington New Jersey, a predominantly Quaker run township during the 18th century, several generations of the Hollinshead family were clockmakers. They were Quakers until Joseph Hollinshead Snr. (a second-generation clockmaker) was disowned for 'marrying out', however it appears they remained close to the ideals they had been brought up in. It was Joseph Hollinshead Jnr. who is remembered today for training America's first African American clockmaker – Peter Hill of Burlington, born in 1767 the son of one of the slaves working on the Hollinshead family estate. Peter Hill was apprenticed to Joseph Hollinshead Jnr. aged 14, then employed as a paid journeyman, eventually being freed from slavery c1794. Peter Hill set up in business on his own account around this date in premises almost opposite the Friends Meeting House in Burlington, marrying Tina Lewis in 1795 (the Acting Committee of the New Jersey Abolition Society reported Peter Hill could accomplish his own purchase and that of his wife). They moved to nearby Mount Holly, another Quaker settlement in 1814 and was buried in the Quaker burial ground at Burlington. At a time when it was not easy for an African American to be an independent trader, (despite the help he received among the Quaker community) Peter Hill was well regarded as a clockmaker and built a successful business, today one of his 8 day tallcase clocks is part of the Smithsonian collection.

Image 13: An superb example of a Thomas Wagstaffe 8 day clock movement bought in London from the clockmaker by a visiting American Quaker, who then had an American Chippendale tall case made for it by Francis Gottier. Image Courtesy of Bernard & S. Dean Levy, Inc., New York.

In contrast to the 8 day and 30-hour duration tallcases that formed the "stock in trade" output of most clockmakers during the 18th century, a Quaker clockmaker from Buckingham, Bucks County, Pennsylvania was working at a much greater level of complexity. Joseph Ellicott, of Devonshire stock like Abel Cottey became one of America's greatest clockmakers. Born in 1732 he was a mathematical and mechanical genius, who as a young man showed his early exceptional promise as a designer of mill machinery in Pennsylvania and Maryland. His great masterpiece (no.32 of his output) is one of the most complex year- going astronomical clocks ever made. It is a four-dial clock showing the usual seconds, minutes, hours and date - it also displays the phases of the moon, the year, high tide, and there is a musical carrillion, an automaton and an orrery. He trained his son Andrew Ellicott as a clockmaker, and Andrew eventually turned to surveying, becoming the Surveyor General of the United States in 1792.

No account of American Quaker clockmaking could ignore the cross Atlantic trade with the mother country – the most eminent London clockmaker who engaged in this trade was Thomas Wagstaffe, a Quaker originating from North Oxfordshire, working in Gracechurch Street. His reputation for first class work and his location close to the London Yearly Meeting ensured good business with visiting American Quakers attending the Yearly Meeting during the second half of the 18th century; irrespective of the War of Independence, many dissenters and men of science & industry sympathised with the colonists rather than the English establishment, in some respects it was 'business as usual'. Wagstaffe's standing among his American customers certainly transcended the war, not only supplying clocks and watches but also tools, weights and scales, plate and jewellery; he was highly regarded and a good friend to the Pennsylvania Quakers, presenting a large gallery wall clock to the Pennsylvania Hospital in 1764 which is still reliably ticking away today. Thomas Wagstaffe is also well known for his book 'Piety Promoted', an account of the lives of some notable early Quakers published in the 1750's. He retired to Stockwell in Surrey and then finally to his native North Oxfordshire in 1802 where he died.

The 19th Century

As the 18th century entered its last quarter it seems clear that unlike a century earlier, dissenting men of mechanical nature were being drawn to other forms of Protestantism outside the established church, particularly Methodism. While Wesley (though still a vicar in the Church of England) was preaching, and drawing crowds across England, Quakerism appeared inward looking and retrospective, lacking the evangelical zeal of the 17th century pioneers in sharp contrast to Wesley and his followers. This state of affairs did not go unnoticed by the London Quaker clockmaker Thomas Wagstaffe who wrote to the North Oxfordshire circuit Meetings warning of the dangers of Quaker religious 'drowsiness' and languor, this combined with the strict application of disownment for 'marrying out' had a distinct negative effect.

Nevertheless, here at least, the Quaker clockmaking tradition and network remained robust until the end of provincial clockmaking in England. Like so many other clockmakers in the 19th century they had to adapt to competition from cheap foreign imports. Reliable and far less costly clocks and watches from the USA and Europe forced many English clockmakers to diversify – from makers to retailers and purveyors of jewellery and plate. The Wells family from Shipston on Stour and especially the Simms family from Chipping Norton are good examples of Quaker clockmakers coping with change. From the 1770's they had been used to buying in ready painted dials from the dial manufacturers in Birmingham for fixing to their own movements. (Cast iron painted dials were first produced by the firm of Osborn and Wilson in 1770, were seen as a great advantage over brass faces, often subject to tarnishing, the clear white dials - one of the first products of the industrial revolution to affect clockmaking had more or less replaced the brass face by the 1780's). By the early 1830's and 1840's their stock would have comprised of mercury barometers, pocket watches, fusee wall clocks and longcases (still popular among rural population) and silver jewellery mostly from the larger manufacturing bases of London and Birmingham until by the second half of the 19th century the majority of their stock of clocks would be foreign imports.

It was much the same story in that other distinctive centre of Quaker clockmaking in the north west of England, although by now there was just one Quaker family clockmaking business left – the Simpsons of Wigton. Here by the 1840's, they too had diversified somewhat more dramatically, the last two brothers Stephen and Isaac Simpson were both engaged in manufacturing machinery - Stephen made gas meters at Mansfield in Nottinghamshire and Isaac patented a machine to make gold thread.

Elsewhere the story was much the same, as the clockmaking craft shrank, so did the Quaker involvement. Among the dwindling number of clockmakers (as opposed to watchmakers, retailers and repairers) there remained a small number of highly skilled craftsmen, mostly based in London and few other major centres, who were engaged in making high quality precision spring clocks for a discerning customer base. The Pace family, Quakers from London and Bury St Edmunds fit into this select group in the person of John Pace of Bury St Edmunds in Suffolk, clerk of the Bury Monthly Meeting from 1827 to 1832. He was a noted skeleton clockmaker who made a number of exhibition quality timepieces including a three-year duration skeleton clock that he exhibited at the Great Exhibition of 1851, but this was very much the exception rather than the rule, by the 1870's or so the craft of an individual clockmaker actually making a clock from scratch had all but gone.

Image 14: A 19th Century 8-day skeleton clock by John Pace of Bury St. Edmonds c.1840, made for Robert Ladd of Cambridge (who may have been the retailer.) Image courtesy of Campbell & Archard.

Over a period of 200 years, when English clockmaking was pre-eminent and thousands of clockmakers plied their craft up and down the country, the Quakers could probably be counted in their hundreds, had an impact far outweighed their numbers.

The appendix lists some, but by no means all, Quaker clockmakers.

Appendix

Joseph Atkins	Chipping Norton	Late 18th century early 19th century son of William Atkins. Member of Chipping Norton Preparative Meeting.
William Atkins	Chipping Norton	18th century. Born at Brailes. Trained in London. Moved to Chipping Norton. A member of the Chipping Norton Preparative Meeting. Apprentices: His son Joseph Atkins & Richard Coles of Buckingham.
Thomas Bagley	London	Mid 17th century lantern clock maker. Appeared before Surrey Quarter Session on 27 July 1662 for "unlawfully departing from their several habitations and assembling themselves together under pretence of journey in a regular workshop", and later required to appear and "answer for a Quaker".
Benjamin Bagnall Snr.	Boston USA	From Staffordshire, arrived in Boston C.1772. Died 1773.
Benjamin Bagnall jnr.	Boston USA	son of Benjamin Bagnall Snr.
John Bagnall	West Bromwich then Walsall	Late 18th century
Samuel Bagnall 3	Boston USA	son of Benjamin Bagnall jnr.
Thomas Baker	Blandford, Dorset	Late 17th century early 18th century. Represented Purbeck Quaker Meeting between 1680-1715. 8-day longcase known.

Hilkiah Bedford	London	Born 1632 at Sibsey Lincolnshire. Apprentice to John Thompson London mathematical instrument maker. Became a free brother of the Clockmakers Company in Feb 1667. Longcase, spring and lantern clocks (one signed Hilkiah Bedford in Fleete Streete"). Died May 1689.
Thomas Bevan	Marlborough	Early 18th century from London. Member of Westminster M.M.
Isaac Bispham	unknown	Trained by Isaac Hadwen Snr. in 1727. Married Hadwen's daughter Eleanor
James Blancher	Attleborough, Norfolk	Born 1724. Married a Quaker. Died 1793. Obituary refers to letters in the Royal Society's Philosophical Transactions.
James Bolt	London	Early 18th century
William Bower	Chesterfield	Early 19th century
John Bradshaw	Manchester	Born 1765. Worked in Common Street then Deansgate. Friend of Dr. John Dalton. Died 1832.
William Brewer	Philadelphia	Early 19th century listed as residing at Friends Alms House
Robert Brownless	Staindrop	c.1710. Probably app, to John Ogden of Askrigg Early clocks with religious or morbid verse dials.
Ezekiel Bullock	Lurgan Co. Armagh	b.1650 working 1680's-1714. Lantern and Longcase clocks.
George Canby	Selby	b.c.1634. London trained. Lantern clocks known.
Daniel Catlin Snr	Kings Lynn	Early 18th century from Godmanchester Huntingdonshire. Maker of good quality longcase and bracket clocks. Founder of family clock and watchmaking business in King's from 17th century to 20th century.
Daniel Catlin 2	Kings Lyn	Son of Daniel Catlin Snr. b.1738 d.1812
Daniel Catlin 3	Kings Lyn	Late 18th century. Son of Daniel Catlin 2. B.1771 d.1818 (thought to have been a Quaker).
Elizabeth Caitlin	Kings Lyn	Late 18th century. Sister to Daniel Catlin 3. B1783. m. John Burlington 1819.

Jonathan Chambers	Shefford	Probably London trained, working in Shefford by 1665. Maker of Lantern and longcase clocks. Died 1693 and buried in the Quakers burial ground on his property.
Benjamin Chandlee Snr.	Philadelphia	b.1685 Kilmore, Co. Kildare. Ireland. app. To Abel Cottey in Philadelphia. m.Sarah Cottey (Abel's daughter) in 1710. Moved to Wilmington in 1741. Died 1745. Longcase clocks.
Benjamin Chandlee Jnr.	Nottingham. Maryland	1723-1791 Trained by his father Benjamin in Philadelphia
Ellis Chandlee	Nottingham. Maryland	1755-1816 son of Benjamin Jnr. In partnership with brother Isaac.
Goldsmith Chandlee	Nottingham. Maryland	b.18.8 1751 son of Benjamin Jnr. Moved to Winchester Virginia in 1783. Clockmaker and instrument maker.
Isaac Chandlee	Nottingham. Maryland	1760-1830's son of Benjamin Jnr. In partnership with brother Ellis.
Peter Clare Snr.	Manchester	Born at Hatton, Cheshire. Recorded in Hatton Meeting register 14.12.1729. Moved to Deansgate Manchester. Made Acton St. Mary Church Clock in 1788. Public lecturer in Electricity, lightening, pneumatics and mechanics. Member of Hardshaw Q.M. Died 30.07.1799.
Peter Clare Jnr.	Manchester	Son of Peter Clare Snr. 6.14.4. 1781 registered in Hardshaw MM. Eminent clockmaker. Smokejack maker and house bell hanger. Worked at 50. Quay Street. Honorary member of the Literary and Philosophical Society – Secretary in 1821. Fellow of the Astronomical Society. Honour member of Manchester's Portico Library. Maker of Longcase clocks inc. musical, Watchmans clocks. Clock movements for wholesale. Regulator clocks House Bell Systems and Smoke Jacks. Died 24.11.1851. buried in Mount Street Quaker burial ground.
Samuel Clare	Hatton. Cheshire	18th century Brother to Peter Clare Snr. and Thomas Clare.
Thomas Clare	Hatton. Cheshire	18th century Brother to Peter Clare Snr. and Samuel Clare.

John Clark	Sudbury	18th century.
William Clark	Kendal	18th century Apprentice to Isaac Hadwen & Sedbergh.
Richard Coles Snr.	Buckingham	Born in Buckingham 20.6.1757. App. To William Atkins at Chipping Norton 1771. Moved to Buckingham 1784. Father to Richard Coles Jnr.
Richard Coles Jnr.	Buckingham	b.c. 1792 son of Richard Coles Snr. Clerk of Buckingham M.M from 1851. Died 30.11.1853.
John Cook	Manchester	18th century. Death recorded at Hardshaw QM.
James Cooper	Manchester	Late 18th century inc. by virtue he was briefly in partnership with John Bradshaw of Manchester.
John Cooper	Warrington	Late 17th century working at 'at the sign of the Swan at Boughton' Chester in 1698. His illegitimate son James was baptised – presumably disowned, then moved to Warrington.
Abel Cottey	Crediton, Devon & Philadelphia	Pioneer American clockmaker. Born c. 1655. Sailed with William Penn aboard the 'Welcome' to Philadelphia in 1682. Returned to Devon in 1695 then back to Philadelphia in 1700. Lantern clocks signed from Crediton. Then known as a maker of tallcase clocks in Philadephia. Trained Benjamin Chandlee, who later married Cottey's daughter Sarah. Died in 1711, his inventory witnessed by Peter Stretch of Philadelphia.
John Cutte	Taunton	Disowned at Somerset Quarterly Meeting 26.9.1695.
Arthur Davies	Westleigh. Devon	Working at Westleigh between 1685-1700 then Tiverton. Described in documents referring to Quaker land at Cullumpton as "of Cullumpton" from 1708 to 1712, then Kentisbeare in 1723. Made Lantern clocks and musical posted movement thirty hour clocks.

John Davis	London	Born c.1671 App. To Daniel Quare in 1685. He took the following apprentices of his own who may have been Quakers- John Hoddle 1697 John Cooke 1700 (from Newport Pagnell) Francis Britten 1702 (from Newport Pagnell) Richard Scroope 1709.
Samuel Davis	London	Born c. 1626 app. To William Selwood 1641. Probably not a Quaker (his children were baptised) but included for his close ties to Quaker clockmakers. As beadle (appointed 1674) was responsible for placing apprentices with Quaker clockmakers. Died ante 1698. Longcase and lantern clocks known.
William Debenham	Sudbury	19th century clockmaker.
Thomas Elems (Elms)	Wareham	Late 17 century clockmaker who then moved to Dorchester Represented Purbeck Meeting in 1692 then Dorchester Meeting between 1693-1704. Will dated 1. October 1706.
Thomas Eayre	Kettering	1691-1758. Ingenious country clockmaker, chimes maker, bell founder, surveyor and cartographer. Cast bells for St. Botolph's Boston Lincs. (Boston Stump). Birth registered at Kettering Quaker Meeting but later left the Society of Friends.
Joseph Eayre	St Neots	Son of Thomas Eayre. Ingenious provincial clockmaker who made equation of time clocks. Probably did not attend Quaker Meeting's beyond childhood.
Andrew Ellicott	Buckingham. Bucks County. Pennsylvania	Joseph Ellicott's eldest son b.24.1.1754. Trained as a clockmaker, became an instrument maker and eminent surveyor. Appointed by President George Washington as principal surveyor for the boundary lines for the new capital Washington DC. Appointed Surveyor General of the United States in 1792. Died 28.8.1820.

Joseph Ellicott	Philadelphia	One of America's greatest clockmaker's he was a mathematical and mechanical genius. Born 1732 at Buckingham. Buck County. Pennsylvania. Son of Andrew and Ann Ellicott (Andrew Ellicott came from Cullumpton Devon). Trained by Samuel Bleaker repairing old grist mills. Married Judith Bleaker (Samuel's daughter) in 1753. Visited England in 1767 to claim his legacy from his grandfather, keeping a journal of the trip. Moved to Maryland in 1774. Maker of one of the most complicated clocks ever made (No.32 of his output). A year, musical, moon phase, automaton, orrery, four dial longcase clock.
Ezra Enoch	Sibford Gower	Born 16.7.1799 Sibford Gower. Died 11.4.1860. Buried in Sibford Gower Quaker burial ground. One of the last North Oxfordshire Quaker clockmakers. Longcases recorded.
Thomas Etherington Snr.	York	Watchmaker made free in York in 1684. Died 1728. Lantern clock known.
Thomas Etherington Jnr.	York	Watchmaker. Son of Thomas Etherington Snr. died 1693
William Everleigh	Beominster	Late 18th century clockmaker, ironmonger, cutler, locksmith brazier, tinman, toolmaker and finisher of bath and pantheon bells, who became a Quaker representing Bridport Meeting in 1778. Probably disowned by 1798 when he served as a corporal in the corps of infantry.
John Fardon Snr.	Deddington	Founder of the Fardon family dynasty of North Oxfordshire Quaker clockmakers. Born 13.2.1700 at North Newington. Trained by Thomas Gilkes Snr. at Sibford Gower. Father of John Fardon 2. Died in 1744. Maker of hoop and spike clocks in the North Oxfordshire Quaker tradition.

John Fardon 2	Deddington	Son of John Snr. born at Deddington 11.7.1736. Apprentice to John May of Witney then London. Returned to Deddington c.1756. Disowned in 1758. Father to Thomas Fardon 1 and John Fardon 3. Died 6.12.1786 and buried in Adderbury Quaker burial ground despite being disowned.
John Fardon 3	Deddington	Son of John Fardon 2. Born 1758 a Quaker, but baptised into the Church of England in 1781 prior to his marriage. In partnership with his brother Thomas at Deddington until his death by suicide in 1801.
Thomas Fardon 1	Deddington	The son of John Fardon 2, born 1757 a Quaker, but baptised into the Church of England in 1777 prior to marrying out. Re-admitted to the Adderbury Meeting in 1810, widowed then remarried at Deddington parish church in 1814 and disowned. Received back into Adderbury Meeting with his wife Lydia in 1823. Left the Society of Friends again after Lydia's death, eventually became a church warden at Deddington. Died 6.12.1838 and buried in Deddington churchyard.
Benjamin Ferris	Philadelphia then Wilmington	Born 1780 at Wilmington. Delaware. Apprentice to Thomas Parker of Philadelphia in 1794. Freed then worked in Philadelphia until 1813 then returned to Wilmington. Died 1867.
John Foster	London	Born 1666. Apprentice to Daniel Quare 1680, free c.1689/90. His own apprentices were – Jacob Foster in 1691 and Edward Jagger in 1694.
Samuel Frotheringham	Holbeach	18th century. Died 1745

John Fry	Sutton Benger	An important Quaker and clerk to the London Yearly Meeting in 1746, 1751 and 1756. Born in 1701, apprenticed in London and moved to Knaresborough then settled at Sutton Benger in 1726. A leading member of Chippenham Meeting. Traded with other Quaker clockmakers including the Hadwen's of Liverpool and the Gilkes family in North Oxfordshire. His son Joseph Fry founded J.S. Fry & Sons the famous chocolate firm. John Fry died at Melksham in 1755 "an eminent preacher among the people call'd Quakers, very deservedly and extensively lamented." Sold North Oxfordshire hoop and spike clocks.
George Gailor (Golor)	Philadelphia	Apprentice/Journeyman to Peter Stretch in Philadelphia. Made at least 23 clocks signed Peter Stretch. Died intestate in Philadelphia in 1759.
Benjamin Gilkes	Devizes	Born 8.11.1783. Son of Richard Gilkes of Devizes. Moved to Nailsworth c.1808 where in 1810 he is recorded as a Schoolmaster. Died 20.1.1860.
John Gilkes	Shipston on Stour	Born 1707 Son of Thomas Gilkes Snr. of Sibford Gower. Moved to Shipston 1737. Trained his son Thomas Gilkes and fellow apprentices – John Bretell 1752, Thomas Hutchings 1761. Represented Shipston Meeting on numerous occasions at the Quarterly Meeting. Died c.1790. Maker of hoop and spike clocks in the North Oxfordshire tradition for wholesale and retail.
John Gilkes	Sibford Gower	Born 21.1.1748 the son of Thomas Gilkes 2 of Sibford Gower. Apprentice to his father 7 Sept,1764. Died ante 1773
John Gilkes	Chipping Norton	Born c.1775 the son of Thomas Gilkes of Shipston, apprentice to John Wells of Shipston 1789. Moved to Chipping Norton 10.6.1799. A member and then trustee of Chipping Norton QMH in 1809.

Richard Gilkes	Adderbury	Born 18.1.1715 the youngest son of Thomas Gilkes Snr. of Sibford. Moved to Adderbury c.1744 to become the most famous of the North Oxfordshire Quaker Clockmakers. Apprentices – Richard Tyler 1747, John Millard 1752, William Harris 1755, Matthias Padbury 1764, Joseph Soden 1766, Thomas Eaton 1768, Joseph Williams 1778, Charles Saunders 1780, Richard Gilkes (great nephew) 1780. A member of Adderbury Meeting, represented Banbury MM. at the London Yearly Meeting in 1753. He died at 14.2.1787 and was buried in Adderbury Quaker burial ground. The most prolific maker of hoop and spike clocks in the North Oxfordshire tradition.
Richard Gilkes	Devizes	Born 15.12.1745 the second son of Thomas Gilkes 2 of Sibford. Moved to Devizes and became a leading member of that Meeting. Father of Benjamin Gilkes of Devizes. Died 1822.
Richard Gilkes	Sibford Gower	Born 19.6.1767 the son of Thomas Gilkes 3 of Charlbury. Apprentice to Richard Gilkes of Adderbury in 1780. Returned to Sibford where he died 1.2.1855 and is buried in Sibford Quaker burial ground albeit he was no longer a member of the Religious Society of Friends.
Thomas Gilkes Snr.	Sibford Gower	Born c.1675 at Sibford Gower. Founder of Gilkes family clockmaking dynasty in North Oxfordshire. Trained each of his three sons – Thomas 2., John and Richard and John Fardon of Deddington as clockmakers. He was an important Quaker 'minister' within the Banbury division, representing them at the London Yearly Meeting six times between 1725 and 1737. Died in 1757, his testimonial is recorded at Sibford MM 4.4.1757. Maker of hoop and spike clocks in North Oxfordshire Quaker tradition.

Thomas Gilkes 2	Sibford. Gower	Born 8.1.1704 the son of Thomas Gilkes Snr. of Sibford. Trained his 3 sons Thomas 3, Richard and John and William Green of Milton as clockmakers. Membership of Sibford PM_ eventually becoming clerk. Represented the Banbury division at the London Yearly Meeting in 1751 and 1764. Died in 1772 and buried in Sibford Quaker burial ground 4.10.1772. Maker of hoop and spike clocks in North Oxfordshire Quaker tradition.
Thomas Gilkes	Charlbury	Born 25.5.1736 the son of Thomas Gilkes 2 of Sibford. Moved to Charlbury in 1764. Took John Wells of Shipston as apprentice in 1766. Represented Charlbury at the Quarterly Meetings between 1770-1778. Died 14.2.1779. Maker of hoop and spike clocks in North Oxfordshire Quaker tradition.
Thomas Gilkes	Shipston	Born c.1740's the son of John Gilkes of Shipston and trained by him. He took his own apprentice William Hackall in 1779. Retired to Adderbury in 1786. Died c.1798.

George Graham	London	The most eminent clockmaker of his time. Born c.1673 in Kirklington of Irthington parish Cumberland the son of George Graham, a farmer who became a Quaker after George's birth. Apprentice to Henry Aske of London in 1688. Worked for Thomas Tompion whose niece Elizabeth he married in 1704. In partnership with Tompion until Tompion died in 1713, then took over the business at the Dial and Three Crowns from is old master. He became a Warden of the Clockmakers Company and then Master in 1722. He was a fellow of the Royal Society and is credited with several important inventions - the deadbeat escapement (1715), the mercury pendulum (1726) and perfected the cylinder escapement (1726). As well as the high-quality clocks and watches he was also an important scientific instrument maker. He died in 1751 and is buried in Westminster Abbey. There is no evidence that he remained a Quaker after moving to London.
William Graham	London	Born 1692 the nephew of George Graham. Worked in Lombard Street. Married Anne Bedford daughter of Thomas Bedford. Moved to St. Michael's Cornhill and then to Philadelphia. Died 1759.
Jacob Goodger	Manchester	Late 18th century. Member of Hardeshaw Quaker Meeting
John Greaves	Newcastle	Born c.1725 the eldest son of Richard Greaves. Working in Newcastle by 1746. Premises on the Quayside c.1780-1794. Ceased to be a Quaker during adulthood. Died 1794.
Peter Greaves	Newcastle	Son of Richard Greaves. Working in Newcastle 1747-1755.
Richard Greaves	Newcastle	From Halifax, was working in Newcastle c.1730. His sons John, William & Peter Greaves all became clockmakers in Newcastle. Died 1741.

Thomas Greaves	Newcastle	Born 1763 the son of William Greaves who worked at 52 Quayside. Owned land which later became a Quaker burial ground known locally as "The Quicks Burying Plas in Sidgatt." Died c.1830.
William Greaves	Newcastle	Born 1733 the son of Richard Greaves. Worked at the foot of Plummer Chare Quayside in 1778. A prosperous clockmaker whose dials were engraved by the renowned firm of Bielby & Bewick between 1772 and 1775.
James Green	Gloucester	18th century married at Tewkesbury Q.M.H. in 1721. Longcase clocks known.
William Green	Milton under Wychwood	Born Tadmarton near Banbury 1722. Apprentice to Thomas Gilkes of Sibford. Moved to Milton under Wychwood 1752. Member of Milton P.M. and Witney MM. Died c.1802. A prolific maker of North Oxfordshire hoop and spike clocks.
John Grundy	Manchester	Apprentice to Peter Clare Snr. 1761
William Gunn	Wallingford	Married Mary Fuller at Shutford MH on 19.5.1714. Apprentices - Robert Buller (Banbury) 19.3.1719 and Richard Fowler from Shutford in 1724. Maker of 30 hour and 8 day clocks.
Isaac Hadwen Snr.	Sedbergh & Kendal	Born at Burton – in – Kendal, Westmorland in 1687. Apprentice to John Ogden of Askrigg, Wensleydale from 1701-1708. Worked at Sedburgh from c.1710 producing clocks in the north western Quaker tradition with verse engraved dials. Married Sarah Moore the daughter of Dr John Moore of Eddroth Hall, Clapham, a prosperous local Quaker. Moved to Kendal 1722 then to Over Gayle, Tunstal, Lancashire. Trained his son Isaac Bispham 1727. Thomas Fawcett 1727, William Clark 1730 and Fryer Rider 1733. Made two trips to America firstly 1719 and then again in 1737 where he died of fever at Chester, Delaware on 29.7.1737.

Isaac Hadwen 2	Liverpool	Born 1723 at Kendal, the son of Isaac Snr. Moved to Liverpool c.1737. Made 8 day clocks for retail and wholesale. Died 1767.
Isaac Hadwen 3	Liverpool	Son of Isaac 2. Retired from clockmaking in 1799 to spend the rest of his life campaigning against slavery.
Joseph Hadwen	Liverpool	Born 1725 at Liverpool, the son of Isaac 2. Left clockmaking to go into the grocery and drapery trade. Died 1807.
Sarah Hadwen	Liverpool	Widow of Isaac Hadwen Snr. Moved to Liverpool and managed business until son Isaac 2 was able to take over. Died in 1761.
Joseph Hall	Alston	Born 1767 moved to Alston c.1800. Later ran the Quaker School at Wigton from c.1826. Known for two complicated long duration clocks.
William Hargreaves	Settle	Born c.1705. Trained sons William Jnr. & Thomas as clockmakers at Settle. All three were prolific makers of 30-hour longcase clocks. Died 1779.
William Hargreaves Jnr.	Settle	Born c.1734 died 1809
Thomas Hargreaves	Settle	Born 1741 died 1813
Thomas Harris	Deddington	Born 1732 at Sibford Gower. Married Mary Fardon from North Newington at Banbury QMH in 1762. Son William became a clockmaker at Witney. Member of Adderbury P.M. & Banbury MM. Clocks signed at North Newton (Newington) Bloxham and Deddington. Retired to Milton (a hamlet of Adderbury). Died 1.8.1797 and buried in Adderbury Quakers burial ground. Made North Oxfordshire Quaker hoop and spike clocks.
William Harris	Witney	Born c.1760's son of Thomas Harris of Deddington. Moved to Witney 1793. Disowned by Witney MM. on 8.9.1794 for marrying outside the Society of Friends.

William Harrison	Charlbury	Said by Beeson "Clockmaking in Oxfordshire" to be a Quaker. Mid 18th century.
Jeremiah Henderson	Scarborough	Born 1718 the son of Robert Henderson.
Robert Henderson	Scarborough	Born in 1678 at Oughterby near Wigton Cumberland. Moved to Scarborough in 1708. Prolific maker of 8 day and 30 hour clocks, some early examples with blank dial corners in the Quaker style of the north west of England. Apprentices Joseph Oxley of Brigg c.1730. Richard Ward 1742. Robert Henderson died 1756.
Stephen Horseman	London	Born Brayton, Yorkshire c.1688, the son of Stephen Horseman a wheelwright. Apprentice to Daniel Quare of London 1702. Freed c.1709. Married Quare's niece Mary Savage in 1712. Went into partnership with Quare c.1721 and took over the business when Quare died in 1724. Went bankrupt in 1730.
Richard How 2	Dorchester	Born 1667. Represented Dorchester Meeting. Father of Richard 3. Apprentice – Ralph Norman (Poole) in 1707. Died 29.10.1714. Maker of distinctive 30-hour longcase clocks with blank dial corners favoured by some early Quaker clockmakers.
Richard How 3	Dorchester	Succeeded his father in 1715. Appears to have been disowned for marrying outside the Society of Friends.
Benjamin Huntsman	Doncaster	Born 1704 at Epworth, Lincolnshire of German parents. Famous as the inventer of crucible steel. Worked in Doncaster from c.1725 until 1742. Moved to Handsworth, Sheffield 1742 and set up as a steelmaker there in 1751. Died 20.6.1776.

John Ismay	Wigton	Born in 1699 at Thursby. Apprentice to John Ogden at Bowbrigg Hall. Askrigg in 1711. Worked at Oulton near Wigton from c.1718 to c.1737. Died 1755. Made 30 hour clocks in the distinctive early 18th century Quaker style unique to north west England – lantern style movements with blank or religious verse engraved dials. Also, made a brass quadrant.
William Johnston	London	Born c.1677. Inc. in list for being a Daniel Quare apprentice 1690. Free 1702.
Larkum Kendall	London	Famous chronometer maker. Born at Charlbury in 1721. The son of Moses Kendal, a leading member of the Charlbury P.M. and Witney MM. Apprentice to John Jeffreys of London in 1735, then worked for George Graham before setting up in business at 6, Furnival's Inn Court. A member of the panel appointed by the Board of Longitutde in 1765 to whom John Harrison was obliged to reveal the construction of his fourth marine timekeeper - H4. Contracted by the Board of Longitude to make an exact copy of H4. (for £450) which became known as K1 and was delivered to the Board in 1770; after trials at Greenwich it was assigned to Captain Cook for his second voyage to the South Seas aboard HMS Resolution in July 1772; it accompanied Cook on his final voyage in 1776. Kendall made two other marine chronometers known as K2 and K3, K2 was with Captain Bly at the time of the mutiny on board HMS Bounty and K3 was on board the Discovery on Cook's final voyage to the Pacific in 1776. In contrast to his precision watches, a hooded wall clock by Larkum Kendal has also been noted. Kendal died 22.11.1790.
James Kenway	Bridport	Born 1742. Member of Bridport Meeting. Died 1821.

Ann Kirk	Nottingham	Took over her father Joseph Kirk's business. Married out of the Society of Friends and was disowned by Nottingham Meeting on 1.1.1738.
Joseph Kirk	Hardstoft	Born 1673 at Hardstoft, where some clocks are signed. Had moved to Skegby Derbyshire by 7.5.1723 when he took Robert Willis as apprentice, he moved to Nottingham by 29.5.1731 when he took Patrick Cook as apprentice. The local Quaker M.M. minutes include a marriage consent certificate in 1708.
John Knight	Great Coggerhall	Early 19th century
Theodore Lamb	Sibford	Born 6.2.1881 known as the Sibford Hermit, who lived by the road side near Sibford. Much respected 20th century clock and watch repairer. Died 1951 and buried in Sibford Quaker burial ground.
Stephen Levitt 1	Sudbury	Late 17th century "Sudbury Quakers 1655-1953" S.H.G. Fitch. tells us he was listed among Friends imprisoned in the town for their beliefs prior to 1685. Lantern clock maker.
Stephen Levitt 2	Chelmsford	A Quaker clockmaker of this name, aged 45 is recorded in the Middle Row, Chelmsford in 1734. Presumably the son of Stephen Levitt of Sudbury.
Jacob Littlemore	Frodsham	Born 1689 Frodsham, the son of Joseph Littlemore. Working at Frodsham in 1718 when he took William Whitaker apprentice. Married 1713. Leased a quay in 1726 and bankrupt by 1728 and presumably disowned. Moved to Bersham (Wrexham) then Ruoban where he died in 1745, described as a gentleman.
Joseph Littlemore	Frodsham	Born Frodsham c.1650. Lived at Kinsley and became a Quaker. Married Hannah Williamson at Newton QMH in 1687. Moved to Frodsham c.1690 then to Preston on the Hill c.1712. Described as a clockmaker, smith, gunsmith and whitesmith. Died 23.4.1721 and buried in Newton Quakers burial ground. Longcase and lantern clocks known.

John Marshall	London	Born c.1668. First apprentice to Samuel Rasse in 1682 then Daniel Quare. Free 1689. Advertised as a 'watchmaker at Rainbow Coffee House in Cornhill Nr. Birchin Lane' in 1694, then in 1695 as 'watchmaker against the Royal Exchange in Cornhill.' Apprentices – Thomas Stevens 1693. Free 1702, Wasteneys Law 1694, John Hewitt 1694, Ephraim How 1716 (passed over to George Graham). High quality month duration and 8 day longcases known.
Edward May Snr.	Witney	Born 1701 at Milton near Abingdon, the son of Edward May a miller and Quaker minister. The Witney M.M. minute book records he was living at Witney by 13.2.1724. Trained sons John and Edward as clockmakers. Apprentices Benjamin Thorpe 1726, John Lord 1739. Trustee of Milton under Wychwood QMH in 1735.
Edward May Jnr.	Witney Henley on Thames Ampthill	Born 25.9.1732 the second son of Ed May Snr. Moved to premises in the Market Squaer Henley on Thames 1754. Thought to have moved to Ampthill Bedfordshire c.1784 where he died 19.1.1805 and was buried in the Quaker burial ground there.
John May	Witney	Born 5.10.1726 the eldest son of Edward May Jnr. Apprentices – John Fardon 2 (Deddington) 1750, Benjamin Ward 1753, Richard Pocock 1760, also trained his son Thomas May. Long serving member of Witney Meeting (minute book records 1749 - 1794). Died 14.4.1800. Prolific maker of 30 hour longcases. Also, made spit engines and carried out engraving.
Thomas May	Witney	Born 25.2.1750 son of John May of Witney. Moved to Henley on Thames to take over his uncle's clockmaking business in 1784. Thought to have given up clockmaking to become a school teacher in Henley. Died 1820 and was buried in the local Quaker burial ground (Warborough Division).

Mark Metcalfe	Askrigg	Born Askrigg 1693. Thought to have been an apprentice to John Ogden of Askrigg by virtue of his use of blank dial corners in his earliest clocks.
James Mogg	Basingstoke	Late 17th century and early 18th century. Died 1722. Longcases & bracket clocks.
John Nethercott	Long Compton	May have been born a Quaker at Long Compton c.1665. He was baptised into the Church of England as an adult in 1686 prior to marriage. Two sons John Jnr. & William became clockmakers. Died 1735. Produced hoop and spike clocks and 30 hour clocks with ring and zig zag engraved dials in the North Oxfordshire Quakers tradition.
James Norman	Charminster	Born c.1671. His son Ralph became a clockmaker. 30 hour longcases known.
Ralph Norman	Poole	Born 1690 at Charminster, the son of James Norman. Apprentice to Richard How of Dorchester 1705. Moved to Poole c.1714. known for high quality longcase clocks inc. quarter striking examples.
Bernard Ogden	Darlington, Newcastle, Alnwick, Sunderland	Born 1707 at Askrigg the son of John Ogden. Died 1750. Longcase clocks.
John Ogden	Askrigg	Born 1665 the third son of James Ogden Snr. clockmaker of Soyland. Moved to Bowbridge Hall, Bainbridge a hamlet of Askrigg in Wensleydale. Trained sons John Jnr. & Bernard. Apprentices – John Isaac, Isaac Hadwen, John Sanderson, Robert Brownlow and Mark Metcalfe. Moved to Darlington between 1711 and 1715 where he died in 1741. Pioneer of the distinct north west of England Quaker style of 30 hour clocks.
John Ogden Jnr.	Darlington	Born at Askrigg 1704 the son of John Ogden snr.

Thomas Ogden	Halifax	Born at Soyland near Ripponden in 1693 the son of Samuel Ogden Snr. clockmaker. Moved to Halifax by 1740. Apprentices – John Barlow, 1733, William Anderson 1750, John Ellis 1754. Died without issue 1769. An eminent provincial clockmaker. Known to have supplied movements to George Graham of London.
Joseph Oxley	Fakenham Norwich	Born 1715 at Brigg (Lincs). Apprentice to Robert Henderson of Scarborough c.1730. then moved to London to learn watchmaking. Set up in business at Fakenham then moved to Norwich c.1744. Apprentice – Thomas Wilkins 1749. Gave up clockmaking to go into worsted manufacturing at Norwich during the mid 1750's (see a Journal of the Life and Gospel Labours of Joseph Oxley of Norwich. 1837).
Charles Pace	London	Born 1816 the son of Thomas Pace Jnr. In partnership with brother Henry and then took over the premises at 128 Whitechapel High Street. Had given up clockmaking by 1851.
Edmund Pace	London	Born 1813 the son of John Pace at Bury St. Edmunds. Moved to London by 1841 at 21 Thavies Inn Holborn. Had given up clockmaking by 1844 and later set up the Phoenix Match Co. of Pace& Son at Bow Common.
Henry Pace	London	Born 1809 the son of Thomas Pace Jnr. Took over the business at 128 Whitechapel High Street, then in partnership with brother Charles. Moved to Exmouth in 1837. Returned to Clerkenwell in 1842, then moved to West Ham by 1861.
Henry John Pace	Bury St. Edmunds	1814-1842 son of John Pace (the skeleton clock maker)
Henry John Pace Jnr.	Ottowa	Son of Henry Pace. Moved to Canada c.1862 then to St. Paul Minnesota c.1880. Died 1899 in Lethbridge. Northern Territories (Alberta)

John Pace	London	Born 1748 worked c.1774-1794 at 19 Broad Street Ratcliffe then 19 Cock Hill Ratcliffe. Elder Brother of Thomas Pace Snr.
John Pace	Bury St. Edmunds	Son of Quaker Thomas Pace Snr. Active 1804-1857. Moved from London to 19 Abbeygate Street Bury St. Edmunds then to Chelmsford in 1857. Sons - Edmund and Henry became clockmakers. A famous 19th century maker of high quality skeleton clocks.
Thomas Pace Snr.	London	Born 1752. Worked at 128 Whitechapel High Street. Sons Thomas Jnr. And John became clockmakers. Retired to Chelmsford. Died 1819 & buried at Whitechapel.
Thomas Pace Jnr.	London	Born 1777 son of Thomas Pace Snr. Worked at 128 Whitechapel High Street. Trained sons Henry & Charles. Died 1829.
Matthias Padbury	Burford	Born 3.8.1751 at Sibford Gower. Apprentice to Richard Gilkes of Adderbury 1764. Set up in business in Burford High Street 1773. Married first wife Sarah at Milton under Wychwood QMH in 1774. Became a prosperous business man owning a paper mill in the town. Member of Burford P.M. and Witney M.M. Died c.1806. Maker of hoop and spike clocks in the North Oxfordshire Quaker tradition.
John Paine	Banbury Hook Norton	Born 1801 at Milton in the parish of Adderbury. In business on Parsons Street Banbury then moved to Hook Norton in 1826. Disowned on 1.1.1851 for embezzling Quaker funds.
Samuel Parrott	Killington (Westmorland)	Born c.1719 died 1783. Longcase clocks.
Isaac Pearson	Burlington New Jersey	1685-1749. Clockmaker & Goldsmith. His daughter Sarah married his apprentice Joseph Hall.

Daniel Quare	London	One of the most famous of all clockmakers, born c.1647 in Somerset. Unwilling to swear an oath he became a free Brother in the Clockmaker Company in 1671. He worked from premises in St. Martin's Le Grand in the 1670's by 1681 he was at Allhallow Lombard Street, then at the sign of the king's Arms in Exchange Alley. Apprentices – John Beck 1673, George Heady 1675, Faith Leak 1684, John Foster 1680 Robert Todd 1684, John Davis 1685 John Marshall pre-1689, William Johnson 1690, John Zachary free 1694, John Kirkton 1696, John Nolson free 1697, Stephen Horseman 1701, Richard Vick free 1702, Joseph Appleby 1705, Daniel Quare (son of Robert Quare) 1707. Around 1721 he went into partnership with his former apprentice Stephen Horseman. A prolific maker of longcase and spring (bracket) clocks, some of the very highest quality. Awarded a patent for a portable weather glass (barometer) in 1695. He was a Clockmakers Company Assistant from 1700, Warden from 1705 and Master in 1708. Despite not swearing an oath he was Royal Clockmaker to King. Died 21.3.1724 and was buried in the Quaker burial ground Bunhill Fields.
Benjamin Reeve	Philadelphia	Mid 18th century. Journeyman for Thomas Stretch.
Francis Richardson	Philadelphia	1765-1782 Clockmaker & Goldsmith
John Richardson	Bridlington	c.1690.
Richard Roe	Epperstone Notts.	Born c.1637. Trustee of Long Croft in Oxton QMH. Died 22.3.1720 and buried in Oxton Quaker burial ground. Lantern clocks & Turret clocks.
Emanuel Rowe	Philadelphia	18th century. Apprentice/journeyman for Peter Stretch.

John Sanderson	Wigton	Born 1671 and thought to have been apprentice to John Ogden of Askrigg. Married Elizabeth Pearson a Quaker. Died 1755. Prolific maker of lantern posted 30 hour clocks with verse engraved dials in the unique North Western Quaker tradition.
Jeremiah Sewell	London	Apprentice to Thomas Pace 1786. Worked at Tottenham c.1799.
Thomas Savage Snr.	Clifton Westmoorland	m.1699 sons Thomas Jnr & Jonathan were clockmakers.
Thomas Savage Jnr.	Clifton	Born 1700 died 1731. Longcase clocks.
Jonathan Savage	Clifton	Born 1712. Died after 1745. Longcase clocks.
Benjamin Simms	Witney Chipping Norton	Dates unknown.
Charles Price Simms	Chipping Norton	Born 1820 son of Samuel Simms. Clerk to Chipping Norton P.M. Died 1910.
Daniel Rutter Simms	Chipping Norton	Born 1864 son of Charles Price Simms. Died 1954.
Frederick Simms	Chipping Norton	Born 1816. Died 1894.
John Simms Snr.	Chipping Norton	18th century. Father of John Simms Jnr.
John Simms Jnr.	Chipping Norton	Born 1757. Apprentice Richard Lamb 1794. Died 1823.
Samuel Simms	Chipping Norton	Born c.1784 son of John Simms Jnr. Died 1869.
William Simms	Chipping Norton	Active c.1790.
Daniel Simpson	Carlisle	Son of John Simpson of Wigton. Moved to Workington c.1810. Died 1841.
Edmund Simpson	Preston	Born 1794 son of Stephen Snr.
Isaac Simpson	Chorley & Preston	Born 1800 son of Stephen Snr. Worked at Chorley before moving to Preston. Married outside the Society of Friends and was disowned. Gave up clockmaking and patented a machine for making gold thread. Died 1859.
John Simpson 1	Wigton	In business with brother Joseph c.1758. Died 1796.
John Simpson 2	Wigton	Son of Joseph Simpson of Wigton. Died 1837.

Joseph Simpson	Wigton	In business with brother John c.1758
Stephen Simpson	Kirkby Lonsdale Preston	Born 1752 Gisburn Yorks. Worked at Kirkby Lonsdale then moved to Preston by the the sign of the Tup's Head. Longcase & Turret clockmaker. Died 1821.
Stephen Simpson Jnr.	Preston	Born 1791 son of Stephen Simpson Snr. Took over business in 1822. Moved to Mansfield to manufacture gas meters. Died 1840.
William Simpson	Preston	Born 1781 son & journeyman of Stephen Simpson Snr.
William Smith	Dorchester	Active c.1684-1730. Member of Dorchester Meeting 1677 to 1730.
Jeremy Spurgin	Colchester	Born 1666. Noted maker of longcase clocks. Died 1699.
Francis Stamper	London	Born 1655 at Allhallows near Wigton Cumberland. Apprentice to Samuel Davis London 1675, free 1682. Apprentices: Joshua Penford 1684, Daniel Moore 1689, Joseph Foster 1684, Thomas Hymans 1696. A very prosperous Quaker clockmaker who worked in Lombard Street, with property at Doncaster, Stanford, Tottenhoe, Torpenhow and Allhallows in Cumberland. He owned land in Pennsylvania, mining shares in Cumberland and Lancashire and a half share in the trade of the East India Company held jointly with Daniel Quare. Maker of Longcases, spring (bracket) and lantern clocks. His widow went into partnership with Joshua Wilson. Died 1698 and buried in the Quaker burial ground at Winchmore Hill.
John Stokes	Saffron Walden	From Dunmow (Essex). Working at Saffron Walden c.1660. Apprentice Thomas Pilbrow 1717. Died c.1723.
Batty Storr	York	Born Selby 1710 the son of Marmaduke Storr. Working at York c.1730. Son Isaac became clockmaker. Apprentice Joseph Champney 1745, William Vincent 1751. Died 1793.
Isaac Storr	York	Born 1750. Son of Batty Storr. Worked for Batty Storr. Died 1775.

Jonathan Storr	York	Born 1739 the son of Batty Storr. Moved to London by 1769. Left the Society of Friends. Died 1812 and buried at Acomb near York.
Marmaduke Storr Snr.	Selby	Born 1667 Owstwick, East Riding. Moved to Selby 1691. Also, owned a tannery. Sons Marmaduke Jnr. And Batty Storr became clockmakers. Married the daughter of George Canby an early Quaker clockmaker.
Marmaduke Storr Jnr.	Selby London	Born 1702 at Selby the son of Marmaduke Snr. Said to have been apprentice to Stephen Horseman of London. A partner in Storr & Gibbs of London working c.1741-1750. Died 1750.
Benjamin Stretch	Bristol	Born c.1700 son of Samuel Stretch of Leek. Moved to Bristol c.1723. Apprentice Samuel Stretch 2. Died 1764. Buried Bristol Quaker burial ground. Longcase clocks and watches.
Daniel Stretch	Salem County	Born 1694 at Leek, emigrated to Philadelphia with his father Peter Stretch in 1703. Moved to Salem County in 1714. Died c.1735.
Isaac Stretch	Birmingham	Born 1696 son of Samuel Stretch of Leek. Moved to Birmingham with his father c.1712. Apprentice Walter Sturley 1715. Died at "the Watch out of Doors" 97 High Street. Birmingham.
Isaac Stretch	Philadelphia	Peter Stretch's grandson born 1714, the son of Daniel Stretch. Worked as a journeyman for his uncle Thomas. Disowned in 1751 for enlisting in the militia. Died after 1770.
James Stretch	Birmingham	Son of Samuel Stretch Snr. Worked from c.1735-1770.
John Stretch	Leek Bristol	Born 1668 at Tatton Cheshire, brother of Samuel and Peter Stretch. Moved to Bristol by 1703.
Joseph Stretch	Birmingham	The son of Samuel Stretch. Born c.1691 (after another infant brother of that name died in 1690) Apprentice: John Walker 1717.

Peter Stretch	Leek Philadelphia	Born 1670 Harpers Gate, Horton near Leek, Staffordshire. Worked at Leek with brother Samuel Snr. Emigrated to Philadelphia in 1703 (arrival). His clockmaker sons Daniel (b.1694), Thomas (b.1697) and William (b.1701) were all born in Leek and trained by Peter Stretch in Philadelphia. In business on the corner of Front Street and Chestnut Street which became known as "Peter Stretch's Corner". Apprentices: John Davis and Emmanuel Rose. Peter Stretch made Lantern and longcase clocks at Leek and was a prolific maker of American tallcase clocks in Philadelphia. Became a Philadelphia common councilman in 1708. One of America's most famous clockmakers. Died 1746.
Samuel Stretch Snr.	Leek Wolverhampton Birmingham Bristol	Born 1657 at Tatton Cheshire, elder brother of John and Peter Stretch. Worked in Stockwell Street, Leek. Sons Benjamin and Samuel Jnr. Became clockmakers. Moved to Rotten Row, Wolverhampton 1697 where the building was licenced as a Meeting House. Moved to Birmingham 1712 and then finally to Keysham Bristol by 1714 to join Brother John. Died 1732. Longcase and Lantern clocks.
Samuel Stretch Jnr.	Bristol Philadelphia	Son of Samuel Stretch Snr. Left England in c.1711 to join his uncle Peter Stretch in Philadelphia where he died in 1732.
Thomas Stretch 1	Philadelphia	Born 1697. Leek the son of Peter Stretch. Took over his father's business. Made the turret clock for the State House in 1753. Disowned by Philadelphia M.M. for marrying outside the Society of Friends in 1743. Died 1765. Prolific maker of Tallcase clocks.
Thomas Stretch 2	Philadelphia	Born 1741. Peter Stretch's grandson, trained by his uncle Thomas Stretch in Philadelphia. Moved to Burlington, New Jersey. Disowned by Philadelphia M.M. in 1765 for drinking and neglect of his business. Died 1770.

William Stretch	Philadelphia	Born 1701 Leek. Worked as a journeyman for his father Peter Stretch. Died 1746.
Daniel Tantum	Nottingham Derby	Born c.1690. Apprentice: William Barnard of Newark. Worked at Nottingham from c1714 then moved to Derby c.1741. Disowned by Society of Friends for marrying outside. Longcase and spring (bracket) clocks.
Francis Tantum	Loscoe	Born 1674 Loscoe. Brought up by his Quaker uncle. Appears to have been disowned for marriage outside the Society of Friends. Apprentices: Thomas Norman 1706, James Woolley 1712. Died c.1729. A well-known maker of good quality longcase clocks.
Jonathan Tantum	Derby	Son of Daniel Tantum. Died 1732.
John Terry Snr	York	Thought to have been a Quaker. Worked at York between 1706 until his death in 1757. Trained each of his sons as clockmakers.
John Terry Jnr.	York	Born c.1696 son of John Snr. Died 1783.
Reuben Terry	York	Son of John Terry Snr. Free 1713 and worked in York until at least 1724.
Thomas Terry	York	Born c.1705 son of John Terry Snr. Apprentice to his father 1720. Free 1733.
Robert Todd	London	Born c.1670. Apprentice of Daniel Quare 1684. Working until c.1740.
William Tomlinson	London	Born c.1673. Free 1699. Worked in Miles Lane, then near Royal Exchange then White Hart Court, Gracechurch Street. Apprentices: James Snelling 1703, Jonathan Newton 1708, Deveraux Bowby 1710, Joseph Taylor 1714. Master of Clockmakers Company 1733. The famous Quaker Physician Dr John Fothergill lodged with him in White Hart Court from 1741. taking over the premises in 1747, describing his lodgings as "Tis a watchmaker in Whitehart Court next door to the meeting house".
Edward Thorp	Colchester	Born 1752 son of Thomas Thorp. Moved to Bethnal Green London c.1785. Returned to Colchester c.1786. Died 1831.

Thomas Thorp	Colchester	Born 1717. Made clocks and watches from premises in St. Runwald's parish. Elected overseer of the poor in 1748. Died 1804.
Richard Tyler	Wallingford	Born 1733. Apprentice to Richard Gilkes of Adderbury. Moved to Wallingford 1756. Apprentices Daniel White 1769, Robert Keate 1775, William Panter 1781. Retired to Adderbury. Died 11.6.1800 – buried in Adderbury Quaker burial ground. Longcase clocks.
Thomas Virgo	London	Born c.1660 Thetford. Apprentice to Samuel Davis 1674. Free 1682. Apprentice Robert Baldwin 1682. Died 1685. Lantern clocks.
Thomas Wagstaffe	London	Born 1724 at Banbury. Moved to London. Worked in Gracechurch Street. Famous Quaker clockmaker who traded widely with American Quakers visiting the London Yearly Meeting. Gave gallery clock to Pennsylvania Hospital. Wrote "Piety Promoted" published in the 1750's. Retired to Stockwell Surrey then finally to Chipping Norton in 1802 where he died. Longcase & spring (bracket) clocks inc. automaton bracket clocks.
Richard Wall	Bristol	Free 1631. Clockmaker and goldsmith
John Wells Snr.	Shipston on Stour	Born 1749 at Byfield, Nortants. Apprentice to Thomas Gilkes 3 of Charlbury in 1766. Worked at Sibford Gower. Apprentices: John Gilkes (Chipping Norton) 1789, Thomas Heydon 1794. Member of Armscote and Shipston PM's Trained sons John Jnr. & Thomas. Died 1810. Maker of hoop and spike clocks in the North Oxfordshire Quaker tradition.
John Wells Jnr.	Shipston on Stour Chipping Norton	Born 1787 son of John Wells Snr. In partnership with brother Thomas before moving to Chipping Norton, where he was disowned at Charlbury M.M. for immoral behaviour in 1820. Returned to Shipston in later life & re-admitted to Shipston P.M. Died c.1847.

Thomas Wells	Shipston on Stour	Born 1786 son of John Wells Snr. Took over family business in 1810, then in partnership with brother John. Died 1855.
Joseph Williams	Adderbury	Born Adderbury 1762. Apprentice to Richard Gilkes of Adderbury. Son William became a clockmaker. Died 1835 and buried in Adderbury Quaker burial ground.
William Williams	Adderbury	Born 1793 son of Joseph Williams. Baptised into the Church of England as an adult in 1820. Re-admitted to Adderbury PM in later life. Died 1862 and buried in Adderbury Quaker burial ground. Longcase and fusee wall clocks.
Joseph Williamson	London	Thought to have been a Quaker. Working in Clements Lane. Apprentices: Joseph Grove 1681, Isaac Johnson 16989, Samuel Jenkins 1712 and William Williamson 1717. Master of the Clockmakers Company 1724. Well known for his equation of time clocks and most probably supplied that element to other clockmakers.
Joshua Wilson	London	Born c.1675. Apprentice to William Fuller 1688. Apprentices Benjamin Rouse 1698, Joseph Reckless 1702. In partnership with the widow of Francis Stamper in 1699. Died c.1714. Longcases and lantern clocks.
John Whitfield	Clifton Near Penrith	Born 1706. Worked at Clifton from c.1743 Disowned 1744. Died 1789.
Joseph Wilkinson 1	Wigton	Born 1710. Thought to have been apprentice to John Sanderson of Wigton c.1724. Died 1790.
William Wilkinson	Wigton Penrith	Born 1758, son of Joseph Wilkinson. Moved to Penrith c.1790, finally to Eamont Bridge c.1818. Died 1824.
Joseph Williamson 2	Penrith Eamont Bridge	Born 1788 son of William Wilkinson. Succeeded father of Eamont Bridge before moving to Annan in Scotland. Died 1855.

Bibliography

Bates, K. 1980. *Clockmakers of Northumberland and Durham*. Morpeth: Pendulum.

Beeson, C.F.C. 1989. *Clockmaking in Oxfordshire 1400-1850*. Oxford: University of Oxford Museum of the History of Science.

Beeson, C.F.C. 1971. *English Church Clocks 1280-1850*. Chichester: Phillimore.

Bird, C&Y. 1996. *Norfolk and Norwich Clocks and Clockmakers*. Chichester: Phillimore.

Camerer-Cuss, T.P. 1967. *The Country Life of Book Watches*. London: Country Life.

Davies, E. 2007. *Greater Manchester Clocks and Clockmakers*. Ashbourne: Mayfield.

Dowler, G.1984. *Gloucestershire Clock and Watchmakers*. Chichester: Phillimore.

Eckhardt, G. 1955. *Pennsylvania Clocks and Clockmakers*. New York: Devon-Adair.

Fennimore, D. & Hohmann, F. Ill. 2013.*Stretch America's First Family of Clockmakers*. Winterthur. Delaware: Winterthur Museum.

Haggar, A. & Miller, L. 1974. *Suffolk Clocks and Clockmakers*, Ticehurst: Antiquarian Horological Society, and *Supplement* 1979.

Howse, D. 1969. 'Captain Cook's Marine Timepieces Part 1: the Kendall Watches', *Antiquarian Horology* Vol. 6/4, pp. 190 – 205.

Loomes, B. 1976., *Country Clocks and their London Origins*. Newton Abbot: David and Charles.

Loomes, B. 1997. *Clockmakers of Northern England*. Ashbourne: Mayfield.

Loomes, B. 2014. *Clockmakers of Britain 1286-1700*. Ashbourne: Mayfield.

Marshall, T. 2013. *The Quaker Clockmakers of North Oxfordshire*. Ashbourne: Mayfield.

Mason, B. 1969. *Clockmakers and Watchmakers in Colchester*. London: Country Life.

Moore, A.J. 1998. *The Clockmakers of Somerset*. Self-published.

Moore, D. 2003. *British Clockmakers & Watchmakers Apprentice Records 1710-1810*. Ashbourne: Mayfield.

Pace. D. 2013. 'The Pace Family of Quaker Clockmakers' *Antiquarian Horology* Vol.34. March, pp. 60 – 71.

Ponsford, C. 1985. *Devon Clocks and Clockmakers*. Newton Abbot: David and Charles.

Tribe, T., & Whatmoor, P. 1981., *Dorset Clocks and Clockmakers with a Supplement on the Channel Islands*. Oswestry: Tanat Books.

Turner, G. L'E. 1967. 'The Auction Sale of Larcum Kendall's Workshop, 1790.' *Antiquarian Horology* Vol.5 (8), pp. 269-75.

White, G. 1989. *English Lantern Clocks*. Woodbridge: Antique Collectors Club.

Wilbourn, A. & Ellis, R. 2001. *Lincolnshire Clock, Watch & Barometer Makers*. Lincoln: Hansord, Ellis and Wilbourn.

Young, J. 2004. *Wiltshire Watch and Clockmakers Vol. 1*. Trowbridge: Sedgehill.

Young, J. 2006. *Wiltshire Watch and Clockmakers Vol. 2*. Trowbridge: Sedgehill.

Young, J. 2012. *Wiltshire Watch and Clockmakers Vol. 3*. Trowbridge: Sedgehill.

GLOSSARY

Arbor:	An axel on which is mounted a wheel or pinion (or other rotating part).
Automaton:	A clock with animated figures, usually located in the arch of the dial, triggered by the going, striking, musical, or repeating train.
Balance:	A horizontal wheel (usually iron) pushed alternatively backwards and forwards by the clock wheel train, regulating its speed.
Bracket Clock:	Spring driven clock normally displayed on a mantel piece, on furniture or a wall bracket.
Crown Wheel:	The escape wheel of a verge escapement, its teeth are parallel to its length.
Crutch:	A thin iron or steel rod attached to the escapement-pallet arbor, which connects it the pendulum.
Escapement:	That part of the movement, which controls the release of motive power.
Anchor Escapement:	A type of recoil escapement of anchor or lunette shape where the escape wheel recoils after the pallet has arrested the wheel tooth, mounted on a horizontal arbor in the same plane as the escape wheel; from one end of this the long pendulum receives its impulse through a crutch attached to the anchor arbor. Used on weight driven clocks after 1670.

Deadbeat Escapement:	An escapement whereby the escape wheel does not recoil, used in regulatory timepieces.
Verge Escapement:	Early form of escapement, in which two pallets at 90 degrees on the verge staff are pushed alternatively aside by the teeth of the crown wheel to impart oscillatory motion to a balance or pendulum.
Foliot:	The earliest type of regulator used in English clocks before c.1700. Consists of a horizontal bar placed across the top of an upright verge, toothed at each end which oscillates first one way then the other, small weights are attached each end and moved along for regulation.
Fusee:	A mainspring equalizer in the form of a spirally grooved truncated cone with the great wheel mounted upon it.
Hoop & Spike Clock:	A posted frame 30-hour duration clock with an iron hoop, riveted to the top plate for hanging from a hook and iron spikes projecting from the back posts for stability.
Lantern Clock:	The 19th century name given to a brass four posted short duration or 30-hour weight driven clock with decorative castings, variously described as Chamber, House or Balance clocks in the 17th century.
Pallet:	The part of an escapement acting upon the teeth on a wheel.
Passing Strike:	A simple striking mechanism where the bell hammer is operated direct from the motion work (the gears which drive the hands).
Remontoire:	A devise (usually a spring) wound by the train and discharged at regular intervals, to secure a more constant force to the escapement.
Ring & Zig Zig:	A pattern of radial dial engraving, comprising alternate concentric circles and free hand engraving in the form of zig zags or wrigglework, exclusive to the North Oxfordshire Quaker clockmakers of the 18th century.

Skeleton Clock:	A mantle style spring clock where the frame is cut away in a decorative manner, exposing the movement, housed beneath a glass dome. Popular during the 19th century.
Train (Going):	The set of wheels and pinions driven by a power source (weight or spring) regulated to rotate at a constant speed by an escapement.
Train (Striking):	The set of wheels and pinions driven by a power source, weight or spring, which when released by the motion work causes the hour to strike.

3| George Bradshaw, 1801-1853: Publisher and Compiler of Timetables

By Colin Mckenzie

George Bradshaw was born at Windsor Bridge, Pendelton, Salford, on 29th July, 1801 (*Manchester Guardian*, 17 Sept. 1853, p. 7). His parents, Thomas Bradshaw and Mary Rogers, had their only son baptised at a Congregational Chapel in Salford, near to the family home at Windsor Bridge (see his baptismal certificate held at Friends House). His education started with home-tutoring supplied by a Swedenborg Minister of Religion, a Rev. Coward, who was based in Salford. Three years later, Bradshaw was moved by his parents to study under a Mr. Scott at Overton School in Lancashire until he reached the age of 14 (Boase and Bagwell 2015). He was then apprenticed to John Beale, who ran a business in St. Anne's Gate in the centre of Manchester, where George learned the skill of map making, specialising in maps of newly constructed canals across northwest England.

He is also reported as completing the art work and maps contained in a work by Duncan Smith called 'the Art of Penmanship Improved,' which was published in 1817. In 1820, his parents moved to Belfast, and George traveled with them. He opened a business involving the manufacture and sale of maps, but this was not financially successful, so he returned to Manchester in 1822. We do not know if his parents came with him at the time (Bracegirdle 1994, 201).

Returning to Manchester, he was employed immediately by John Beale, his earlier trainer and employer, where he had been an apprentice in St. Anne's Gate, Manchester. Bradshaw's skills in map making were obviously excellent as he immediately acquired work with John Beale who employed Bradshaw in connection with his firm's production of cartography and publishing of maps. It is known that his employer had established links with Ackworth School (Ackworth School Records, '1830s developments,' Friends' House Library see also http://archive.org/stream/ackworthschoolca00ackw/), but it is not known if Beale was in membership. During the time of his employment with Beale, his skills in map making increased, and he soon produced a series of three maps covering the canal system of northwest England. There followed other maps of transport systems.

However, it was the newly developing railway system that was to prove most beneficial to Bradshaw in his working life. With the rapid development of railways, especially in northwest England, Bradshaw identified a need for up-to-date travel data, especially on newly opened lines which were soon to become valuable transport links for business people who were not familiar with many services to and within their destinations. With an increasing railway network nationally, the area to be covered reached nearly every corner of the country, and Bradshaw seems to have risen to meet that need from 1846 (Boase and Bagwell 2015) until his death in 1853; and thereafter the work was continued by the organisation that he had set up and which continued to use his name until at least 1939. He made several attempts to encourage local railway operating companies to publish travel data, but they were afraid of the local competition, especially where rivals were operating on parallel routes. Bradshaw's solution was to become a shareholder of as many of the operating companies as was possible. Being a shareholder, he was privileged in having advance notice of changes to operating times, etc., and was able to publish constantly updated train times and fares for many operators' services. This data was included, as each edition of his timetables reached production. The regular publications continued through to 1939, with a relatively short gap regarding the data for the European mainland between 1914 and 1918 when travel for most people to the European mainland was disturbed by other events. An examination of later editions of Bradshaw's Continental Guide (from 1811 onwards) shows that the detailed research had continued after Bradshaw's untimely death.

A comparison of Bradshaw's 1847 European Guide (the first) and his 1853 European Guide (published for second month 1853 just at the time of his death) give a clear indication in the rise of interest in Britain for details of European travel. This has already been examined in Seaton (2015). It also shows the rapid expansion of rail services to and from the mainland of Europe, corresponding with the vast, rapid development of European rail travel across Europe and beyond, during that period.

The 1847 European Bradshaw Guide, dated '5th month,' offers connecting services between London and several European cities and holiday destinations on the mainland. In Tables E1 to E5 below, are listed connecting services between London and many European destinations on a daily basis. Fares and connections are detailed for the duration of the timetable. In Tables R1 to R5, the equivalent return details are given. Timings and fare options are displayed in the 1853 editions with the possible options of different outward and return routes available, including different channel crossings, with costs. All services are fully bookable and prepaid, and are available with full advanced bookings, including seat reservations. For the early nineteenth century, it does appear to be quite a sophisticated service offered by Bradshaw for the traveling public. The guides also include adverts for hotels available in most locations listed in the timetables and the possibility of advanced room bookings being in place before setting off. The 'Bradshaw' provided the guide to be carried on holiday. Large resorts had a 'Bradshaw Agent' resident, and there was a senior European agent located in Paris to coordinate updates to the guides, as needed. To many, it might seem the forerunner of the complete package holiday was being provided by Bradshaw in the nineteenth century across much of Europe.

In the 1853 European Guide dated '3rd. month' (which was the last to be personally compiled by Bradshaw) the range of similar possible services is somewhat more vast, compared with 1847, and also illustrates both the development of European railways during that period and also the wider choice then available to the European traveler, both business people as well as those on holiday alone or with family. The development of services between 1847 and 1853 was considerable, as can be seen in a comparison of similar routes, as well as new locations available by 1853, as European railway development expanded rapidly.

By 1859, there was an increasing need for travel data in respect of travel from Britain to the mainland of Europe and beyond. In terms of accuracy, the contents do illustrate the complexity of the data over 160 years ago for the traveler abroad and the research undertaken by Bradshaw and his staff to produce the publications.

The ongoing service, through 'Agents' located across the mainland of Europe and available to the traveler, is impressive for the mid-nineteenth century.

The European Bradshaw, as it became known, lists all the relevant data for rail travel from England to every European country, and beyond, giving full details of services from London termini using cross-channel ferries and ongoing rail transport from the European channel ports to every country in Europe and beyond, including cities in Russia, the Middle East, and parts of Africa.

As in all of Bradshaw's guides, the Continental Bradshaw provides up-to-date times, fares, and alternative train operations, where relevant and available, in addition to details of local train operators, also where relevant and available, and their services available to the public, with Bradshaw's assurance that the data was as up-to-date as possible. Local contact details of Bradshaw's agents would reassure British travelers that any changes to travel data, while they were there, could be made available to them while at their holiday destination, and they would know that the information was current and accurate.

It seems that Bradshaw provided a new service, for British travelers abroad, either on business or on family holidays, which allowed them to venture onto the mainland of Europe without a 'human' travel guide; they just took with them their copy of the European Bradshaw. Perhaps, this was to be the start of regular European holidays for travelers – long before the package holiday was 'invented' by Thomas Cook.

Bradshaw's death was untimely, at a time when his work was rising in importance. He contracted cholera while acting as a consultant on railway matters to the Swedish Government, while planning a railway extension to Oslo alongside his friend and fellow railwayman Robert Stephenson, with whom he had worked on many foreign railway development projects across Europe. His burial in the grounds of the cathedral in Oslo is one mark of respect shown by an appreciative foreign government to a visitor working as a consultant in their developing railway network. Had he not died of cholera and been buried in haste in a foreign land, his grave would probably have become a shrine for 'railway' pilgrims to this day, including perhaps Michael Portillo.

Comparison of European Timetables from Bradshaw European Guides

For 1847	from Bradshaw's European Guide
Table E1	London to European destinations (by cross-channel routes)
Table R1	Return routes using outward connections in Table E1
Table E2 crossings	London to Northern European destinations using North Sea
Table R2	Return routes using outward connections in Table E2
Table E3	London to Mediterranean destinations and beyond
Table R3	Return routes using outward connections in Table E3

For 1853	from Bradshaw's European Guide
Table E11	London to European destinations (by cross-channel routes)
Table R11	Return routes using outward connections in Table E11
Table E12 crossings	London to Northern European destinations using North Sea
Table R12	Return routes using outward connections in Table E12
Table E13	London to European destinations (by cross-channel routes)
Table R13	Return routes using outward connections in Table E13

Bibliography

Boase, G.C. revised by P.S. Bagwell. 'George Bradshaw'. *Oxford Dictionary of National Biography*, accessed May 2015.

Bracegirdle, C. 1994. 'George Bradshaw and his Timetables' *Backtrack* 8 /4, pp 210-211.

Bradshaw's Continental Railway Guide, London/ Manchester: Henry Blacklock. Also available online at the University of Michigan Library.

Minutes of Proceedings of Institution of Civil Engineers (1854), xiii. 145-9;

Athenæum, 27 Dec. 1873, p. 872,

17 Jan. 1874, p. 95,

24 Jan. p. 126;

Notes and Queries, 6th ser. [viii. 45, 92, 338; xi,15]

Milligan, Edward H. 2007. *British Quakers in Commerce & Industry 1775-1920*

York: Sessions.

Seaton, T. 2015. "Travel and Touring in England by Elite Quaker Industrial Families in the long 19th. Century," *Quaker Studies*, vol. 20 (1), pp. 117-44.

Smith, G Royde, 1939. *The History of Bradshaw, a Centenary Review of the Origin and Growth of the Most Famous Guide in the World*, London/Manchester : H. Blacklock.

Appendices

Bradshaw Continental Guide 1847 6th. Month							
Summary of FARES for connecting services London – Paris & RTN							
London to Paris and RTN		Single Fares to destination		Length of through journey using connecting trains			
London – Paris	Channel Crossing		1st.	2nd.	Hrs.	Mins.	
	Dover	Calais	£1.6.0	£1.4.0	14	0	
	Dover	Bologne	£1.6.0	£1.4.0	14	0	
	Newhaven	Dieppe	£1.4.0	£1.0.0	16	0	
	Southanpton	Le Havre	£1.3.0	£1.4.0	16	0	
	Dock @ St. Catherine's	Le Havre	£1.3.0	£1.0.0	24	0	
	Dover	Ostend	£2.18.9	£2.2.6	20	0	
for example using connections for destinations further afield							
London – Venice	Dover	Bologne	£ 11:19:5	£ 6.3.6	84	0	
London – Zurich	Dover	Calais	£ 6. 7. 9	£ 4.14.5	90	0	
Service and fares extracted from Bradshaw Continental Guide 6th. Month 1847							
Examples of cross-channel connections			Bradshaw European Guide 6th. Month 1847				

London – Vienna Bradshaw Continental Guide 5th. Month 1847

OUT   Through trains 1st. & 2nd. class Paris – Vienna

dep.	London Bridge	20:35 via Dover/Calais ferry
arr.	Paris	07:20
dep.	change station	11:35]
arr.	Strasbourg	18:45] through
dep.	(Buffet @ Station)	19:00] train
arr.	Salzburg	01:15] Paris
dep.		02:00] to
arr.	Vienna	10:00] Vienna no catering on board train

RTN   Through trsins 1st. & 2nd. class Vienna – Paris

dep.	Vienna	21:30] through
arr.	Salzburg	09:00] train
dep.		09:50] Vienna
arr.	Strasbourg	12:05] to
dep.	(Buffet @ Station)	13:15] Paris - no catering on board train
arr.	Paris	14:45]
dep.	change station	16:45 via Calais/Dover ferry
arr.	London Bridge	07:30

Single Fare (1st. class) £9: 6: 6 Single Fare (2nd. class) £8: 5: 6 by this route

Return fare twice Single fare by this route

London – Basle Bradshaw Continental Guide 5th. Month 1847

OUT - Through train - 1st & 2nd class Ostend – Basle

dep.	London Bridge	20:30
arr.	Dover	22:30 - **via Dover/Ostend ferry**
dep.	Ostend	07:15
arr.	Brussels	09:30
dep.		09:45
arr.	Cologne	21:00
dep.		21:30
arr.	Strasbourg	05:45 - no catering on board train
dep,	Buffet @ Station	06:20
arr.	Basle	09:40

1847	Bradshaw		
		Channel	Crossing
LONDON to	PARIS		
1	via	Dover	Calais
2	via	Dover	Bologne
3	via	Newhaven	Dieppe
4	via	Southampt'n	Le Havre
5	via	Dock @ St Catherine's	Le Havre
6	via	Dover	Oostende
LONDON to	VENICE	Dover	Bologne
London to	Zùrich	Dover	Calais

European		
Fares		length of
SNG	RTN	journey
1st. Class	2nd. Class	Hrs. Mins.
£1. 6. 0	£ 1. 4. 0	14. 00
£1. 6. 0	£1. 4. 0	14. 00
£1. 4. 0	£1. 0. 0	16. 00
£1. 3. 0	£1. 0. 0	16. 00
£1. 3. 0	£1. 0. 0	24. 00
£2. 15. 9	£2. 2. 6	20. 00
£11. 19. 5	£6. 3. 6	84. 00
£6. 7. 9	£4. 14. 5	50. 00

Timetables & Fare Comparison		
		Journey
Fare	Fare	Hrs. Mins.
£1. 6. 0	£1. 4. 0	14.0
£1. 6. 0	£1. 4. 0	14.0

OUT		
London station	Liverpool Street	
dep.	20:30	
PORT	Harwich PQ.	
arr.	21:30	
dep.	22:00	
PORT	Hook van	Holland
onward travel to Northern Europe destinations		
arr.	05:15	»»»»»»»»»»»»»
dep.	05:40	05:18
Rotterdam	06:11	- - - - -
Amsterdam	07:30	- - - - -
Cologne	>>>>>>>>>>	11:15
Berlin	——————	16:54
RTN	>>>>>>>>>>	>>>>>>>>>>
return travel to Hook van Holland then to UK >>>		
Berlin		13:05
Cologne	>>>>>>>>>>	19:21
Amsterdam	21:45	- - - - -
Rotterdam		- - - - -
PORT	Hook van	Holland
arr.	23:27	23:15
dep.	23:50	<<<<<<<<<<
PORT	Harwich	
arr	06:20	
dep	07:00	
London station	Liverpool Street	
arr	08:00	

Bradshaw	European	Timetables		London &
OUT	London stn.	Charing X	Charing X	Waterloo
	dep	09:00	10:00	10:00
	PORT	Dover	Folkestone	Newhaven
	arr	10:15	11:15	11:30
	dep	11:05	11:55	12:00
	PORT	Calais	Boulogne	Dieppe
	arr	12:25	13:41	15:00
	dep	13:15	14:12	15:35
	Paris station	NORD	NORD	St. Lazare
	arr	16:40	17:20	18:54
++++++	+++++++++	+++++++++	+++++++++	+++++++
FARES	route > >	Dover/ Calais	or Boulogne	
1st. Class	Single	£ 6 : 15: 2		
	Return	£10: 13 ; 9		
2nd Class	Single	£ 4: 12: 11		
	Return	£ 7 : 15 : 2		
++++++	+++++++	+++++++++	+++++++++	+++++++
RTN	Paris station	NORD	NORD	St, Lazare
	dep	08:25	09:55	10:18
	PORT	Bologne	Bologne	Dieppe
	arr	11:25	13:10	13:00
	dep	11:45	13:53	13:53
	PORT	Folkstone	Dover	Newhaven
	arr	13:10	14:35	15:00
	dep	13:40	15:00	16:00
	London stn.	Charing X	Charing X	Victoria
	arr	15:25	17:10	19:05
	London to &	from Paris		

Paris	Summary	1853	with fares
Victoria	Charing X	Charing X	Waterloo
11:00	14:20	20:45	21:50
Dover	Folkestone	Newhaven	So'hamptn
12:15	15:40	22:45	00:00
12:55	16:10	00:15	08:00
Calais	Boulogne	Dieppe	Havre
14:20	18:17	02:30	06:30
14:40	18:25	02:50	08:00
NORD	NORD	St. Lazare	St. Lazare
18:54	21:16	06:20	11:22
+++++++++	+++++++++	+++++++++	+++++++++
Newhaven /	Dieppe	So'thampton	/ Havre
£ 5 :17 : 3		£5: 18: 7	
£ 9 : 4 : 6		£ 9: 6: 3	
£ 4 : 1: 8		£4 : 1 : 1	
£ 6:12 : 7		£6 :12: 6	
+++++++++	+++++++++	+++++++++	+++++++++
NORD	NORD	St Lazare	St. Lazare
12:00	16:00	21:20	19:48
Calais	Bologne	Dieppe	Havre
15:22	18:58	00:51	23:20
15:45	19:10	01:25	24m
Dover	Folkstone	So'thampton	So'thampton
16:40	20:35	05:30	06:10
17:25	21:05	06:00	08:05
Victoria	Charing X	Victoria	Waterloo
22:45	22:45	07:30	10:11
Bradshaw	European TT	5th. month 1853	European Bradshaw

111

London to/fr.	Southern Europe –	
OUT	Charing X	09:00
	Dover arr.	10:40
	dep.	11:05
	Calais dep.	13:15
	Paris Nord	16:40
	PLM	19:00
	Marseilles	08:30
	F.O sail	10:00
	Cairo arr WO	17:05
	Journey time	- six days
RTN	Cairo dep.	FO - 12:00
	Marseilles	WO - 04:00
	dep.	11:56
	Paris PLM	04:55
	Nord dep	09:55
	Calais arr.	13:10
	sail	13:30
	Dover arr.	14:35
	dep.	15:30
	Charing X arr	17:40
Sailings to Cairo from Marseilles weekly		

London to Mediterranean and beyond		
OUT	Victoria	11:00
	Dover arr	12:45
	dep.	12:55
	Calais arr	14:37
	dep.	14:57
	Paris Nord	19:19
	dep. PLM	20:05
	Milan dep.	12:25
	Venice arr	16:40
	service	daily
RTN		
	Venice dep	08:00
	Milan	- - - - - - - - - -
	Paris PLM	06:45
	Paris Nord	dep 08:25
	Bologne sail	11:25
	Folkestone	dep. 14:40
	Charing X	arr. 15:25

113

OUT and	RTN		
	FARES from	1st. Class	2nd Class
	London to –		
	Marseilles	£20:17:3	£11: 1: 5
	Alexandria	£23:13:3	N/A
	Cairo	£20:15:0	£14: 3: 0
	Venice	£12: 0: 5	£8:10: 7
	Milan	£6:12: 0	£4:11: 6
European Bradshaw 5th. Month 1853			

4 | Joseph Wharton: American Hicksite Quaker "Captain of Industry"

By Jean Mulhern and Cathy Pitzer

Joseph Wharton (1826 - 1909), an American Hicksite Quaker, was a wealthy Philadelphia industrialist and educational benefactor during the Second Industrial Revolution (1870 - 1914). Today he is remembered for establishing the essential zinc and nickel metal industries in the United States, his success in the iron and steel industry, and his roles in founding Swarthmore College and the Wharton School of the University of Pennsylvania.

In the late 19th century, Joseph Wharton competed in a business and industrial arena dominated by "robber barons" and "captains of industry," so labeled in the popular press and categorized by later historians. Recently, the National Endowment for the Humanities (2016) has challenged students to research American capitalists of this time period and determine whether each might be considered a robber baron or a captain of industry. Following the NEH study template, students will find, as outlined in this article, that Joseph Wharton was not motivated by personal power or self-aggrandizement. He was first and foremost an enterprising industrialist, driven toward product and process improvement through scientific investigation and technology and chemical process innovations (National Mining Hall of Fame 1997). This article will explore to what extent Wharton's grounding in the Quaker faith and heritage informed his life choices, his business and career decisions, and the ways in which he spent his time and wealth to solidify his rank among the American captains of industry.

According to Wharton biographer W. Ross Yates, the six integral aspects of his worldview were his love of mining and refining metals, family, politics, scientific inquiry, agriculture, and the sea (1987, 341-9). In a privately printed biography of her father, Joanna Wharton Lippincott wanted his grandchildren to know that, in addition to his business and industrial successes, "this rather stern-looking man [was] a genial and entertaining host, a most charming and

115

affectionate father, a friend to the deserving, besides being an athlete, an engraver, a chemist, a poet and writer, a linguist, and a scientist" (1909, Preface, 4). She highlighted his life-long Quaker affiliation and attributed his good health and vigor to abstinence from tobacco and avoidance of strong alcohol. At the time of his death in 1909 at age 82, Wharton was a member of the Green Street Monthly Meeting in Philadelphia and his death was so noted in the meeting minutes (Green Street 1909, 38).

Background

Wharton was a privileged birthright Quaker, born to William and Deborah Fisher Wharton, who came from many generations of successful American Quaker merchant shipping families based in Philadelphia and Newport, Rhode Island. The Quaker Fishers had arrived in America on the same boat as William Penn and the Quaker Whartons followed soon after. Both of Joseph's grandmothers came from wealthy shipping families in Newport, Rhode Island. These Quaker families "cherished simplicity but were not bound by any vow of poverty" (Yates 1987, 16; Philip S. Benjamin 1976). In fact, 17th and 18th century Philadelphia Quakers developed mercantile enterprises based on their Quakerly reputations for honesty, thrift, and fair dealing. Building wealth came easy to them in colonial times and they interpreted their Quaker responsibilities for this wealth to create jobs for others, to provide for those less fortunate by providing education and resources to help themselves, and to live in a manner similar to their non-Quaker peers but without ostentation (Yates 1987, 16, 228).

Joseph's father, William Wharton, lived on an inheritance and chose a simple lifestyle and plain dress. He and his wife Deborah were Quaker ministers devoted to serving their community and caring for their own and extended families. Using the typology of Benjamin (1976), William and Deborah were "weighty" Quakers. They knew the controversial minister Elias Hicks and joined the Hicksite Friends who separated from the Orthodox Friends from 1827 in the Middle Atlantic, Ohio, and Indiana regions. Joseph, fifth among their ten children, was reared within the close-knit Philadelphia Hicksite Spruce Street Meeting, which had erected what author Frederick Tolles called a "hedge" to protect and preserve their faith and culture, separate from the Orthodox Quakers (1948).

Compared with the Orthodox Quakers, the Hicksites sought a simpler, more disciplined life with less class differentiation, a more rural focus, less government intrusion, and a more activist stance against slavery. They opposed evolving religious doctrine in preference for a focus on their interpretation of the Friends discipline (Yates 1987, 24). Thomas D. Hamm said they espoused "plain living," "...unprogrammed meetings, the centrality of the Inner Light,

116

continuing revelation, nonpastoral ministry..." (2000, 17). Notably, they opposed education in the liberal arts in favor of the learning of practical skills (Yates 1987, 24).

The Hicksite founding community in Philadelphia, including William and Deborah Wharton, was determined to prove the worthiness of the Hicksite interpretation of Quakerism. From 1827 forward for a hundred years, Hicksites lived separately from the Orthodox, avoiding contact in business and society. Yates (1987) and Benjamin (1976) observed that members of the two Quaker societies did not intermarry. In fact, Joseph Wharton had close friends and business associates from many religions, including Episcopalians, Methodists, Jews, Roman Catholics, and lapsed Quakers, but not Orthodox Quakers. His generation was the last to be sheltered within that protective enclave, with the next generations marrying outside the Hicksite community more frequently, including Wharton's own nephew (Yates). Hamm (2000) observed that by 1900, Hicksites had retained the foundations of their faith while responding to their changing world, becoming more open to music, art, and philanthropy. Even their definition of the "plain life" had become less rigid (Hamm 2000, 17).

Farming

True to Hicksite Quaker values, when Joseph Wharton turned 16 years of age, he ended his private education through tutors and private schools and chose farming as his intended occupation. While his academic talent and education had prepared him for college, none of his siblings had attended college and nor did he. His education continued throughout his life in the form of apprenticeships, first in farming, then in accounting and metallurgy, self-guided reading, institutes, lectures, applied work in chemical laboratories, travel, and interviews with experts (Yates 1987; Lippincott 1909).

Wharton spent three years within the household of Hicksite farmer Joseph Walton, a member of the Fallowfield Meeting in Chester County, Pennsylvania. Wharton later said he traced his passion for science and chemistry to his reading of Walton's copy of *The Muck Manual for Farmers*, a book of agricultural chemistry by Samuel L. Dana. He reported in letters, however, that he preferred city life to the isolation of rural life. Thus, in the early 1840s, Wharton returned to Philadelphia and began a series of strategic and increasingly productive career moves in industries related to ore processing and manufacturing, many energized by recent European chemical or technical improvements. His earliest industrial ventures were in partnerships with family members and other Hicksite businessmen (Lippincott 1909; Yates 1987).

Business and Industry in the Philadelphia Area

Hicksite Quakers in Philadelphia faced challenges to their intent to observe strict religious discipline and a simpler life. Those doing business found themselves becoming wealthy and having more power and influence in the external business world than could be imagined in 1827. Thus, they adapted themselves to the burgeoning economy, especially in areas not directly addressed in the discipline. The accounting and business management skills that Wharton acquired during this period became essential as he began to assist his older brother Rodman in handling their family's extensive properties and households. After Rodman's early death in 1854, Wharton became the quasi-head of the extended family, responsible for its financial affairs as well as for the various enterprises and proposed ventures. In the historical tradition of the Wharton and Fisher families, various business ventures and their attendant risks were financed through gifts, loans, and advances on inheritances, not through banks, mortgages, or loans from external individuals. External debt was considered very bad practice, as was leveraging company assets in lean times, a Quaker principle that saved Wharton's companies several times during financial crises (Yates 1987).

Rodman Wharton, Joseph's mentor, had recognized a financially promising future in the emerging field of applied chemistry, already established in Germany but new to Philadelphia. Rodman formed a successful partnership with other Hicksite Quakers to manufacture white lead used to make paint. This partnership ended when Rodman formed a new company with Joseph, now of age. That business expanded to include an infusion of capital from a brother-in-law and another product, refined cottonseed oil. Despite intensive efforts to improve the chemical processing of the oil, profitability eluded them and that enterprise ended, with lessons on supply chain economics, product improvement, and global competition well learned. Wharton later made good use of the principles of vertical integration, continuous quality improvement, and protectionist tariffs (Yates 1987).

Wharton's next enterprise, funded by his stake in previous ventures and money from his father, was in brick manufacturing using improved machinery. He attempted to sell not only the bricks but also patent rights to the machinery, especially in Southern states. There he observed first-hand slaves working in manufacturing and predicted economic disaster if slavery were suddenly abolished. Unlike Hicksite Quaker abolitionists, he held a position of incrementalism, believing that slavery, while certainly abhorrent, must be ended by southerners themselves while also assuring that former slaves were prepared for independence in life and earning a livelihood (Yates 1987, 58, 109).

Because of the sagging economy in 1854, Wharton gave up the brick business, based on profit/loss analysis. He then began managing the Pennsylvania and Lehigh Zinc Company, formed with his brother Charles. He developed this company by improving the manufacture of zinc oxide and spelter. He rechartered the company and worked out a clever side arrangement to become the first manufacturer of metallic zinc, used in the production of copper. He turned a substantial profit from that venture, riding the rising demand for brass during the Civil War and demonstrating his business acumen in the "art of the deal."

Ironically, while a Quaker, Wharton's most profitable ventures depended on military contracts and applications. He was not a public pacifist in the Civil War or the Spanish-American War. Ever the American patriot, he contended that having a strong defense (and protected manufacturing) helped assure a nation's peace. He was willing to support American war efforts with his products and money, and even flew the United States flag over his factory, but was not willing to serve in the military or bear arms (Yates 1987, 110). While living near his operation in Bethlehem, Pennsylvania, he wrote to his mother Deborah 60 miles away in Philadelphia about these issues to reassure her of his stance. Both his mother and his wife worried for his personal safety if he were suspected of being a pacifist. Although too old to serve and married, he strengthened his case to avoid the Civil War draft by seeking election as a school director in 1862 (Yates 1987, 110).

Later, Wharton enterprises included a highly profitable 40-year venture in New Jersey nickel production, for which he held an American monopoly and a substantial percentage of international trade. Through aggressive lobbying based on scientific data, he persuaded the federal government to purchase his copper/nickel 75/25 alloy for the five cent coin, a coin still called the "nickel" (Wharton 1877). Perfecting nickel production led Wharton directly into the iron and steel industry where he became a major stockholder in the Bethlehem Iron Company. His investigations of steel processing in Europe enabled him to convert that American company to the first manufacture of high strength steel to fulfill a valuable US government contract for steel plate used for warships and guns in 1885. He marketed his armament products to Germany and Japan as well. He sold the company now named Bethlehem Steel Company in 1901 but continued to build wealth from the steel industry through his holdings in coal and ore mining and pig iron manufacturing. He also diversified his investments with gold, silver, and ore mines in the American West.

Joseph Wharton was a hands-on manager, regardless of his role within a particular business or the size of the business. He conducted daily walk-abouts of Bethlehem Iron and his Camden, New Jersey Nickel Works. His working pace was full-bore and high energy with frantic daily races by carriage to keep to his tight schedule. He combined his work and home lives as natural complements, bringing scientists and business experts home to dinner and relatives to work alongside him (Lippincott 1909; Morris 1909). He paid workers prevailing wages but provided no benefits and was unresponsive to their single attempt to strike at one of his factories. Wharton was loyal and supportive to plant supervisors who supported him and recruited supervisors and workers based on their expertise.

Wharton paid attention to the activities of his north Philadelphia industrialist peers. Of note was mechanical engineer and efficiency expert Frederick Winslow Taylor, whose parents had deep American Quaker roots. Unlike Wharton's parents, Taylor's parents had reared him in a secular world of international travel and an Exeter Academy education, rounded out with a shop floor apprenticeship at Midvale Steel Works. Taylor's mother had been disciplined for her non-Quaker wedding ceremony and eventually espoused transcendentalism. His mortgage lawyer father was a nominal Quaker. (Copley 1923). Open to new business practices, Wharton invited Taylor to implement his differential piece-rate pay system in the Bethlehem Iron Works, a short-lived experiment that did not improve worker morale but did identify a way to streamline steel processing (Yates 1987, 283).

Family and the Sea

Family was a high priority for Wharton. Nevertheless, he delayed marriage, intent on building his business and distracted by the excitement of making inroads in the metal industry. Finally, in 1854, Wharton married his long-time fiancée Anna Lovering, his ideal bride of modest manner and bright intelligence, from a Hicksite Quaker family with wealth derived from the invention of an improved sugar manufacturing process. His extended family included wife Anna and three daughters (reared mostly in a Spruce Street house gifted from Anna's father), plus his brothers and sisters and their families. Except for a few years when he first worked at Bethlehem Iron, he and Anna never lived separately as he found sanctuary in his home life.

For many years Wharton managed the family wealth on behalf of his father William, who died in 1856 (Deborah died in 1888) and then in the interest of the extended family. He oversaw the family land estates, gifts, loans, and advances to family members for business ventures (not all successful but an acceptable risk of doing business). He advised Anna in the management of her own property. As guardian, he assumed responsibility for the education of the sons of his brother Rodman who died in 1854. He also respected and supported the charitable and educational causes of his mother, sister, and sister-in-law, who were weighty (or practicing) Quakers to his nearly nominative Quaker status in the meeting (Yates 1987; Benjamin 1976). While the Whartons were faithful in attending meetings, Joanna observed that she and her sisters never attended First Day School as Wharton preferred their time at home in family activities (Lippincott 1909).

In the interests of family life and to accommodate their hosting of Quaker committee meetings as well as his frequent meetings with the leading business, political, and scientific leaders of the day, Wharton built two large functional homes. *Ontalauna* was built near other Hicksite families on Old York Road, Philadelphia in 1881. *Marbella*, a summer residence on the Atlantic Ocean, was constructed among other Hicksite Quaker retreats at the more secluded island of Conanicut, west of the showier Newport, Rhode Island. Both spacious homes featured high-quality amenities with architecture of simple elegance and natural landscapes. These homes were frequent gathering places for Wharton's extended family and friends and the scene of many a sleigh ride or stroll in the gardens or along the coast. It was at Marbella that the Whartons indulged their Newport ancestral-inspired love of the sea, with its rugged coastal views, boating, and hiking in annual summer retreats (Lippincott 1909; Yates 1987). There, Wharton switched his scientific inquiry to sea life, rushing specimens to his friend Louis Agassiz, biologist and geologist, who lived nearby (Morris 1909).

Politics

Frederick Tolles (1956) outlined the history of American Quakers in public office, ranging from the early domination of Pennsylvania colonial government by Quakers to the threat of Meeting disownment for seeking elective office, emerging in the late 18th century. Tolles said that even as late as the 1950s, Quakers continued to avoid elective office (1956, 20). He also discussed Quaker disapproval of lobbying government for personal gain.

Wharton, in addition to his major business enterprises and his devotion to family, found time, albeit at a hectic pace, to pursue his other loves, as his biographer Yates (1987) has called them. One love was politics, not as an elected official, but as a lobbyist. Lippincott (1909) showed how her father was mindful of this 19th century American Quaker concern with compromising spiritual integrity when pressed by the conflicting interests of public office. She said that he turned down a sure offer to be elected to Congress as a Republican from the Pennsylvania 2nd District. His son-in-law Harrison Morris (1909) said that

Wharton had been considered by his friends for Secretary of the Treasury, an opportunity also waived.

Nevertheless, Wharton became active in the American Iron and Steel Association as a lobbyist of Presidents and congressmen. He advocated for strong tariff protection for certain industries, especially nickel, iron and steel, based on his public service argument that internal peace was best assured through a strong country with a vigorous industrial economy (Yates 1987, 184). To be sure, these tariffs also were good for American industrial profit. His daughter wrote that he thrived in the political arena in Washington D.C., as co-organizer and chief lobbyist for the Industrial League that coordinated the lobbying efforts of numerous industries, calling for strength through united effort (Lippincott 1909; also Sass & Copperman 1980). This group actually drafted tariff legislation that was passed by Congress, beginning with the Schenck Tariff Act of 1870 (Yates 1987, 150).

Science

Joseph Wharton, always with an inquiring mind, was passionate about putting the scientific method to work to help answer his questions about the natural world (Yates 1987; Morris 1909). Hicksite Quakers found no conflict between the spiritual realm and scientific investigations into nature, continuing the long history of scientific achievements by Quakers in both England and America (Raistrick 1950). Wharton's publication record was wide-ranging, from scientific papers to commencement speeches to a particularly controversial Hicksite Quaker pamphlet in 1892 (*The Creed in the Discipline*).

Of special note was Wharton's scientific paper on the pumice fallout from the eruption of the Krakatoa volcano in 1883 presented before the American Philosophical Society, of which he was a member. He had devised an experiment in which he proved that particles obtained from Philadelphia snowfall were from Krakatoa and not from local pollution (Yates 1987, 211). Another Wharton scientific paper described using the Doppler effect on the color of light from stars to determine their distance from Earth (Wharton 1865). He rarely gave papers on metal processing because he did not want to reveal proprietary information to competitors.

In the early 1890s, Wharton took notice of a movement to revise the Hicksite discipline to include a statement of belief in the Holy Trinity. Conservative in his faith, he opposed all statements of creed. He decided to weigh in on the issue by applying his scientific research method in a textual analysis of historical documents related to the Bible and early Quaker disciplines. Albert J. Edmunds, writing in *The Westonian* about the 1892 pamphlet, contends that "...Wharton's essay practically contends that Friends of all bodies could unite under the Discipline of 1762, and that discord-breeding elements were introduced into the printed editions by copying the English; whereas our American Discipline had grown up in complete independence of London..." (Edmunds 1909, 196), without mention of the Trinity. Wharton's sister Esther Smith, after reading a draft of the essay, wrote him a letter, pleading that he temper his arguments and avoid language seeming to be intolerant of those arguing for change in the Discipline. Wharton proceeded to publish his essay as a pamphlet for distribution, an aggressive move that drew criticism as an act of public incivility and intolerance (Yates 1987, 347-348).

Agriculture

Joseph Wharton diversified his land holdings by purchasing extensive acreage in New Jersey and investing in gold, silver, and other mineral mines in the American West. He enjoyed several trips West in his later years, hiking into undeveloped areas to inspect his property. His lifelong interest in agriculture was indulged at Conanicut Island, where he raised turkeys for gifts. He also purchased extensive New Jersey property through a number of transactions with the intent of first exploiting any remaining mineral deposits, later for its potential for timber, a possible railroad route, a commercial beet growing operation, and as a water supply to nearby Camden or Philadelphia (never realized). Although the New Jersey property was never profitable, he enjoyed owning and preserving it and growing cranberries and sweet potatoes (Yates 1987). Eventually his 96,000 acre "gentleman's farm" in the Pine Barrens ecosystem formed the core of the 110,000 acre Wharton State Forest, the largest state park in New Jersey (New Jersey State Park System).

Charitable Contributions

Although Joseph Wharton focused his energies on growing his businesses, his family and intellectual pursuits, being a wealthy man he made several noteworthy donations, all with an intent to improve the lot of others. Throughout his life, he was a private donor to numerous Quaker charitable projects promoted publicly by his mother, wife, sisters, and family. One such public project was St. Joseph's Chapel, built in 1884 on land he donated in South Bethlehem, near his Bethlehem zinc and iron works, for use by immigrant employees. This chapel, an Episcopal mission, was a project initiated by his nephew William Thurston, an officer of Bethlehem Iron. Thurston, a former Quaker who had become an Episcopalian for business reasons, had compassion for his workers and saw to their needs. In addition to the chapel, Thurston himself financed an orphanage for the children of workers who died in a smallpox epidemic (Yates 1987). Wharton, by the way, was not pleased that his nephew became the first grandchild of William and Deborah Wharton to leave the Hicksite Quakers, an apostasy. Wharton wrote to him: "...I confess the step does not please me, for the drawing away from us of those we love cannot be a pleasant thing. Still, in these matters each one must think and act for himself" (Yates 1987, 206). Their relationship continued to be amicable.

In 1908, just before his death, Joseph Wharton donated 25 acres of forest land in the Olney neighborhood of North Philadelphia to the city to be known as Fisher Park, honoring his mother's family (Yates 1987, 357). It is still in use today.

Higher Education

Joseph Wharton was involved in two major ventures in higher education, the establishment of Swarthmore College and the founding of the Wharton School of Business at the University of Pennsylvania. Wharton's interest in higher education was typical of Quakers with wealthy antecedents; both his mother and sister were active in charitable and educational causes, with a particular interest in former slaves and in Native Americans in New York state and on the American Plains (Sass 1982, 3). Involvement in higher education was also consistent with Wharton's scientific pursuits. An active member of the Academy of Natural Science, the American Philosophical Society, and the Franklin Institute, Wharton gave lectures before various professional societies and published a number of papers in scientific journals (Yates 1987, 209, 230). Later, in 1895, he was honored to chair the Committee of the Overseers to Visit the Chemical Laboratory at Harvard. Of course, he recommended more emphasis on practical technical instruction (Yates 1987, 208).

Friends lagged behind other religious groups in the latter part of the nineteenth century in establishing colleges. Both Hicksite and Orthodox Friends believed education should be useful and provide preparation for work. Hicksites put a greater value on practicality and simplicity, particularly emphasizing farming, manufacturing, commerce and the trades, careers for which a college education was not necessary. Orthodox Friends were more accepting of higher education, establishing Haverford College outside of Philadelphia in 1833 and Earlham College in Indiana a few years later.

Swarthmore College, located west of Philadelphia, was founded in 1869 as the first American college funded by Hicksite Quakers. Its establishment was spearheaded between 1854 and 1860 by the Baltimore, Philadelphia, and New York Yearly Meetings, and the women in Wharton's family were enthusiastically involved in this effort. Joseph's parents William and Deborah actively advocated for the college in their Philadelphia Yearly Meeting. His mother and sister, Hannah Haydock, were charter members of the Swarthmore Board of Managers (which today would be called the Board of Trustees). Deborah contributed time, bought 220 shares of college stock, and endowed a scholarship. Hannah, from the New York Yearly Meeting, traveled to meetings at her own expense. The Board selected Edward Parrish, brother of Rodman's widow Susanna, as its first president and two of Susanna's children were students in the first entering class (Sass 1982, 213).

Wharton, in actuality, had little to do with the opening of Swarthmore College other than purchasing stock in 1864 at the request of his mother. In 1870 he replaced his mother on the board of governors, eventually serving as president of the governing board from 1883 to 1907 (Swarthmore 1920). He provided funds for a chapel, a science building, and an endowed Professorship of History and Political Economy. He approached Swarthmore activities as an astute businessman, giving commencement addresses, serving on committees, and supervising construction projects. He and his daughter Joanna Lippincott, who became a board member in 1894 (Sass 1982, 219), were successful in overcoming Hicksite objections to the teaching of religion as part of the "history of civilization." In his will, Wharton gave Swarthmore $100,000 to complete Wharton Hall, a men's dormitory (Yates 1987).

Joseph Wharton devoted much more personal passion to founding the now well-known Wharton School of the University of Pennsylvania. He brought to bear on this new concept of education all that he learned as an entrepreneur and industrialist and all that he believed in with regard to the knowledge and qualities needed for success in late 19th century business and industry.

The Wharton School of Finance and Economy was Wharton's brainchild, the first collegiate school of business in the country. During the latter part of the 1800s it was customary for boys interested in a career in business to be apprenticed to learn the trade (Sass 1982, 19). Businesses were becoming too large and complex, however, and the heads of companies far too busy for the apprenticeship system to work. The only business-related schools were "commercial colleges" where subjects such as penmanship were taught. These colleges turned out clerks rather than heads of companies.

While there were professional schools of medicine, law, engineering and dentistry, there were no comparable schools of business. Wharton envisioned a school where boys of good character would graduate with a social science background and business related instruction in taxation, money, industry, commerce, and transportation. The emphasis on the social sciences was consistent with Claude Henri de Saint-Simon's belief in "positivism," popular at that time, which postulated that social outcomes could be predicted by scientific methods. In 1881 Wharton sent a letter to the Board of Trustees of the University of Pennsylvania proposing a "School of Finance and Economy," to be funded by his $100,000 donation. The school was to be called the Wharton School of Finance and Economy to commemorate his historic family name (Yates 1987, 221). While Wharton had rarely interfered with Swarthmore's curriculum, he was quite specific as to what the Wharton School curriculum should include and specified that each student had to write a thesis before graduation. Graduates would also display the personal characteristics of accuracy, honesty, and a conservative outlook towards debt (Sass 1982, 37). He emphatically insisted that faculty advocate protectionism, in which he passionately believed.

When Wharton died in 1909, it was widely assumed that the Wharton School would be a major beneficiary of his estate. Wharton's will originally included a $500,000 contribution to the school but that sum was taken out of his will in 1906, prior to his death in 1909. The $500,000 was to be distributed among any living grandchildren along with other additional funds (Joseph Wharton will as probated, 1909). The change was the result of a personal disagreement between the Wharton family and the "Philadelphia establishment" that controlled the Board of Trustees (Lippincott 1909; Rzeznik 2013; Sass 1982, 118).

The Wharton School awarded its first undergraduate degrees in 1884 and its first undergraduate degrees to women in 1909. A leader in the education of women, Wharton School alumni included Frances Perkins, appointed Secretary of Labor by Franklin D. Roosevelt, becoming the nation's first female cabinet member. Dorothy Swaine Thomas, PhD, became Wharton's first female faculty member in 1948 and Jean Andrus Crockett, the first female departmental chair, became the first woman to head the Federal Reserve Bank of Philadelphia. The Wharton School continued to expand its programs and degrees offered with MBA and PhD offerings, executive education programs, business journals, research institutes, and other innovations in business education. Today the Wharton School is one of the world's best known schools of business with almost 100,000 alumni worldwide (Wharton School 2016). In recognition of the centennial of the founding of the Wharton School, Joseph Wharton's contribution to management education was honored with the issuance in 1981 of an 18 cent US postage stamp bearing his image (Tower 1981).

There is some question as to what extent the Wharton School of today reflects Quaker values, if, in fact, it ever did. The school's early focus was "to apply rigorous scientific methods, modeling and analysis to business studies" ("Wharton History"). While this objective reflects the emphasis of Joseph

Wharton upon scientific efficiency, it is not particularly reflective of Quaker values. In fact, Wharton was characterized in one media account as an "old boy club for would-be financiers" ("Politico"). The recent rebranding initiative (2009) "Knowledge for Action," reflects a commitment to "social impact" and "global initiatives", objectives that are more consistent with Quaker testimonies (Slavon 2012).

Joseph Wharton's presence lives on in the Wharton School primarily in name. There is a Joseph Wharton fellowship program in the graduate program ("Wharton Fellowship Program") and a J.W. Scholars program for undergraduates ("Joseph Wharton Scholars"). The Alumni Clubs of Boston ("Boston Joseph Wharton Award"), Washington D.C. and New York give Joseph Wharton Awards each year; interestingly, one of these was recently awarded to Ivanka Trump, daughter of President Donald Trump, as well as to Trump himself. ("Wharton Club of New York...") All four of Trump's adult children graduated from Penn. The school's literature makes no mention of Trump, arguably its most famous alumnus, who received his undergraduate degree in 1968 after transferring from Fordham. Penn administrators have made no public mention of Trump and numerous letters of protest against Trump's immigration policies have been written by students and alumni ("You Do Not Represent Us").

Conclusion

Joseph Wharton was a brilliant, energetic and successful entrepreneur. However, as Malcolm Gladwell (2008) has pointed out in his book, *Outliers*, extraordinary success cannot be explained by talent alone. In the same way that Bill Gates could not have founded Microsoft were he born two decades earlier or later, Wharton could not have parlayed his interests in metallurgy into Bethlehem Steel were he not born at the start of the Second Industrial Revolution or not in the burgeoning Philadelphia mining/industrial region with its history of highly regarded entrepreneurial Quaker businessmen. Like other business leaders of that time, Wharton came from a privileged background (Gladwell 2008) and he had a mother who valued education and learning (Goertzel 1962). He was thus well-equipped and well-positioned by his family and faith, time and location, to leverage these assets in a new world. Sass and Copperman described it as a "new world of wage-laborers, corporations, power machinery, and scientific equations" (1980, 51).

Wharton greeted this new world as a Quaker, faithful in Meeting attendance and sensitive to supporting and valuing the Quaker activist women in his family while making strategic choices related to pacifism and public office, striving to balance Quaker testimonies on those topics with the needs of his industry. As a Quaker, he avoided debt, spent money practically, and took only carefully calculated risks. He was a scientist curious about the natural world, empowered by a spiritual faith unthreatened by the scientific method, eager to learn and apply the new fields of chemistry to metallurgy and sociology to labor practices. He was a husband of nature, using his wealth to preserve land for parks and protected aquifers and his time to explore such diverse topics as volcanoes, the stars, and marine life. While living a life privileged by old and new wealth, he embodied the Quaker equalitarian ethos, putting in countless hours daily on the shop floor and in the laboratory, solving problems, improving processes, and creating jobs.

Wharton must be understood in the context of the times in which he lived. The Protestant Ethic, the predominant religious ethos of the day, stated that the probability of going to heaven could be predicted by financial success on earth. Wharton can be criticized for producing and profiting from munitions; although these activities met his own principled tests of logic they would not satisfy the peace testimony as understood by most Quakers today.

As a successful industrialist, Wharton blended his focus on financial prosperity with the emerging Hicksite Quaker acceptance of charitable contributions toward causes that promised some demonstrable societal benefit. He donated his money anonymously to Hicksite Quaker projects and is credited with founding and supporting two institutions of higher education, Swarthmore College to prepare Hicksite Quaker youth for productive service to their community and the Wharton School to elevate the quality of business and industrial leaders in the burgeoning world economy. The achievement record of Joseph Wharton, demonstrably well-grounded in his Hicksite Quaker faith and culture, inspires us to celebrate him as an American "Captain of Industry."

Bibliography

Benjamin, Philip S. 1976. *The Philadelphia Quakers in the Industrial Age 1865 - 1920.* Philadelphia: Temple University Press.

"Boston Joseph Wharton Award", Whartoboston.com/boston_joseph_wharton_award

Copley, Frank Barkley. 1923. *Frederick W. Taylor, Father of Scientific Management.* New York: Harper and Brothers.

Edmunds, Albert J. 1909. "Quaker Literature in the Libraries of Philadelphia." *The Westonian: A Monthly Magazine for Friends* 13 9, 182-203.

Gladwell, Malcolm. 2008.*Outliers.* New York: Little, Brown.

Goertzel, Victor and Mildred George. 1962. *Cradles of Eminence*. Boston: Little, Brown.

Green Street Monthly Meeting. 1909. *Monthly Meeting Minutes, 1909 - 1915*. Philadelphia, PA. *United States Quaker Meeting Records, 1681 - 1935*. Ancestry.com

Hamm, Thomas D. 2000, Fall. "The Hicksite Quaker World, 1875 – 1900." *Quaker History 89* 2, 17-41.

"Joseph Wharton Scholars", https//undergrad_insidewharton.upenn/ edu/Wharton.history/

Lippincott, Joanna Wharton. 1909. *Biographical Memoranda Concerning Joseph Wharton, 1826 - 1909*. Philadelphia: privately printed and circulated by J. B. Lippincott, 1909; available through HathiTrust Digital Library.

Morris, Harrison S. 1909. "Joseph Wharton, Sc.D., LL.D." *Proceedings of the American Philosophical Society 48*: 71-76. Digitized by Google Books.

National Endowment for the Humanities NEH. 2016. The Industrial Age in America: Robber Barons and Captains of Industry. Study resources. http://edsitement.neh.gov

National Mining Hall of Fame. 1997. *Joseph Wharton* Induction citation. Leadville, CO: National Mining Hall of Fame and Museum. www.mininghalloffame.org/inductee/wharton

New Jersey State Division of Parks and Forestry. no date. *Wharton State Park* online brochure. http://www.co.burlington.nj.us/DocumentCenter/View/1324

Raistrick, Arthur. 1950. *Quakers in Science and Industry, being an account of the Quaker contributions to science and industry during the 17th and 18th centuries*. New York: Philosophical Library.

Rzeznik, Thomas F. 2013. *Church and Estate: Religion and Wealth in Industrial-Era Philadelphia*. University Park, PA: Pennsylvania State University Press.

Sass, Steven A. 1982. *A History of the Wharton School 1881-1981*. Philadelphia: University of Pennsylvania Press.

Sass, Steven A. & Copperman Barbara. 1980. "Joseph Wharton's Argument for Protectionism." *Business and Economic History 9* 2nd series, 51-60.

Slavon, Susan 2012 *"Wharton Brand Refresh Isn't Just Academic"*. /up=content/uploads/innovation/History

Swarthmore College. 1920. *"The Register of Swarthmore College, 1862 - 1920; Being a Biographical Director of the Board of Managers..."* Pennsylvania: The College. Digitized by Google Books.

Tolles, Frederick Barnes. 1948. *Meeting House and Counting House: The Quaker Merchants of Colonial Philadelphia, 1682-1763*. Institute of Early American History and Culture at Williamsburg, VA / The Univ. of North Carolina Press.

Tolles, Frederick Barnes. 1956. "Quakerism and Politics." The Ward Lecture, Guildford College, North Carolina. http:www.quakers.org/pamphlets/ward1956.pdfwharton

Tower, Samuel A. 1981, June 21. "Stamps; For the Man Who Started Business Education." *The New York Times* online.whartonny.com/article.html

"Wharton Club of New York" – 2016 Wharton Awards Dinner Previous Awards" , Whartonny.com/article.html?aid=1135

"Wharton Fellowship Program", mba.wharton.upenn.edu/Financing-mba/grants-Fellowships-shcolarships/Wharton-fellowship-programs/

"Wharton History", Wharton.upenn.edu

Wharton, Joseph. 1865. "Speculations Upon a Possible Method of Determining the Distance of Certain Variably Colored Stars." *American Journal of Science and Arts: Series II*, Vol 40:190–192. Digitized by Google Books.

Wharton, Joseph. 1877. *Memorandum Concerning Small Money and Nickel Alloy Coinage with Illustrations and Descriptions of Existing Nickel Alloy Coins*. Philadelphia: Collins Kessinger Legacy Reprints.

Wharton, Joseph. 1893. "Dust from the Krakatoa Eruption of 1883." *Proceedings Commemorative of the 150th anniversary of the American Philosophical Society Held at Philadelphia for Promoting Useful Knowledge*, May 22–26, 1893. American Philosophical Society, 1894, 343-345. Digitized by Google Books.

Wharton, Joseph. 1909. "Will Papers" Image 69. *Philadelphia Wills, No. 141 - 164, 1909* in *Pennsylvania, Wills and Probate Records, 1683 - 1993*. Ancestry.com

Wharton School. University of Pennsylvania. 2016. "About Wharton." Wharton.upenn.edu/about Wharton

Yates, W. Ross. 1987. *Joseph Wharton: Quaker Industrial Pioneer*. Bethlehem, PA: Lehigh University Press.

"You Do Not Represent Us Wharton Students Tell Donald Trump", usnews.com/news/articles/2016-07-11/Wharton-students-post-open-letter-to-Donald-Trump.

PART III
Theorising Quaker Commerce

5 | Early Quakers and 'Just Debt'

By Karen Tibbals

Current knowledge among today's Quakers about debt and borrowing money focuses on two main points – the early writings against borrowing money quoting Romans 13:8 from Fox's Journal and the Balby Elders writings, and that Quakers were disowned for debt. But an intensive study of the Advices from London Yearly Meeting and other early Quaker writings reveals a concept that has been lost to us, 'Just Debt.'

In order to understand 'Just Debt' and how early Quakers developed it, one needs to first understand the context into which Quakerism arose and how thoughts about borrowing money had evolved over time. This chapter will provide that context, starting with a review of Roman Catholic usury theory and how it changed over time, and then move on to John Calvin's very different view of usury. Next, it will look at the evolution of English thought about usury prior to the establishment of Quakerism. After that, it will move to a similar analysis of Quaker thought about debt and how it changed over time, from the initial total prohibition to the later establishment of the concept of 'Just Debt' in the Advices of London Yearly Meeting. It will examine the characteristics of 'Just Debt' and also give examples of how Quakers lived out their commitment to 'Just Debt'. Further, it will argue that the shift from the responsibility of debt from the lender in usury theory to borrower in Quaker 'Just Debt' reflects the outsider status of Quakerism. Finally, this chapter will make the point that the shifts in Quaker theology about debt are similar shifts as that seen in Catholic and broader English usury theology as the faith communities worked to make their theology relevant to how the world of that day worked.

Religious and Economic Context

Quakerism was born into the middle of the seventeenth century, a time of much turmoil and change. The development of the Seekers, from whom Quakers sourced many of its members, was a direct result of disillusionment that the

133

religiously based English Civil Wars had not changed society and had not brought on the second coming of Christ. In fact, the upheaval and disruption of the Civil Wars had challenged established social norms and societal frameworks been destroyed making things worse, these war-related changes came after a period of more gradual but still far reaching change (Gwyn, 2006, 82-115).

Under the political stability of Queen Elizabeth I's reign and, at least partially, the result of England discovering, colonizing and exploiting lands abroad, society had begun to be transformed from an agrarian based economy to one with a greater emphasis on trade. While the agrarian countryside did still contain the bulk of the population and of the economic activity, London took on increasing importance as an urban trade center and attracted a growing number of people from the rural areas. London's population rose from an estimated 50,000 in 1530 to about 225,000 in 1605. As people moved in from rural centers, they needed to learn a new trade and how to deal in an economy based on money as opposed to one based on barter and paying rent to one's lord (Hunt 1996; Earle 1989).

Learning how to live in close quarters such as an urban environment with many other people also posed a problem. Sanitation practices needed to change, and until then, disease ran rampant, resulting in epidemics of the black plague (both in 1603 and the Great Plague of 1665) as well as epidemics of such diseases as cholera and yellow fever. The Great Fire of 1666 was another consequence of the poor living conditions in London (Hunt, 1996; Earle 1989).

Religious Context about usury and debt

Not only was there upheaval in the social and economic order in this period, the role that religion played in economics was changing, as illustrated by the change in thought about usury between the sixteenth and seventeenth centuries. As many are aware, the Roman Catholic Church prohibited usury beginning in the eighth century, in order to protect the poor from being exploited, defining it as any taking of interest. Usury was a complicated concept; it did not mean just charging a high interest rate, but also meant any way in which the lender took advantage of the borrower. That said, it should be noted that a common rate of interest at the time was 43% an extremely high rate which certainly could damage the borrower (Noonan 1967, 40). Over the centuries, the Church realized that an outright prohibition was hampering trade (which wasn't their intent), so various exceptions were developed such as for partnerships and mortgaging properties. The Church also developed exceptions that allowed for interest to be charged if the borrower didn't pay back the loan on time, or if damaged were caused. By the time of the Reformation, these exceptions were well developed, although preachers (including cleric Martin Luther) were still clearly anti-usury (Noonan 1967, 34-51).

However, under John Calvin, founder of Reformed theology, religious thought about usury shifted, which affected English religious thought a century later.

Calvin's Thought About Usury

The majority of John Calvin's ministry work was as a pastor in the city of Geneva, Switzerland. Geneva was an urban city in transition at the time Calvin was ministering there and was a magnet for migrants from Europe, especially from France. The Genevan populace was dependent on the food produced outside the city, and trade for that food was a crucial part of the city's economy. As part of his pastoral duties, Calvin participated in the Consistory, a panel composed of both lay and clergy, which ruled the city in a theocracy, hearing cases of trade-related conflicts, including fraud and broken contracts, and especially focused on cases which represented new economic developments. His was the dominant voice in the Consistory, and, as such, the findings of the Consistory can be seen as reflecting his views, in addition to usually cited writings, letters and sermons. A further source of insight into his views can be found in the fact that he also chaired a committee in 1543 to set the highest allowable interest rates at 5% and then supported a later increase to 6.67%. Thus, he participated broadly in the Genevan theological conversation about usury (Valeri 1997, 129, 131; Wykes 2003, 41).

A review of Calvin's works demonstrates that Calvin brought three main concerns to his view of usury, treatment of the poor, honesty, and the effect of usury on the fabric of society. Calvin was not as concerned about loans between merchants as about how usury might be used to exploit the poor. In this, he reflected the concerns of the Catholic scholars who had come before him. Concern for the poor was one of his major principles informing his criteria of when usury should be permitted (Valeri 1997, 132-33).

Despite Calvin's agreement with the Catholic scholars that preceded him on the importance of protecting the poor, he broke from them on a number of points. Catholic views of usury had built on Aristotelian thought that money was sterile, that itself had no use but was only a medium of exchange. Instead, Calvin believed that money was productive, and in fact he arranged funding for cloth manufacturers and in other ways supported loans to help develop of commerce in Geneva. Further, Calvin refuted the confusing scholastic Catholic belief about the transfer of ownership of money. The Roman conception of a loan (*muutum*) held that money's ownership transferred when a loan was made and that the lender had no claim on the money once it was loaned, at least until the term of the loan was up. Thomas Aquinas and other scholastics had incorporated that thought into their view of usury, which had become the dominant Catholic belief. In contrast, Calvin believed that "the lender continues to own his money after it had been lent out." Calvin's interpretation allowed for a more complex and more accurate picture of the amount of assets a person had under their control, and captured the difference between lending money and spending money (Munro 2011).

Another key to understanding Calvin's thoughts about usury can be found in his pronouncement that ethical judgment of usury should be based on whether the parties mutually benefited. Calvin only condemned usury if it was against "equity or charity." In this interpretation, he was relying on the Golden Rule in Matthew 7:12 for this interpretation and made it clear that he did not want to condemn anything that God had not condemned, another thought that broke with the Catholic interpretation (Wykes 2003, 42-5).

Calvin's doctrine of usury set out seven principles of when usury could be allowed. These were,

1. Usury not be used against the poor
2. That the lender not be "addicted to gain and profit"
3. No condition of the loan be against Christ's teachings
4. The borrower must benefit as well as the lender
5. Only God's word used to judge the equity
6. Contracts must be for the good of society
7. Cannot exceed the maximum rate set by the law (Calvin 2002, 94-6).

English and Puritan views of Usury

The Puritan movement developed in England during Queen Elizabeth I's reign. Puritans were English Calvinists who insisted on "the need to purify the Church through a return to biblical religion." (Gonzalez 2010, 194) Puritanism developed as a result of Protestant clerics' exposure to Calvinism, when they fled to Continental Europe (and Calvin's Geneva) during the five-year reign (1553-1558) of Mary, a Catholic and Elizabeth's older sister. A century later, the Puritan movement was so strong that conflicts between the English King and Puritan dominated Parliament ultimately culminated in the English Civil Wars in the middle of the seventeenth century. But English society was not dominantly Puritan or Calvinistic, which complicates an analysis of thought about usury (Gonzalez 2010, 203).

The economic environment of England of the time was more diverse than the solely urban Geneva in which Calvin lived and ministered and underwent much change in the period.

Eric Kerridge claims that sixteenth century English views (i.e., during Mary and Elizabeth's reigns) concerning usury reflected the ancient Catholic views, despite the break with the Catholic Church under King Henry VIII, and that they almost universally "condemned usury in the generally accepted meaning of the word" (Kerridge 2002, 53). Given that Henry VIII's break from the Roman Catholic Church was only a political break with Rome and not a theological break, this consistency is not surprising (Gonzalez 2010, 92).

Nevertheless, this universal condemnation of usury in England did not last. Early twentieth century economic and religious historian R.H. Tawney noted the change in sentiment from total condemnation of usury at the beginning of the sixteenth century to a later acceptance. Tawney attributed this change to the attempt "to meet the needs of the increasingly commercial civilization." (Tawney 1962, 108) Mark Valeri elaborates on Tawney's statement, explaining the necessity of allowing loans in the national interest, claiming that "Protestants transformed the morality of credit as a means of protecting their churches in the midst of a transatlantic contest for empire that began in the 1650s" (Valeri 2011, 150). In his analysis, Valeri focused on the "bills of exchange" that British merchants relied on in order to facilitate trade. These "bills of exchange" were in essence IOUs, written by a buyer of goods instead of payment when they didn't have actual currency. These notes would then be sold by the recipient of the note for hard currency. These "bills of exchange" could go through several hands before finally being settled by the original parties, having been traded between multiple unknown people, potentially across country lines or an ocean. In earlier days, this entire process would have qualified as usury, since each buyer was guaranteed a profit (the percentage or fee that each 'discounted' the note by) and exchange rates might have been perceived to be manipulated (which could happen if the note was sold across country lines). Valeri concluded that in order to keep pace with the change in commerce, the traditional prohibitions against usury needed to be removed or else the entire merchant class would be in violation (Valeri 2011, 148-151). Norman Jones studied the sentiment behind the passage and repeal of the English 1571 law against usury, and agrees that bills of exchange were not routinely condemned in this time (Jones 1989, 140).

Beyond the need for new forms of exchange to aid in changes to business, there was also a shift in the terms in which usury was evaluated. While the negative effect on the poor continued to be a concern as it was for both the Catholic scholars and Calvin, usury began to be considered as a matter of individual conscience instead of law. In his 1613 work entitled, *Cases of Conscience*, William Perkins argued that conscience was "placed in the middle between man and God," and that obedience needed to be linked with conscience. Writing slightly earlier, Andrew Willet stated that usury was not unjust when it was "not against charity in conscience." Willet echoed some of Calvin's thoughts when he declared that the way to judge loans was by Golden Rule, and that loans to the poor should not be allowed (Jones 1989, 150-154).

Walter Howse incorporated even more of Calvin's thought in his early seventeenth century manuscript. He closely restated Calvin's criteria for an ethical loan with nine criteria,

1. Lend not from greed
2. Contract for certain gain but willing to return it
3. Inwardly resolved to lose principle
4. Hew to legal interest rates
5. Never take biting interest
6. Lend freely, without concern for the return of the principle
7. Be ready to forgive debtor if in need, and help a debtor in need
8. Thank God for blessings
9. Only loans when compatible with the common good (Jones, 1989, 157).

Howse's prohibition on 'biting interest,' the keeping to legal rates, and the concern for the 'common good' echo Calvin's principles. Calvin's principle concerning lack of addiction to gain can be seen in Howse's criteria concerning a lender's willingness to return the gain, lend freely and willingness to forgive the debtor and provide help to a needy debtor.

Drawing from these sources, and particularly from Howse, was one of the most influential works about usury from the middle of the seventeenth century. The author of this work, Robert Filmer, concluded that usury was not prohibited by God, that one needed to obey the laws of the land, to have concern about charity and that whether something was usury should be determined by following one's conscience. Filmer's view became the dominant thought in the late seventeenth century, just as Quakerism was becoming established (Jones 1989, 159).

As early twentieth-century religious and economic historian RH Tawney noted, this was a transition time from dominance of religious principles over economic matters to one where government dominated as demonstrated by this history of usury thought (Tawney 1962, 279).

Early Quaker Thought on Usury

The earliest Quaker publications from the 1650s and 1660s that mention borrowing money, debt or usury all are consistent with the religious thought prohibiting usury common in England a century earlier.

The Balby Elders were first in 1656, saying "That all Friends that have callings and trades, do labour in the thing that is good, in faithfulness and uprightness; and keep to their yea and nay in all their communications; and that who are indebted to the world, endeavor to discharge the same, that nothing they may owe to any man but love one another" (Barclay 2010, 64). The phrase "owe to no man but love one another" was a direct reference to Romans 13:8. In one of his three pamphlets addressed to traders and in his Journal, George Fox concurs. He also rails against usury, echoing the Puritan preachers of a century earlier. For both Fox and the Balby Elders, the prohibition against borrowing was stated as an absolute – do not run into debt, although Balby has the additional thought that, if debt exists, one should pay off it off (Fox 1991 Vols. 7 & 8, 194).

Stephen Crisp, seventeenth century missionary to the Netherlands, explained in more detail why it was so important to not take on debts in an undated letter to a Friend. If the Friend was imprisoned for his faith, which was common for early Quakers, he would not be able to pay back the debt and thus injure those he borrowed from. This would violate the Golden Rule from Matthew of treating others the way you wish to be treated (Crisp 1850, 247).

As Quakers tried to put this into practice, the thinking about debts took a different direction. By the late seventeenth century, the phase 'Just Debt' began to be used the conveyed a different concept about debt, that there were some debts that were justified.

'Just Debt'

The second advice about Trade developed by London Yearly Meeting in 1692 was the first recorded mention of the topic of 'Just Debt' and starts with the following phrase: "It is advised and earnestly desired, that the payment of just debts…." Since the advice starts with 'just debt', the concept must have been well established and doesn't explain it. We can determine what must have been part of 'just debt' by analyzing the elements mentioned in the full passage (reproduced below) in the context of other Quaker writings and the society as a whole.

It is advised and earnestly desired, that the payment of just debts be not delayed by any professing truth beyond the time promised and agreed upon, nor occasion given of complaint to those they deal with by their backwardness of payment where no time is limited; nor any to overcharge themselves with too much trading and commerce, beyond their capacities to discharge with a good conscience towards all men; and that all friends concerned be very careful not to contract extravagant debts to the endangering the wronging of others, and their families, which some have done, to the grieving the hearts of the upright; nor to break their promises, contracts, or agreements, in their buying or selling, or in any other lawful affairs, to the injuring themselves or others, occasioning strife and contention, and reproach to truth and friends. And it is advised, that all friends that are entering into trade, or that are in trade, and have not stock sufficient of their own to answer the trade they aim at, be very cautious of running themselves into debt, without advising with some of their ancient and experienced friends among whom they live, and more especially such trading as hath its dependence upon sea-adventures. 1692. P. E. (London Yearly Meeting 1802, 195)

Here we can see that, unlike the prohibition seen in the Balby Elders' and Fox's earlier writings, the shift to acceptance of borrowing money if one was entering into trade and didn't have stock sufficient for the trade being entered. This was the first criterion of a 'Just Debt'. To understand more about why this concept was probably developed, it is important to understand the context of those times. Similar to today, in order to open a business, one needed to invest money in stock/inventory or raw materials and, for a store, in shop fittings. Wholesalers would advance some stock if the would-be merchant had other start-up capital (another form of debt), but seed money was still needed. Wages of the working class were so low that those in the working class would barely earn enough to live on, and were unlikely to be able to save any money. An apprenticeship had to be paid for by a relative, and an apprentice did not earn any money until journeyman status. Thus, at the end of an apprenticeship, a prospective tradesman would probably not have been able to save enough to afford to start out on their own. The options were usually to borrow that seed money, either from family or from a money lender. Families felt an obligation to assist young relatives to start out in the world, and so they would have been a primary source of start-up capital for the fledgling entrepreneur of the 17th century (Hunt 1996; Earle 1989). William Stout, a Lancashire Quaker, was an example of a well-to-do relative who felt provided money to numerous relatives and even to a former apprentice so they could get a start in the world (Marshall 1967).

But Quakers were outside of regular society. A convinced Friend could not count on non-Quaker family members for their support. Some meetings took up collections to pay for the apprenticeship, when no relatives were available (Gwyn 2006; Tibbals 2012). Even though it was allowed to borrow money to buy stock for trade purposes, London Yearly Meeting says to get advice beforehand. If a wise Friend agrees, then it becomes a 'Just Debt', another key criteria. There are two issues that a Friend can help with here, knowing one's self and one's abilities and the temptation for riches.

Even though one can use borrowed money to buy stock, it was not a 'Just Debt' to buy too much stock to "over charge themselves." This was one reason why it was so important to consult a wise Friend, because it was easy to fool one's self about one's abilities. Stephen Crisp warned against enlarging trade beyond what could be handled. He went further, speaking about recognizing the differing abilities of people, and that it was dangerous to not realize that, because disaster may sneak up unawares (Crisp 1850, 247).

It was also tempting to spend money extravagantly. Fox warns again and again about extravagance of the world, and covetousness, in various pamphlets as well as in one of pamphlets addressed to merchants particularly (Fox 1991, Vols. 7 & 8, 196). A search of the Digital Quaker collection turns up 38 mentions of the word covetousness in the collection of Fox's works. Covetousness was an easy trap to fall into and was often mentioned in early Quaker pamphlets addressed to all sorts, not just those in trade. Success in the world then, just like today, was judged by the exterior trappings of life, and a new tradesman starting out might be tempted to appear more successful than he was in order to attract potential customers and to be able to assure suppliers that they would get their money for their goods. Later admonishments for a plain way of living from London Yearly Meeting in 1724 were particularly appropriate for young merchants, which were then amplified several times in later years (London Yearly Meeting 1802, 196).

Ambrose Rigge, sometime traveling companion of Fox, published on this issue in a pamphlet addressed to Friends specifically. He graphically described the "Snares, Temptations and… hurtful Lusts" that those who are "spending above what they are able to pay for, or run into great trade beyond what they can in Honesty and Truth manage" can be led into (Rigge 1678).

Stephen Crisp was eloquent on the issue of the temptations of riches in another essay, warning that the dangers of riches and greed were great, saying that "some have too much set their minds after the things of this world, they have erred from the faith, and have placed their trust in uncertain riches." He instructed that merchants were to obey God in all things, even in their business and should only trade "if the Lord will.... (God should be) the ruler of your trading and dealing" (Crisp 1850, 247).

Selling goods to the New World and other far off places represented a particular temptation. Crisp, Rigge and London Yearly Meeting all warned against trading that relates to "sea-adventures" (Crisp 1850, 247; Rigge 1678; London Yearly Meeting 1802, 196). This was a special example of trade that could be a temptation to what Crisp called "uncertain riches". As this advice was being given, trade had been opening up to the New World and to Africa, all places that were or would become colonies. Goods were needed in these places, but sea adventures were risky. Ships could be lost at sea, and trading with goods at a distance carried other risks such as pirates, unscrupulous captains and crews and even unknown markets abroad. A trader did not know if the goods sent would be needed or even if they would be paid for in cash (Hunt 1996; Earle 1989; Tibbals 2012).

So to summarize some of the major elements of 'Just Debt', the advice implies that was a 'Just Debt' to buy needed stock, but not to buy stock intended to trade above one's abilities or to help one achieve "uncertain riches" or to trade in risky enterprises. Nor was it a 'Just Debt' to buy goods to enhance status or due to covetousness. One would know if it was a "Just Debt' if a wise Friend agreed.

There is a little more we can learn about 'just debt'. The next major concept, "endangering the wronging of others, and their families", related to the effect of not paying back debt to the people from whom the money was borrowed from. Not only does it emphasize how important it was to pay back the debt and that to not pay it back was to violate the Golden Rule, it also provided a clue about who one should borrow from. Presumably, a Quaker should only borrow from people who would be hurt if they were not paid back, that is private lending, and not from public money lenders. Because Quakerism was a society of its own, outside of the mainstream society, Quakers borrowed from each other. If one person defaulted on a debt, this could have a domino effect on the interlocking web of debt among Quakers. Quakers were obliged to settle arguments among themselves and not go to court (at first because they refused to swear an oath and later due to advices about dealing with disputes internally). If money was borrowed from outside the Society of Friends, this could have a calamitous effect. If a debt over two pounds wasn't paid, the non-Quaker creditor could sue for repayment, and if the debt was then not paid, the debtor could be thrown into debtors' prison. While the debtor would only go to prison about 10% of the time, Friends were already facing the threat of prison for other religious related reasons – they did not need to expose themselves to other risks, especially risks that would reflect badly on Quakerism (Gwyn 2006; Earle 1989; Tibbals 2012).

Fox's prohibition against mention of usury in one of his pamphlets provides another clue that borrowing from moneylenders was not acceptable (Fox 1991, Vols. 7 & 8, 194). William Stout, that successful ironmonger from Lancashire, recorded lending money to other Quakers, including his apprentices, so that they could start on their own in trade (Marshall 1967). Of course, we know about the banks that were later developed by Quakers, such as Gurney's and Barclays', but banks only began to be established in the eighteenth century and did not lend to individuals and small businesses until later (Ackrill 2001).

Local Meetings and Debt

It wasn't only the Yearly Meeting that had advices about trade and debt, Monthly and Quarterly meetings wrote minutes about trade. Gainsborough Quarterly meeting was one of the first, when it recorded in 1699. "Friends launch not out in to trading and business beyond what they are able to manage nor break their promises in paying their just debts or contracts, and that none practice any clandestine way of trading which is to the great dishonor of Truth and a scandal to religion, which the Testimony of truth is gone forth against" (Brace 1949, 30).

In addition to what they had to say, the Monthly and Quarterly meetings put into practice these advices. By examining the early minutes, we can understand how the different meetings took different approaches with their members, ranging from disowning members for violating the standards to providing practical help so they could meet the standards. Note that nowhere does London Yearly Meeting say it will disown people for not paying 'Just Debts' but the monthly meetings did (London Yearly Meeting 1802, 196).

Gainsborough Monthly Meeting both provided support and disowned members for the two members between 1669 and 1719 who had trouble for paying debts they owed. Members did meet several times with the offenders and gave them very practical business advice. For example, the advice sent to John Odlin in 1689 when his business was in trouble told him to take a true account of what he owed and to whom, collect the money that he was owed, sell everything he owned and make payments to his creditors proportionately. Nicholas Wilkinson, a cordwainer, was given similar advice did not take it, so they wrote him out of the meeting in 1693, citing both his frequenting company of loose women as well has his "running into debt, and taking no care to pay what he owes,... and other ungodly practices as lying for which he is so notorious, that his word in any case cannot be taken" (Brace 1949, 50).

The Somersetshire Quarterly Meeting seems to have either been the harshest or had the worst offenders seen in the minutes of the four monthly and quarterly meetings, which were reviewed. They were the most active in disowning members, numbering 12 over the period from 1668 to 1699. Although they may have also provided help, it was not recorded in their minutes (Morland 1978).

The Men's Meeting of the Society of Friends in Bristol was very pro-business and innovative in how they approached this topic, combining poor relief and business. They provided seed money for a deserted wife to start a business so she could support her family, and creating and running a workhouse so those who didn't have work could be gainfully employed (Mortimer 1977). The Leeds Meeting took a more proactive stance, not just reacting to member's business troubles, but actively stating that they wanted to be helpful to one another. Each time a member declared they wanted to start a business, a committee of experienced businessmen from the Meeting were appointed, and would give very practical advice about how to go about it. Sometimes they would advise waiting to gain more skill or capital or support from relatives prior to starting a business. If a member started a business without their advice, such as John Atkinson did, they still tried to help if they got into trouble, but felt in that case they could be of only limited assistance. While not all enterprises run by their members were successful, the advice seems to have helped, since very few of the members' businesses ended up in trouble for debts. Perhaps because they took such a helpful stance, they did not disown anyone for debts from 1692 to 1712. Those few who did run into trouble expressed the proper contrition and were assisted in paying off as much as possible, and so were not read out of the meeting (Mortimer 1980).

Individual Quaker Experience with Debt
The topic of debt comes up in journal entries when people talk about business matters of their lives, even if they were not in business themselves. Edward Brookes felt he had an unpaid debt when he did not finish an apprenticeship, even though the obligation to do so had been legally terminated on account of the Revolutionary War. In order to clear his obligation, he worked for his master until the debt was paid, which he called the happiest years of this life (Brookes 1839, 331). James Gough, an Irish Quaker who became a schoolmaster, had contracted with a carpenter to build a house, but after it was built found the actual cost was double the estimate. He had saved the original

amount, but now found himself in owing money he did not have. But through "industry and frugality, and through divine assistance, in some time I got over this difficulty and paid every farthing." He went on to reflect on this experience, "Truth has ever led to integrity, punctuality, upright dealings in our outward affairs and to limit ourselves to few wants, and a humble condition in life, rather than invade or risk the property of other men" (Gough 1845, 12). Robert Willis got into financial difficulties through the death of his wife. He quit working to be with his wife in her last days, but then was unable to pay the doctor's bill. In the midst of his grief, he did not know how to handle the debt. He sought the advice of Friends, who advised him to sell his goods to pay the bill, and put his children out to others, which he did (Willis 1836, 295). Being accused of not paying one's debts was a slur, and one needed to defend oneself, as John Richardson wrote in his journal, when an enemy asserted that he could not pay his debts (Richardson 1840, 105).

Joseph Fry, Elizabeth Fry's husband, a tea dealer and banker, was not very successful in trade. After several crises in which his wife's family (the Gurneys) helped him out, his bank and tea business finally went bankrupt during a banking crisis during the late 1820s. This system-wide crisis was so extreme that it took a major intervention so that the entire economy was not disrupted, in which his brother-in-law (head of Gurney's bank) was an important participant. Despite his brother-in-law Samuel Gurney's statement that Joseph's problems were just a reflection of the difficult circumstances, he was disowned for 'unjustifiably' risking other people's money. The disownment minute also stated that the "imprudent manner of conducting ... business had brought 'great and lamentable loss to a large body of creditors and 'reproach upon our Christian profession'". Thus, Joseph Fry was partially disowned due to the attention brought to the bankruptcy by prominence of his wife but also because of his impudence – a temptation which Crisp had both discussed. It was easy to fall in to difficulties, as Joseph Fry could attest. Notably, in the Fry bankruptcy one can see an example of the consequences of the legal system of that time. In bankruptcy, the Frys lost all they possessed and the family was taken in by the Gurneys, Elizabeth's family (Rose 1981).

Banker Thomas Gould lost everything when he speculated in shares of the London Lead Company, "just before its shares fell disastrously". His mother settled with her son's creditors, even though "she had no legal obligation to do so" (Ackrill and Leslie 2001, 14-15).

Accounts of women business people stand out among these accounts of seventeenth and eighteenth century Quaker business people because of their rarity. There were at least two eighteenth century Quaker women who got into trouble with debt. Joseph Oxley recounted the story of a woman entrepreneur who got into trouble in the 1740s with debt, due to her inability to balance shop-keeping and nursing twins. She was troubled by this, so she went to her creditors and had them seize what was left of her assets. This Friend was highly regarded by others in the Society, so that afterwards Friends contributed money to assist her and her family. Notably she was not disowned, probably because of her willingness to follow what was prescribed, the reasons for her troubles and her attitude (Oxley 1837, 460). Another woman in Pennsylvania was required to place her children in the homes of other friends in order to enable her to make restitution for her indebtedness in 1770 (Marietta 1984, 24).

Meetings would sometimes pay the debts of those who owed money, such as when two Friends from Philadelphia Yearly Meeting had their debts paid, one for passage to the New World, the other in the routine course of affairs. Nicholas Waln (a Philadelphia lawyer) was so troubled by the fact that another Friend could not have a certificate of membership until he paid off a debt that he took care of the debt himself. He was often known to give messages in meeting about trade, when he touched on many topics seen in the advices such as fictitious credit, hazardous pursuits and dealing with creditors (Waln 1834, 122).

However, young would-be merchants did not always heed the advices. Joseph Pike tells of young merchants who told him that his advice was fine for him because he was already rich, but that these youngsters believed that they could not follow his advice if they wanted to succeed (Pike 1838, 389).

William Penn represented a special case about debt, because of his prominence, his experience and because he wrote about money. In the 1669 edition of *No Cross, No Crown*, he tied fearing and obeying God and paying debts to the idea of treating their tenants well, saying that this will alleviate much suffering. He too tied the rich and poor together in his statement that excoriated the "small number of men" who experience pleasure, ease and lusts on the backs of the "sweat and tedious labour of the husbandman," calling them to become aware of God's judgment about this injustice (Penn 1726). Penn's *Advice of William Penn to his Children* also contained exhortations to be diligent, and frugal, using the phrase that we tend to associate with Benjamin Franklin, "a penny saved is a penny got" and expanding on it goes on to say "For many got that cannot keep, and for want of Frugality spend what they get, and so come to want what they have spent" (Penn 1726). He also addressed over- trading in *No Cross No Crown*, and brings in yet another Bible verse about the love of money (1 Timothy 6:10) which can be the cause of overreaching (Penn 1726).

Despite these fine sounding statements, Penn had financial trouble during his life, due to a number of factors - his extravagant living style (one that reflected the style in which he was raised in but which was contrary to Quaker practices and which gained him censure from Puritan preacher Richard Baxter), his Irish estates not producing income any longer and becoming worthless, and the lack of return on his investment in Pennsylvania. Penn did not deal well with the debt he incurred. He was sued for 20,000 pounds, and, when the judgement was entered against him, he refused to pay on the grounds that his creditor had falsified his books, entering debtor's prison instead. In essence, one might say that Penn didn't feel it was a 'Just Debt'. The Quaker community offered to pay that debt for him, but Penn refused, saying he did not owe it. Given Penn's prominence, this was a high profile case. Eventually, the Lord Chancellor, Duke of Marlborough, intervened and negotiated a settlement. Penn acquiesed to that offer and, in 1708, was released after seven months in prison (Moretta 2007, 168). This was a very different experience than Joseph Fry experienced when his unpaid debts became public knowledge just a few years later.

Statistics compiled by Jack Marietta about Philadelphia Yearly Meeting from 1682 to 1776 demonstrated that a Quaker with a debt they were unable to pay back were disowned about 50% of the time (Marietta 1984, 6-7). As part of examining the cases to see if the debtor should be disowned, in about half of the cases, the meetings identified other offences that may have been contributing factors, such as drunkeness, neglecting ones' vocation, loose behavior, fraud, prohibited marriage and neglecting the care of one's family (Marietta 1984, 33). The advices of the various Yearly Meetings included specific situations in which one would be disowned included persisting in behavior after having been advised against it, a charge of injustice against the persons' character (perhaps dishonesty) and having affected the reputation of the Society of Friends. As was seen in the local minutes, if one expressed contrition (and were believed) and worked with the meeting to pay back what was possible, a Quaker would probably not be disowned.

This advice from 1692 was just one of many advices developed over the centuries by Quakers about trade and debt, but it was one of the earliest. Notably, various crises developed over the period leading to more advices.

South Seas Bubble

One of the major crises was the South Sea Bubble. In 1711, the English government refinanced their government debt at a lower rate under Queen Anne by rolling it into a chartered limited company. To make it more attractive, they granted the South Seas Company the rights to trade in what we call South America today. Even though Spain and Portugal dominated trade in South America, the potential riches represented by trade in that region caught the imagination of the public. Stock prices of the South Seas Company were bid up to extremely high levels. When it became clear that there wouldn't be riches, the resulting bust in 1720 caused many lost fortunes, including those of Quakers.

The 1692 London Yearly Meeting advice about 'Just Debt' and trade included a brief mention of sea adventures but this was expanded in 1724, four years after the South Seas Bubble burst, with a new advice, emphasizing the riskiness of hazardous enterprises.

> It is earnestly desired that all friends everywhere be very careful to avoid all inordinate pursuit after the things of this world, by such ways and means as depend too much on the uncertain probabilities of hazardous enterprizes; but rather labour to content themselves with such a plain way and manner of living, as is most agreeable to the self-denying principle of truth which we profess, and which is most conducive to that tranquillity of mind that is requisite to a religious conduct through this troublesome world. 1724. P. E. (London Yearly Meeting 1802, 197)

In this one can see clear echoes of the South Seas Company, in the talk about hazardous enterprises and the root cause of inordinate pursuit of the things of this world. But that appeared to not be sufficient, as eight years later, there was another advice issued about the topic,

> How exact in performing their words and promises, without evasive excuses and insincere dealings! How careful to not involve themselves in business dealings which they understood not, nor had stock of their own to manage! How circumspect not to contract greater debts than they were able to pay in due time! But with sorrow we observe, that contrary to their example, and the repeated advices formerly given by this meeting against inordinate pursuit after riches, too many have launched into trades and businesses above their stocks and capacities. … involved themselves and families in trouble and ruin and brought considerable loss upon others. 1732 (London Yearly Meeting 1802, 197)

This advice may reflect a second crisis involving the South Seas Company but one that was limited to the Quaker community. In 1728 a "Quaker conspiracy" was exposed of a group of Quakers who had misappropriated corporate funds from the London Lead Company, invested those funds in the South Seas Company and then lost everything. They had hidden the lost for several years and caused much consternation when it was exposed (Ackrill and Leslie 2001, 13-14).

This did not mean one could not invest in hazardous enterprises; only that one could not borrow to invest in hazardous enterprises. Further, one should not invest if the investment represents a large portion of total net worth. William Stout, the Quaker Lancashire ironmonger, invested in ships several times, mostly with success, but did lose money sometimes. However, he did not borrow money to do so, nor did he invest a large part of his net worth (Marshall 1967).

These South Seas related failures and the exposure of the Quaker conspiracy may have also prompted the shift in 1732 for London Yearly Meeting asking monthly meetings to watch over the individual members. Presumably, since the advices to individual members did not seem to be working (or else these events would not have happened), the Quaker answer was to create a structure to ensure that they were followed. At first, members were to check with members if they saw them getting into trouble paying back their debts or keeping to their contracts. This later got more intrusive, so that meetings were to inspect the accounts of members once a year, even if they were not in trouble. If the member did get into trouble, members of the meeting inspected the accounts and worked with the creditors. The attitude of the member and the cause of the difficulties were crucial – if the cause was not fraud and the member was repentant, then the meeting would work with the member. However, if the member showed any of those signs or refused the meeting's involvement, he or she would be disowned (The Old Discipline 1999).

The Quaker shift from a focus on lending to borrowing

Notably, Quakerism started in a very similar vein to Roman Catholic and pre-Calvinist English thought about usury, with universal condemnation of usury. Usury theory had condemned the lender for charging interest and for making a profit and did not discuss the responsibilities of the borrower. This was perhaps because of the focus on protecting the poor, and the underlying belief that lending money was to take advantage of the borrower, and did not benefit the borrower at all. Calvin shifted to recognizing the benefit of a loan to the borrower, as one condition for acceptable loans but did not lay out any responsibilities of the borrower.

The earliest Quaker writings on debt echo the usury prohibition. However, even then, unlike Roman Catholic thought, Calvin's writings and English clerics' sermons, there was mention of the responsibilities of the borrower and not just of the lender. This probably arises out of the experience of the early Quakers, where the practice of their faith had cast them out of society and where to not pay back debt was to incur consequences above and beyond those they experienced for their faith. Because they were outcasts, their debts would have been to other Quakers, and thus, not paying it back would hurt other Friends. So, this focus on responsibilities of the borrower probably arise from the social location of Quakers. Unlike Roman Catholic, Calvinist or English thought, there are no mentions of the responsibilities of the lenders or of acceptable interest rates in any of the advices collected in the 1802 version of London Yearly Meetings Advices and Extracts. The only thing that comes close to advice to a lender is the advice to not take on another's debt in 1708.

> To prevent the great scandal and reproach which any professing truth may bring on it, by breaking in other men's debt, we remind you to exercise a godly care therein, as much as in you lies, by giving timely caution to any such as either break their promises, or delay the payment of their just debts, or otherwise render themselves suspected. 1708. P. E. (London Yearly Meeting 1802, 196)

The Quaker shift from outright condemnation to practical advices

As was demonstrated, the Roman Catholic prohibition of usury was gradually eroded through creation of exceptions. Later, John Calvin was very pragmatic in developing a rule that would support trade while maintaining a society that was theologically based. English society went through a similar shift from outright prohibition to a pragmatic rule of putting it to one's conscience and creation of a interest rate rule that would not inhibit trade.

Similarly, Quakerism went through a shift from outright prohibition by Fox and the Balby Elders to the creation of the concept of 'Just Debt' in the London Yearly Meeting Advices and enacted by the local meetings, both in England and in the New World. In doing so, they followed a pattern simliar to John Calvin, but unlike Calvin's short lived rule of theocratic Geneva the Society of Friends continued evolving the Advices over a period of centuries.

Conclusion

There is much else that could be discussed on the topic of Quakers, debt and 'Just Debt'. There were advices on how to know what one has and how much one can borrow safely, which is at the core of the first advice for trade in

1675. There were many advices on how to pay back the money that was owed if one couldn't pay it in full and what could and couldn't be done if a 'Just Debt' wasn't paid it back in full.

To summarize, a 'Just Debt' was one that was for a good business purpose, such as to buy stock for a business, but only if that was within your abilities and wise Friend agrees. A 'Just Debt' was also one that is borrowed from someone to whom losing the money would matter. A debt was not 'just' if it was for extravagant purposes, to live above ones' means or to reach for riches by trading above one's ability. A debt was also not 'just' if it was for hazardous enterprises.

These advices represent a shift from consistency with condemnation of usury similar to the Roman Catholic Church and English clerics a century before to one reflecting the lived experiences of a closed Quaker society concerned about its reputation and the effect on other Quakers. It was also a shift from a focus on the responsibility of the lender found in usury theory to the responsibility of the borrower, perhaps reflecting the outsider status of the Quakers of that day.

Bibliography

A Short Memoir of David Cooper. (1836). In J. &. Comly, *Friends' Miscellany* (pp. 337-343). Philadelphia: J. Richards.

Ackrill, M., & Leslie, H. (2001). *Barclays: The Business of Banking 1690-1996*. Cambridge UK: Cambridge University Press.

Adams, T. (1993). *A Far-Seeing Vision: The Socialist Quaker Society (1898-1924)*. Bedford, England: Quaker Socialist Society.

Al-anon Family Groups. (1988). *One Day at a Time in Al-Anon*. NY: Al-anon Family Groups.

Allott, S. (1978). *Friends in York: The Quaker Story in the LIfe of the Meeting*. York: William Session Ltd.

Amazon. (2013, Dec 17). *Integriy*. Retrieved Dec 17, 2013, from http://www.amazon.com/s/ref=sr_nr_n_14?rh=n%3A283155%2Cn%3A3%2Ck%3A%22integrity%22&keywords=%22integrity%22&ie=UTF8&qid=1387293292&rnid=1000

Anderson, A. R. (2012, 11 28). *Success Will Come and Go, But Integrity is Forever*. Retrieved 12 17, 2013, from Forbes: http://www.forbes.com/sites/amyanderson/2012/11/28/success-will-come-and-go-but-integrity-is-forever/

Anderson, A. R. (2012, Nov. 28). *Success Will Come and Go, But Integrity is Forever*. Retrieved Dec. 17, 2013, from Forbes: http://www.forbes.com/

sites/amyanderson/2012/11/28/success-will-come-and-go-but-integrity-is-forever/

Appiah, K. A. (2010). *The Honor Code: How Moral Revolutions Happen*. NY: W. W. Norton.

Bacon, M. (1980). *Valient Friend: The life of Lucretia Mott*.

Bacon, M. H. (1980). *Valient Friend: The life of Lucretia Mott*. New York: Walker and Company.

Barbour, H. (1964). *The Quakers in Puritan England*. New Haven: Yale University.

Barbour, H. (1995). *Quaker Cross Currents: Three Hundred Years of Friends in the New York Yearly Meeting*. Syracuse, NY: Syracuse University Press?New York Yearly Meeting.

Barclay, A. (2010). Advices of the elders at Balby. In T. Hamm, *Quaker writings : an anthology, 1650-1920* (pp. 64-68). NY: Penguin.

Barclay, R. (1692). *Apology For True Christian Divinity*. Retrieved July 7, 2013, from Digital Quaker Collection: http://dqc.esr.earlham.edu:8080/xmlmm/loginB?XMLMMToc=E3603092C-003&XMLMMLanguage=English&XMLMMCollection=/earlham&XMLMMReturnURL=http://esr.earlham.edu/dqc/biblio.html

Barclay, R. (1831). *"Truth Cleared Of Calumnies" In Truth triumphant (Volume 1)*. Retrieved February 18, 2014, from Digital Quaker Collection: http://dqc.esr.earlham.edu:8080/xmlmm/docButton?XMLMMWhat=hitPage&XMLMMWhere=hit&XMLMMHitNumber=2&XMLMMBuilt=Y&XMLMMBeanName=toc1&XMLMMNextPage=/printBuiltPage.jsp&XMLMMCheck=1.223.9.6.2

Bell, J. (2013, June 21). *Call to Action*. (J. Bell, Performer) Catholic Church, Market Harborough, UK.

Benjamin, P. S. (1976). *The Philadelphia Quakers in the Industrial Age 1865-1920*. Philadelphia: Temple University.

Blum, U., & Dudley, L. (2011). Religion and Economics: Was Weber Right? *Journal of Evolutionary Economics*, 207-230.

Brace, H. W. (1949). *The First Minute Book of the Gainsborough Monthly Meeting of the Society of Friends 1669-1719*. Hereford: Lincoln Record Society.

Briggs, A. (1961). *Social Thought and Social Action: A study of the work of Seebohm Rowntree 1871-1954*. London: Longmans.

Brinton, H. (1953). *Friends for 300 Years: Beliefs and Practices of the Society of Friends since George Fox started the Quaker Movement*. London: George Allen & Unwin Ltd.

Britain Yearly Meeting. (2008). *Living faithfully today*. Retrieved 6 1, 2013, from Quaker Faith and Practice: http://qfp.quakerweb.org.uk/qfp20-22.html

Britain Yearly Meeting. (2008). *Living faithfully today*. Retrieved June 1, 2013, from Quaker Faith and Practice: http://qfp.quakerweb.org.uk/qfp20-22.html

Britain Yearly Meeting. (n.d.). *Quaker Testimonies*. Retrieved 6 6, 2013, from Quakers in Britain: http://www.quaker.org.uk/testimonies

Brookes, E. (1839). Life and Journal of Edward Brookes. In J. &. Comly, *Friends Miscellany Vol XII* (pp. 330-333). Philadelphia: J. Richards.

Browning, D. S. (1991). *A Fundamental Practical Theology: Descriptive and Strategic Proposals*. Minneapolis: Fortress.

Budge, F. A. (1880). *Annals of the Early Friends*. Philadelphia: Henry Longstreth.

BYM. (1993). *Questions of Integrity*. London: Britain Yearly Meeting.

BYM. (n.d.). *Faith and Practice 20.22*. Retrieved 2 25, 2013, from http://qfp.quakerweb.org.uk/pdf/QFP_Chapter_20.pdf

Cadbury, D. (2010). *Chocolate Wars: The 150-Year Rivalry between the World's Greatest Chocolate Makers*. New York: Public Affairs.

Cadbury, D. (2010). *The Chocolate Wrs: The 150-Year Rivalry between the world's greatest chocolate makers*. NY, NY: Public Affairs.

Cadbury, E. (1979). *Experiments in industrial organization*. NY: Arno Press.

Cadbury, W. C. (1961). *The Second Period of Quakerism*. Cambridge: Cambridge University Press.

Cave, E. &. (2000). *Faith in Action: Quaker Social Testimony*. London: Quaker Home Service.

Cazden, E. (2011, Jan 7). From slave trader to abolitionist: "Quaker Tom" Robinson of Newport, Rhode Island. Boston: American Society of Church History.

Chalkey, T. (1741). *Journal Of The Life, Labours, Travels Of Thomas Chalkley*. Retrieved 12 27, 2013, from Digital Quaker Collection: http://dqc.esr.earlham.edu:8080/xmlmm/docButton?XMLMMWhat=hitPage&XMLMMWhere=hit&XMLMMHitNumber=3&XMLMMBuilt=Y&XMLMMBeanName=toc1&XMLMMNextPage=/printBuiltPage.jsp&XMLMMCheck=5.6.2.10.3

Child, J. (1964). Quaker Employers and Industrial Relations. *Sociological Review*, 293-313.

Cloud, H. (2006). *Integrity: The courage to meet the demands of reality.* New York: Harper.

Cohen, G. (2012, 4 5). *Shared Values – A New Approach to Business and Capitalism.* (G. Cohen, Performer) Rutgers Business School, Newark, NJ.

Comly, J. &. (1835). Nicholas Waln's Advice. In J. &. Comly, *Friends Miscellany Vol. VI* (pp. 284-5). Philadelphia: J. Richards.

Conference of Al Friendsl. (1920). Minute 27. In C. o. Friends, *Official Report: Conference of All Friends* (pp. 116-118). London: Conference Continuation Committee.

Conscious Capitalism. (2014). *Conscious Capitalism.* Retrieved Feb 19, 2014, from http://www.consciouscapitalism.org/

Cooper, W. (2001). *A Living Faith.* Richmond, IN: Friends United Press.

Cooper, W. A. (1991). *The Testimony of Integrity in the Religious Society of Friends.* Wallingford, PA: Pendle Hill.

Corley, T. (1972). *Quaker Enterprise in Biscuits: Huntley and Palmers of Reading 1822-1972.* London: Hutcinson of London.

Cox, H. (2004). Review of The Kingdom is Always Coming. Grand Rapids: Eerdmans.

Crisp, S. (1850). Life of Stephen Crisp. In W. a. Evans, *The Friends Library Comprising Journals, Doctrinal Treatices, & Other Writings of Members of the Religious Society of Friends Vol XIV* (pp. 244-275). Philadelphia: Joseph Rakestraw.

Crothers, A. G. (2012). *Quakers living in the Lion's Mouth.* Gainsville: University Press of Florida.

Dandelion, P. (2007). *An Introduction to Quakerism.* Cambridge: Cambridge University Press.

Davison, R. A. (1964). *Isaac Hicks: New York Merchant and Quaker, 1767-1820.* Cambridge, MA: Harvard University Press.

Davison, S. (2011, June 30). *Quakerism & Capitalism — Transition (1895-1920): The Limited Liability Corporation.* Retrieved June 24, 2012, from Through the Flaming Sword: http://throughtheflamingsword.wordpress.com/tag/limited-liability/

Defoe, D. (1839). *The complete English Tradesman.* Retrieved 12 20, 2013, from The Gutenberg Project: http://www.gutenberg.org/ebooks/14444

Diaper, S. (1988). J. S. Fry and Sons. In C. Harvey, & J. Press, *Studies in the Business History of Bristol.* Bristol: Bristol Academic.

Dorrien, G. (2003). *The Making of American Liberal Theology: Idealism, Realism and Modernity 1900-1950*. Louisville: Westminster John Knox.

Drake, T. E. (1950). *Quakers and Slavery in America*. New Haven, CT: Yale University Press.

Earle, P. (1989). *The Making of the English Middle Class: Business, Society and Familly Life in London 1660-1730*. Berkely & Los Angeles: University of California Press.

Edmundson, W. (1820). *Journal of the life, travels, sufferings, and labour of love of William Edmundson* . Retrieved May 31, 2013, from Digital Quaker Collection: http://esr.earlham.edu/dqc/index.html

Edmundson, W. (1837). Journal of the Life of William Edmundson. In T. &. Evans, *The Friends' library Vol II* (pp. 96-97). Philadelphia: Joseph Rakestraw.

Eichengreen, B. (2004). The British Economy between the wars. In R. F. Johnson, *The Cambridge Economic History of Modern Britain: Volume II Economic Maturity, 1860-1939* (pp. 315-343). Cambridge: Cambridge University Press.

Elders, B. (2010). In H. Thomas, *Quaker Writings: An Anthology 1650-1920*. NY: Penguin.

Emden, P. H. (1940). *Quakers in Commerce: A record of business achievement*. London: Sampson, Low, Marston & Co, LTD.

Endy, M. B. (1981). The Interpretation of Quakerism: Rufus Jones and his critics. *Quaker History*, 3-20.

Evans, C. (2004). *The Kingdom is Always Coming*. Grand Rapids: Eerdmans.

Evans, E. W. (1920). The Closed Door. In C. o. Friends, *Official Report: Conference of All Friends* (pp. 100-109). London: Conference Continuation Committee.

Evans, J. (1837). Joshua Evans' Journal. In J. &. Comly, *Friends Miscellany Vol X* (pp. 1-67). Philadelphia: J. Richards.

Fisher, S. (1679). *"Burden Of The Word Of The Lord" In Testimony of truth exalted*. Retrieved May 31, 2013, from Digital Quaker Collection: http://esr.earlham.edu/dqc/index.html

Floud, R., & Johnson, P. A. (2004). *The Cambridge Economic HIstory of Modern Britain, Volume II Economic Maturity*. Cambridge: Cambridge University Press.

Foulds, E. V. (1953). *The Story of Quakerism: 1652-1952*. London: The Bannisdale Press.

Fox, G. (1658). A Warning to all the Merchants in London and such as buy and sell.

Fox, G. (1660). *Declaration from the harmless & innocent people of God called Quakers*. Retrieved Feb 20, 2014, from Digital Quaker Collection: http://dqc.esr.earlham.edu:8080/xmlmm/print?XMLMMDocList=1 &XMLMMDocStyle=STYLED&XMLMMStyleFile=&XMLMMBean Name=toc1&XMLMMNextPage=/printFromList.jsp&XMLMMChe ck=1.419.1.0.0

Fox, G. (1661). A Line of Righteousness.

Fox, G. (1831). *"Collection Of Many Select And Christian Epistles, Letters And Testimonies" In Works of George Fox (Volume 4)*. Retrieved 01 28, 2013, from Digital Quaker Collection: http://dqc.esr.earlham.edu:8080 /xmlmm/print?XMLMMDocList=4&XMLMMDocStyle=STYLED &XMLMMStyleFile=&XMLMMBeanName=toc1&XMLMMNextPa ge=/printFromList.jsp&XMLMMCheck=2.30.4.0.0

Fox, G. (1831). *"Collection Of Many Select And Christian Epistles, Letters And Testimonies" In Works of George Fox (Volume 7 & 8)*. Retrieved May 30, 2013, from http://dqc.esr.earlham.edu:8080/xmlmm/print?XML MMDocList=2&XMLMMDocStyle=STYLED&XMLMMStyleFile= &XMLMMBeanName=toc1&XMLMMNextPage=/printFromList.js p&XMLMMCheck=1.2.2.0.0

Fox, G. (1831). *"Collection Of Many Select And Christian Epistles, Letters And Testimonies" In Works of George Fox (Volume 7&8)*. Retrieved May 30, 2013, from http://dqc.esr.earlham.edu:8080/xmlmm/print?XMLMM DocList=2&XMLMMDocStyle=STYLED&XMLMMStyleFile=&X MLMMBeanName=toc1&XMLMMNextPage=/printFromList.jsp& XMLMMCheck=1.2.2.0.0

Fox, G. (1831). *"To The People Of Uxbridge" In Works of George Fox (Volume 4)*. Philadlephia & NY: Marcus Gould.

Fox, G. (1831). *"Collection Of Many Select And Christian Epistles, Letters And Testimonies" In Works of George Fox (Volume 1&2)*. Retrieved Dec 5, 2013, from Digital Quaker Collection: http://dqc.esr.earlham.edu: 8080/xmlmm/docButton?XMLMMWhat=hitPage&XMLMMWhere =hit&XMLMMHitNumber=1&XMLMMBuilt=Y&XMLMMBeanNa me=toc1&XMLMMNextPage=/printBuiltPage.jsp&XMLMMCheck =8.18.13.7.1

Fox, G. (1831). *"Collection Of Many Select And Christian Epistles, Letters And Testimonies" In Works of George Fox (Volume 7 & 8)*. Retrieved May 31, 2013, from Digital Quaker Collection.

Fox, H. (1958). *Quaker Homespun: The Life of Thomas Fox of Wellington Serge Maker and Banker, 1747-1821*. London: George Allen and Unwin Ltd.

Frost, J. W. (1973). *The Quaker Family in Colonial America: A Portrait of the Society of Friends*. NY: St. Martins Press.

Gough, J. (1845). James Gough. In T. a. Evans, *Friend's Library IX*. Philadelphia: Joseph Rakestraw.

Green, R. W. (1973). *Protestantism, Capitalism, and Social Science: The Weber Thesis Controversy*. Lexington, Mass: Heath.

Grubb, E. (1912). *Christianity and Business* . London: T. Fisher Unwin & Headley Brothers.

Grubb, I. (1930). *Quakerism and Industry before 1800*. London: Williams and Norgate Ltd.

Guiton, G. (2012). *The Early Quakers and the "Kingdom of God": Peace, Testimony and Revolution*. San Francisco: Inner Light Books.

Gunderson, G. (1976). *A New Economic History of America*. NY: McGraw-Hill.

Gwyn, D. (1986). *Apocalypse of the Word*. Richmond Indiana: Friends United Press.

Gwyn, D. (2006). *The Covenant Crucified: Quakers and the Rise of Capitalism*. Wallingford, PA: Pendle Hill Publications.

Harley, C. K. (2004). Trade, 1870-1939: from globalsation to fragmentation. In R. F. Johnson, *The Cambridge Economic History of Modern Britain: Volume II Economic Maturity, 1860-1939* (pp. 161-189). Cambridge : Cambridge University Press.

Harris, H. (1938). *American Labor*. New Haven: Yale University Press.

Hart, H. (1928). *Building a New Economic Order*. Philadelphia: Business Problems Group of the Social Order Committee (PYM Orthodox).

Hart, H. (1928). *Industry in a Christian Social Order*. Philadelphia: Business Problems Group of the Social Order Committee of PYM (Orthodox).

Hatton, T. J. (2004). Unemployment and the Labour Market, 1870-1939. In R. F. Johnson, *The Cambridge Economic History of Modern Britain: Volume II Economic Maturity, 1860-1939* (pp. 344-373). Cambridge: Cambridge University Press.

Hawkins, R. (1707). *A brief narrative of the life of Gilbert Latey, comprising some account of the first settlement of Friends' Meetings in London*. London: Soule.

Heath, C. H. (2010). *Switch: How to change things when change is hard*. NY: Broadway Books.

Heron, A. (1995). *Quakers in Britain: A Century of Change 1895-1995*. Kelso, Scotland: Curlew Graphics.

Hicks, E. (1832). *Journal of the life and religious labours of Elias Hicks.* Retrieved February 18, 2014, from Digital Quaker Collection: http://dqc.esr.earlham.edu:8080/xmlmm/docButton?XMLMMWhat =hitPage&XMLMMWhere=hit&XMLMMHitNumber=2&XMLMM Built=Y&XMLMMBeanName=toc1&XMLMMNextPage=/printBuil tPage.jsp&XMLMMCheck=1.223.3.4.2

Hilty, H. H. (1993). *By Land and by Sea: Quakers Confront Slavery and its Aftermath in North Carolina.* Greensboro, NC: North Carolina Friends Society.

Hinshaw, C. E. (1973). *Quaker Values in Today's World: Three Lectures.* Richmond, IN: Earlham .

Hodgkin, J. E. (1918). *Quakerism and industry; being the full record of a conference of employers, chiefly members of the Society of Friends, held at Woodebrooke, near Birmingham, 11th-14th April, 1918, together with the report issued by the conferen.* London: Friends Book Centre.

Hodgkin, J. E. (1920). The Testimony in Personal Life and Society. In C. o. Friends, *Official Report: Conference of All Friends* (pp. 94-100). London: Conference Continuation Committee.

Hodgkin, J. E. (1928). *Quakerism and Industry, being the full record of a confrence of employers, members of the Society of Friends held at Wroodbrooke, near Birmingham.* London: Friends Book Centre.

Hofstadter, R. (1955). *The Age of Reform.* NY: Random House.

Holmes, J. H. (1920). Implications of The Quaker Testimony in Personal Life and In Society. In C. o. Friends, *Official Report: Conference of All Friends* (pp. 1-30). London: Conference Continuation Committee.

Hull, H. (1840). Life of Henry Hull. In W. &. Evans, *Friends Library: Vol IV* (pp. 239-247). Philadelphia: Joseph Rakestraw.

Hunt, M. R. (1996). *The Middling Sort: Commerce, Gender and the Family in England, 1680-1780.* Berkely, Los Angeles, London: University of California Press.

James Gough. (n.d.). In T. a. Evans, *Friend's Library IX.*

Janney, S. M. (1860). *History of the religious Society of Friends (Volume 2).* Retrieved Feb 28, 2014, from Digital Quaker Collection: http://dqc.esr.earlham.edu:8080/xmlmm/print?XMLMMDocList=2 &XMLMMDocStyle=STYLED&XMLMMStyleFile=&XMLMMBean Name=toc1&XMLMMNextPage=/printFromList.jsp&XMLMMChe ck=3.5.2.0.0

Jason, L. A. (2013). *Principles of Social Change.* NY: Oxford University Press.

Jones, P. d. (1968). *The Christian Socialist Revival 1877-1914*. Princeton: Princeton University Press.

Jones, R. (1927). *The Faith and Practice of the Quakers*. London: Methuen & Co. LTD.

Kennedy, C. (2000). *The Merchant Princes: Family, Fortune and Philanthropy: Cadbury, Sainsbury and John Lewis*. London: Hutchinson.

Kennedy, T. (2001). *British Quakerism: 1860-1920: The Transformation of a Religious Community*. Oxford: Oxford University Press.

Killinger, B. (2007). *Integrity: Doing the right thing for the right reason*. Montreal & Kingston: McGill-Queen's University Press.

Klein, M. (2007). *The Genesis of Industrial America, 1870-1920*. Cambridge: Cambridge University Press.

Korn, M. (2013, Feb 6). *Does an 'A' in Ethics Have Any Value?* Retrieved Dec 17, 2013, from Wall Street Journal: http://online.wsj.com/news/articles/SB10001424127887324761004578286102004694378

Langley, M. (2014, Feb 19). Inside Target, CEO Struggles to Regain Shoppers' Trust. *The Wall Street Journal*, pp. A1, A10.

Latey, G. (1660). *To all you taylors and brokers, why lyes in wickedness*. London: printed for Robert Wilson, at the sign of the Black-spread-Eagle and Wind-Mill in Martins.

Lief, A. (1968). *Family business; : a century in the life and times of Strawbridge & Clothier*. NY: McGraw Hill.

London Yearly Meeting. (1802). *Extracts from the Minutes and Advices of the Yearly Meeting of Friends held in London, from its first institution*. London: W. Phillips.

London Yearly Meeting. (1806). *A Collection of the Annual Epistles from the Yearly Meeting in London to the Quarterly & Monthly Meeting of Friends in Great Britainand everywhere*. Baltimore: Cole & Hewes.

LYM. (1802). *Extracts from the Minutes and Advices of the Yearly Meeting of Friends held in London, from its first institution*. London: W. Phillips.

LYM. (1911). Extracts. London: Office of the Society of Friends.

LYM. (1911). *Extracts from the Minutes and Proceedings of London Yearly Meeting of Friends*. London: Office of the Society of Friends.

LYM. (1912). *Extracts*. London: Office of the Society of Friends.

LYM. (1912). *Extracts from the Minutes and Proceedings of London Yearly Meeting of Friends*. London: Office of the Society of Friends.

LYM. (1913). *Extracts*. London: Office of the Society of Friends.

LYM. (1913). *Extracts from the Minutes and Proceedings of London Yearly Meeting of Friends*. London: Office of the Society of Friends.

LYM. (1914). *Extracts*. London: Office of the Society of Friends.

LYM. (1914). *Extracts from the Minutes and Proceedings of London Yearly Meeting of Friends*. London: Office of the Society of Friends.

LYM. (1915). *Extracts*. London: Office of the Society of Friends.

LYM. (1915). *Extracts from the Minutes and Proceedings of London Yearly Meeting of Friends*. London: Office of the Society of Friends.

LYM. (1916). *Extracts*. London: Office of the Society of Friends.

LYM. (1916). *Extracts from the Minutes and Proceedings of London Yearly Meeting of Friends*. London: Office of the Society of Friends.

LYM. (1916-1929). *The Friend*. London: London Yearly Meeting.

LYM. (1917). *Extracts*. London: Office of the Society of Friends.

LYM. (1917). *Extracts from the Minutes and Proceedings of London Yearly Meeting of Friends*. London: Office of the Society of Friends.

LYM. (1918). *Extracts*. London: Office of the Society of Friends.

LYM. (1918). *Extracts from the Minutes and Proceedings of London Yearly Meeting of Friends*. London: Office of the Society of Friends.

LYM. (1919). Extracts. London: Office of the Society of Friends.

LYM. (1920). Extracts. London: Office of the Society of Friends.

LYM. (1921). Extracts. London: Office of the Yearly Meeting.

LYM. (1921). Extracts from the Minutes and Proceedings of London Yearly Meeting of Friends. London: Office of the Yearly Meeting.

LYM. (1922). Extracts. London: Office of the Yearly Meeting.

LYM. (1923). Extracts. London: Office of the Society of Friends.

LYM. (1924). Extracts. London: Office of the Society of Friends.

LYM. (1925). Extracts. London: Office of the Society of Friends.

LYM. (1926). Extracts. London: Office of the Society of Friends.

LYM. (1927). *Extracts*. London: Office of the Society of Friends.

LYM. (1927). *Extracts from the Minutes and Proceedings of London Yearly Meeting of Friends*. London: Office of the Society of Friends.

LYM. (1928). *Extracts*. London: Office of the Society of Friends.

LYM. (1928). *Extracts from the Minutes and Proceedings of London Yearly Meeting of Friends.* London: Office of the Society of Friends.

LYM. (1930). *Extracts.* London: LYM.

LYM. (1930). *Extracts from Minutes and Proceeding of London Yearly Meeting.* London: LYM.

Mackey, J., & Sisodia, R. (2013). *Conscious Capitalism.* Boston: Harvard Business Review Press.

Magee, G. B. (2004). Manufacturing and Technological Change. In R. F. Johnson, *The Cambridge Economic History of Modern Britain: Vol. II Economic Maturity, 1860-1939* (pp. 75-98). Cambridge: Cambridge University Press.

Marshall, J. (1967). *The Autobiography of William Stout of Lancaster 1665-1752.* New York: Manchester University Press/Barnes & Noble.

Martin, M. (2012, 12 10). *Ten Elements of the Quaker Spiritual Journey.* Retrieved 12 30, 2013, from A Whole Heart: http://awholeheart.com /2012/12/10/ten-elements-of-the-quaker-spiritual-journey-2/

McGrath, P. (1971). *Minute Book of the Men's Meeting of the Society of Friends in Bristol 1667-1686.* Bristol: Bristol Record Society.

McGrath, P. (1977). *Minute Book of the Men's Meeting of the Society of Friends in Bristol 1686-1704.* Bristol: Bristol Record Society's Publications.

McKinnon, M. H. (1993). The Longevity of the Thesis: A Critique of the Critics. In H. L. Ross, *Weber's Protestant Ethic* (pp. 211-243). Washington DC: German Historical Insititute/Cambridge University Press.

Meister, J. (2012, June 7). *Corporate Social Responsiblity a leveler for employee attraction and engagement.* Retrieved Dec 17, 2013, from Forbes: http://www.forbes.com/sites/jeannemeister/2012/06/07/corporate-social-responsibility-a-lever-for-employee-attraction-engagement/

Memior of James Emlen. (1836). In J. &. Comly, *Friends Miscellany: Being a collection of Essays and Fragments, Biographical, religious epitolary, narrative nd historial Vol VIII* (pp. 194-195). Philadelphia: J. Richards.

Memior of James Mott. (1837). In J. &. Comly, *Friends Miscellany Vol IX* (pp. 337-371). Philadelphia: J. Richards.

Memiors of James Simpson. (1833). In J. a. Comly, *Friends Miscellany: Being a collection of Essays and Fragments, Biographical, religious epitolary, narrative nd historial Vol IV* (pp. 194-205). Philadelphia: J. Richards.

Milligan, E. H. (2007). *Biographical Dictionary of British Quakers in Commerce and Industry 1775-1920.* York: Sessions Book Trust.

Moretta, J. A. (2007). *William Penn and the Quaker Legacy*. NY: Pearson Longman.

Morgan, W. (1899). *The Freemason's Chronical Vol 49-50*. Retrieved Jan 22, 2014, from books.google.com: http://books.google.com/books?id=I3 otAQAAMAAJ&pg=RA1-PA94&lpg=RA1-PA94&dq=Freemason +doctrine+brotherhood+of+man&source=bl&ots=G9CQHntV9H& sig=19qbsZiQtGSbCTjkbmVm3ww2Jt4&hl=en&sa=X&ei=YXjhUs H0KNH8yAHtp4DQCg&ved=0CFEQ6AEwBQ#v=onepage&q=Fr eemason%20doctrine%

Morland, S. (1978). *The Somersetshire Quarterly Meeting of the Society of Friends 1668-1699*. Somerset: Somerset Record Society.

Mortimer, J. &. (1980). *Leeds Friends' Minute Book 1692-1712*. York: The Yorkshire Archaelogical Society.

Mortimer, J. a. (1980). *Leeds Friends' Minute Book 1692-1712*. The Yorkshire Archaelogical Society.

Mortimer, R. (1971). *Minute Book of the Men's Meeting of the Society of Friends in Bristol 1667-1686*. Bristol: Bristol Record Society.

Mortimer, R. (1977). *Minute Book of the Men's Meeting of the Society of Friends in Bristol 1686-1704*. Bristol Record Society.

Mortimer, R. (1977). *Minute book of the Men's Meeting of the Society of Friends in Bristol, 1686-1704*. Bristol UK: Bristol Record Society.

Moulton, P. (1989). *The Journal and Major Essays of John Woolman*. Richmond, IN: Friends United Meeting.

Musson, A. (1965). *Enterprise in soap and chemicals*. Manchester: Manchester University Press.

Musson, A. E. (1965). *Enterprise in soap and chemicals: Joseph Crosfield & Sons, Limited, 1815-1965,*. Manchester: Manchester University Press.

Newbold, J. W. (1920). Capitalism and War. In C. C. Committee, *Conference of All Friends: Official Report* (pp. 14-20). London: Friends Bookshop.

Newbold, J. W. (1920). Capitalism and War. In C. C. Committee, *Conference of All Friends: Official Report* (pp. 14-20). London: Friends Bookshop.

NEYM. (1809). *Rule For Discipline of the Yearly Meeting held on Rhode-Island for New England*. New Bedford: Abraham Shearman.

Noble, T. (2000). *Social Theory and Social Change*. NY, NY: St. Martin's Press.

Osmer, R. R. (2008). *Practical Theology: An Introduction*. Grand Rapids, MI: Wm. B. Eerdmans Publishing Co.

Oxley, J. (1837-1850). Life of Joseph Oxley. In W. a. Evans, *Friends Library*.

Oxley, J. (1838). Life of Joseph Oxley. In W. a. Evans, *Friends Library Vol II* (pp. 424-460). Philadelphia: Joseph Rakestraw.

Packer, I. (2002). *The Letters of Arnold Stephenson Rowntree to Mary Katherine Rowntree, 1910-1918*. London: Cambridge University Press.

Parnel, J. (1675). *A collection of the several writings given forth from the Spirit of the Lord through that meek, patient, and suffering servant of God, James Parnel, who, though a young man, bore a faithful testimony for God and dyed a prisoner under the hands of a persec.* Retrieved Jan 28, 2014, from Early English Books Online: http://gateway.proquest.com.proxy.earlham.edu:2048/open url?ctx_ver=Z39.88-2003&res_id=xri:eebo&rft_id=xri:eebo:image: 101884:239

Parnell, J. (1675). *A collection of the several writings given forth from the Spirit of the Lord through that meek, patient, and suffering servant of God, James Parnel, who, though a young man, bore a faithful testimony for God and dyed a prisoner under the hands of a persec.* Retrieved Feb. 28, 2014, from Early English Books Online: http://eebo.chadwyck.com.proxy.earlham.edu:2048/search /full_rec?SOURCE=pgthumbs.cfg&ACTION=ByID&ID=13798571 &FILE=../session/1393607899_18047&SEARCHSCREEN=CITAT IONS&SEARCHCONFIG=var_spell.cfg&DISPLAY=AUTHOR

Parnell, J. (1792). A Warning to All People. In *Friends Pamphlets, Vol 1*.

Penington, I. (1784). *"Some Queries concerning the Work of God in the World" In Works of the long-mournful and sorely-distressed Isaac Penington (Volume 2)*. Retrieved Feb 28, 2014, from Digital Quaker Collection: http://dqc.esr.earlham.edu:8080/xmlmm/print?XMLMMDocList=5 &XMLMMDocStyle=STYLED&XMLMMStyleFile=&XMLMMBean Name=toc1&XMLMMNextPage=/printFromList.jsp&XMLMMChe ck=2.28.5.0.0

Penn, W. (1726). *"Address To Protestants Of All Perswasions" In Collection of the works of William Penn (Volume 1)*. Retrieved Feb 28, 2014, from Digital Quaker Collection: http://dqc.esr.earlham.edu:8080/xmlmm/print? XMLMMDocList=5&XMLMMDocStyle=STYLED&XMLMMStyleF ile=&XMLMMBeanName=toc1&XMLMMNextPage=/printFromLis t.jsp&XMLMMCheck=1.28.5.0.0

Penn, W. (1726). *"Advice Of William Penn To His Children" In Collection of the works of William Penn (Volume 1)*. Retrieved Feb 28, 2014, from Digital Quaker Collection: http://dqc.esr.earlham.edu:8080/xmlmm/print? XMLMMDocList=8&XMLMMDocStyle=STYLED&XMLMMStyleF ile=&XMLMMBeanName=toc1&XMLMMNextPage=/printFromLis t.jsp&XMLMMCheck=5.55.8.0.0

Penn, W. (1726). *"No Cross, No Crown" In Collection of the works of William Penn (Volume 1)*. Retrieved May 31, 2013, from Digital Quaker Collection: http://esr.earlham.edu/dqc/index.html

Penn, W. (1726). *No Cross No Crown*. Retrieved 12 27, 2013, from Digital Quaker Collection: http://dqc.esr.earlham.edu:8080/xmlmm/docButton?XMLMMWhat=hitPage&XMLMMWhere=hit&XMLMMHitNumber=4&XMLMMBuilt=Y&XMLMMBeanName=toc1&XMLMMNextPage=/printBuiltPage.jsp&XMLMMCheck=1.2.1.6.4

Philadelphia Yearly Meeting. (1797). *Rules of Discipline and Chrsitian Advices of the Yearly Meeting of Friends for Pennsylvania & NJ*. Philadelphia: Samuel Sandom.

Pike, J. (1838). Life of Joseph Pike. In T. a. Evans, *Friends Library Vol II* (pp. 388-389). Philadelphia: Rakestraw.

Pinker, S. (2011). *The Better Angels of our Nature: Why Violence has declined*. NY: Penguin.

Porter, M., & Kramer, M. (2011). Creating Shared Value. *Harvard Business Review*, 62-79.

Prior, A. &. (1998). The Society of Friends and business culture, 1700-1830. In D. J. Jeremy, *Religion, Business and Wealth in Modern Britain* (pp. 115-45). London: Routledge.

Punshon, J. (1990). *Testimony & Tradition: Some Aspects of Quaker Spritituality*. London: Quaker Home Service.

PYM (Orthodox) Business Problems Group. (1921). Report of Address by B. Seebohm Rowntree on The Human Factor in Business. Philadelphia: PYM (Orthodox) Business Problems Group.

PYM. (1797). *Rules of Discipline and Christian Advice of the Yearly Meeitng of Friends for Pennsylvania and New Jersey*. Philadelphia: Samuel Samsom Jr.

PYM. (1917, Oct 13). Minutes of the Meeting of the Social Order Committee. Philadelphia: PYM (Orthodox).

PYM. (1918, February 11). Minutes of the Meeting of the Social Order Committee. Philadelphia: PYM.

PYM. (1919, February 10). Minutes of the Meeting of the Social Order Committee. Philadelphia: PYM.

PYM. (1920). Bulletin of the Social Order Committee. Philadelphia: PYM.

PYM. (1921). *Minutes of the Meeting of the Social Order Committee*. Philadelphia.

Radnor Monthly Meeting. (1680-1826). Radnor Monthly Meeting Records. Pennsylvania.

Radnor Monthly Meeting. (n.d.). *Minutes.*

Raistrick, A. (1950). *Quakers in Science and Industry.* NY: Philosophical Library.

Rauschenbusch, W. (1907). *Christianity and the Social Crisis.* New York: Hodder & Stoughton.

Reckitt, B. (1952). *The history of Reckitt and Sons, Limited.* London: A. Brown and Sons, Limited.

Rehard, G. H. (2006). *Living our Faith.* Philadelphia, PA : Quaker Press of Friends General Conference.

Richardson, J. (1837-1850). Life of John Richardson. In T. a. Evans, *Friends Library Vol IV.*

Richardson, J. (1840). Life of John Richardson. In T. a. Evans, *Friends Library Vol IV* (pp. 69-105). Philadelphia: Joseph Rakestraw.

Rigge, A. (1678). *A brief and serious warning.* Retrieved 2 1, 2014, from Early English Books Online: http://gateway.proquest.com.proxy. earlham.edu:2048/openurl?ctx_ver=Z39.88-2003&res_id=xri:eebo& rft_id=xri:eebo:image:57551:5

Robert Willis. (1836). In J. &. Comly, *Friends Miscellany: Being a collection of Essays and Fragments, Biographical, religious epitolary, narriative nd historial Vol IX* (p. 295). Philadelphia: J. Richards.

Romanek, C. L. (1969). *John Reynell, Quaker Merchant of Colonial Philadelphia.* Ann Arbor, Michigan: University Microfilms.

Rose, J. (1981). *Elizabeth Fry.* NY: St. Martins.

Rowntree, B. S. (1902). *Poverty: A study of town life.* London: Macmillan and Company.

Rowntree, J. (1905). *Essays and Addresses.* London: Digital Quaker Collection.

Rowntree, J. (1905). *Essays and Addresses.* London: Digital Quaker Collection.

Rowntree, M. (1921). *Social freedom : a study in the application of the ethics of Jesus to modern social and industrial problems.* London: Committee on War and the Social Order : Friends' Bookshop.

Rutgers Business School. (2012, 04 05). *Executive VP of BD Gary Cohen to speak about business strategy and corporate social responsibility in CEO Lecture Series.* Retrieved 12 17, 2013, from Rutgers Business School: http://business.rutgers.edu/news/executive-vp-bd-gary-cohen-speak-about-business-strategy-and-corporate-social-responsibility-ce

Rutgers Business School. (2012, April 05). *Executive VP of BD Gary Cohen to speak about business strategy and corporate social responsibility in CEO Lecture Series.* Retrieved Dec. 17, 2013, from Rutgers Business School:

http://business.rutgers.edu/news/executive-vp-bd-gary-cohen-speak-about-business-strategy-and-corporate-social-responsibility-ce

Shillitoe, T. (1836). Journal of the LIfe of Thomas Shillitoe. In W. &. Evans, *Friends Library V. III* (pp. 78-105). Philadelphia: Joseph Rakestraw.

Simpson. (1920). In W. a. Committee, *Towards a new social order : being the report of an international conference held at Oxford, August 20-24, 1920.* London: War and Social Order Committee;.

Simpson, J. (1833). Memiors of James Simpson. In J. &. Comly, *Friends Miscellany Vol IV* (pp. 195-205). Philadelphia: J. Richards.

Simpson, J. (1838). John Simpson's Letter to Nathaniel Sisson. In J. &. Comly, *Friends Miscellany: Being a collection of Essays and Fragments, Biographical, religious epitolary, narriative nd historial Vol XI* (pp. 372-373). Philadelphia: J. Richards.

Smith, C. F. (1885). *James Parnell.* Retrieved Jan 28, 2013, from Dictionary of National Biography, 1885-1900, Volume 43: http://en.wikisource.org/wiki/Parnell,_James_(DNB00)

Smith, J. (1970). *A descriptive catalogue of Friends' Books.* NY: Kraus Reprints.

Snarr, C. M. (2007). *Social selves and political reforms five visions in contemporary Christian ethics.* NY : T&T Clark.

Social Order Committee of Philadelphia Yearly Meeting. (n.d.). Records, 1917-1969.

Souderlund, J. R. (1985). *Quakers and Slavery: A Divided Spirit.* Princeton, NJ : Princeton University Press.

Story, T. (1846). Life of Thomas Story. In W. &. Evans, *Friends Library Vol X* (pp. 1-201). Philadelphia: Joseph Rakestraw.

Tawney, R. H. (1962). *Religion and the Rise of Captialism: A Historical Study.* Gloucester, Mass: Peter Smith.

The Old Discipline. (1999). Glenside, PA: Quaker Heritage Press.

The Old Discipline: Nineteeth-Century Friends' Disciplines in America. (1999). Glenside, PA: Quaker Heritage Press.

Thomas Hamm, e. (2010). *Quaker writings : an anthology, 1650-1920.* NY: Penguin.

Thoughts on Plainness and Simplicity. (1836). In J. &. Comly, *Friends Miscellany: Vol VIII* (pp. 335-6). Philadelphia: J. Richards.

Tibbals, K. (2012). *Early Quakers and their relationship with the Business World.* Richmond IN: Earlham School of Religion.

Tolles, F. (1963). *Meeting House and Counting House: The Quaker Merchants of Colonial Philadelphia 1682-1763*. NY: WW Norton.

Tolles, F. B. (1960). *Quakers and the Atlantic Culture*. NY: Macmillan.

Townsend, E. (1832). Ezra Townsend's Testimony. In J. &. Comly, *Friends Miscellany* (pp. 373-375). Philadelphia: J. Richards.

Townsend, E. (1832). Testimony concerning John Townsend. In J. a. Comly, *Friends Miscellany Vol II* (pp. 373-375). Philadelphia: J. Richards.

Turford, H. (1772). A Trial of Christianity from the life and nature of Christ and true Christians, with a description of true Godliness and the way by which we may conform our lives thereunto. In H. Turford, *The Grounds of a Holy Life; Or, The Way by Which Many Who Were Heathens, Came to Be Renowned Christians; and Such As Are Now Sinners, May Come to Be Numbered with Saints; by Little Preaching. To Which Is Added, Paul's Speech to the Bishop of Cretia, As Al* (pp. 113-143).

Vernon, A. (1987). *A Quaker Business Man: The Life of Joseph Rowntree*. York: Session Book Trust.

Vernon, A. (1987). *A Quaker Business Man: The Life oF Joseph Rowntree*. York: Session Book Trust.

Wagner-Tsukamoto, S. (2005). An Economic Approach to Business Ethics: Moral Agency of the Firm and the Enabling and Constraining Effects of Economic Institutions and Interactions in a Market Economy. *Journal of Business Ethics*, 75-89.

Wagner-Tsukamoto, S. (2008). Contrasting the Behavioural Business Ethics Approach and the Institutional Economic Approach to Business Ethics: Insights From the Study of Quaker Employers. *Journal of Business Ethics*, 835-850.

Waln, N. (1834). Biographical Memiors of Nicholas Waln. In J. &. Comly, *Friends Miscellany, Vol V* (pp. 106-133). Philadelphia: J. Richards.

Walvin, J. (1997). *The Quakers: Money and Morals*. London: John Murray.

War & Social Order Committee. (1919). *Our Father... Thy Kingdom Come... On Earth*. London: London Yearly Meeting.

War and Social Order Committee. (London). *"Whence come wars?": being papers prepared by members of the yearly meeting's committee on War and the Social order, for their second conference, held at Jordans, 7th-10th April, 1916* . 1916: London Yearly Meeting.

Waring, B. C., Leeds, M. E., & Evans, E. W. (1921, March 25). Report of the Social Order Committee for the year 1920 to 1921 to Philadelphia

Yearly Meeting of the Religious Society of Friends. Philadelphia: Social Order Committee.

Watchman. (1938, 4 29). The Quaker Employer's "Conference". *The Friend*, pp. 349-50.

Watson, A. (1932, 6 10). Christianity in Industry. *The Friend*, pp. 515-6.

Watson, C. E. (1991). *Managing with Integrity: Insights from America's CEOs*. NY, NY: Praeger.

Weber, M., & Kalberg, S. (2001). *The Protestant ethic and the spirit of capitalism*. Chicago, Il: Fitzroy Dearborn.

West, R. (1998). *Daniel Defoe: The Life and Strange Surprising Adventures*. New York: Carroll & Graf Publishers, Inc.

Whitehouse, P. (2009). *Quakers & Business Group Business Principles*. Retrieved Feb 25, 2014, from Quakers & Business: file:///C:/Users/Karen/Downloads/Q&B%20Business%20Principles.pdf

Willis, R. (1836). Robert Willis. In J. &. Comly, *Friends Miscellany: Being a collection of Essays and Fragments, Biographical, religious epitolary, narriative nd historial Vol IX* (p. 295). Philadelphia: J. Richards.

Windsor, D. B. (1980). *The Quaker Enterprise: Friends in Business*. London: Frederick Muller Limited.

Woolman, J. (1971). *The Journal and Major Essays of John Woolman*. New York: Oxford University Press.

6 | The Rowntrees:
Tales from a Chocolate Family

By Paul Chrystal

The story of Rowntrees is well known and well documented; the rise from humble beginnings in York to global chocolate confectioners while at the same time making breath-taking advances in social welfare and education is nothing short of astonishing. What is less well known is how various members of the Rowntree family each achieved fame and success in their own right – not just in the world of confectionery but in other fields too. Rowntree family men, Quakers all, had an impact on a wide range of local and world events ranging from the Irish potato famine, the two world wars, and the Scarborough Riots; they were enlightened pioneers in industrial relations, workers' rights, housing reform and poverty relief; along the way they were embroiled in episodes of industrial espionage and racism. This chapter highlights some of these lesser known aspects of Rowntree family history, including the impact on Joseph on witnessing at first hand the Irish potato famine; Joseph Rowntree and his good causes; the stern regime at the Rowntree shop in Pavement around 1852; early days at Rowntrees' first chocolate factory 1869; Joseph Rowntree and his industrial espionage, 1872; John Wilhelm Rowntree's 'racism'; Joshua Rowntree and the Scarborough Riots, 1900; Seebohm Rowntree and *Poverty* (1901); *The Cocoa Works Magazine* and the exploding bananas; New Earswick: garden village and Nazism, 1904; Joshua Rowntree and the Scarborough Bombardment, 1914; the Rowntrees in World War I; and the Rowntrees in World War II.

Joseph Rowntree and 'the Great Hunger' 1845-1852

If Joseph Rowntree's (1835-1925) time at Bootham School in York was to influence him in various ways in later life, the school trip he took to Ireland during this time was probably much more influential: some seventy years later Joseph Rowntree was still able to describe his experiences, in a memorandum written in 1924 (Rowntree & Co 1925, 3). Sold to him as a botanical trip he was accompanied by his brother John and by John Ford, the head at Bootham.

Joseph Rowntree senior would be only too aware how seeing at first hand the lamentable conditions that were 'an Gorta Mór', or the 'Great Hunger', would affect his boys. Joseph would have already witnessed poverty, soup kitchens and destitution in Hungate and Bedern in York, but nothing there would have prepared him for his experiences in Ireland.

What started badly enough as a natural catastrophe of biblical proportions was exacerbated by the bungling indecision and inertia of Lord John Russell's laissez faire-obsessed Whig government between 1846 and 1852. It is reliably estimated that a million or so Irish died of starvation or disease – cholera, dysentery, scurvy, typhus, and infestations of lice – one eighth of the population – and two million more were forced to emigrate. Potato blight – *phytophthora infestans* – wiped out the means of subsistence for more than one third of the population over a four or five-year period. The tendency to explain it away by providentialism ('the Irish were being judged by God') or moralism ('the Irish had it coming – they are lazy, violent, filthy and devoid of self-reliance') – racial stereotyping – further inflamed the situation (Donnelly 2002). Here are examples of the sort of thing the Rowntree group would have witnessed, as seen by other visitors. Quaker William Bennett described the situation in Mayo: *'three children huddled together, lying there because they were too weak to rise, pale and ghastly, their little limbs ... perfectly emaciated, eyes sunk, voice gone, and evidently in the last stages of actual starvation'* (Bennett 1852). The Revd Dr Traill Hall, a Church of Ireland rector in Schull, described *'the aged, who, with the young — are almost without exception swollen and ripening for the grave'* (Hall, 1849). Quaker Joseph Crosfield saw numerous marasmic children: *'A heart-rending scene [of] poor wretches in the last stages of famine imploring to be received into the [work]house ... Some of the children were worn to skeletons, their features sharpened with hunger, and their limbs wasted almost to the bone'* (Kennedy et al 1999, 106) . William Forster, Quaker abolitionist and prison reformer who inspired Elizabeth Fry, wrote that in Carrick-on-Shannon *'the children exhibit the effects of famine in a remarkable degree, their faces looking wan and haggard with hunger, and seeming like old men and women'* [6] (*Central Relief Committee* 1852, 146). Thousands of corpses were buried without coffins in shallow graves only to be eaten by dogs. Nicholas Cummins, the magistrate of Cork, saw this in Skibbereen:

> I entered some of the hovels and the scenes which presented themselves were such as no tongue or pen can convey the slightest idea of. In the first, six famished and ghastly skeletons, to all appearances dead, were huddled in a corner on some filthy straw, their sole covering what seemed a ragged horsecloth, their wretched legs hanging about, naked above the knees. I approached with

horror, and found by a low moaning they were alive – they were in fever, four children, a woman and what had once been a man. It is impossible to go through the detail. Suffice it to say, that in a few minutes I was surrounded by at least 200 such phantoms, such frightful spectres as no words can describe, [suffering] either from famine or from fever. Their demoniac yells are still ringing in my ears, and their horrible images are fixed upon my brain. (Cummins 1846)

Joseph's haunting memories will have been kept alive by the Irish immigrants who fled from the famine and populated the poorer parts of York, notably Walmgate (Finnegan 1982, 35ff).

Joseph Rowntree and the Good Causes

Joseph Rowntree was actively involved in an impressive number of other local good causes. His interests in religious education extended to include The Bible Society and The Religious Tract Society. His social work took in the Soup Kitchen, City Mission, York Penitentiary Society, set up by the Gray family of lawyers, York County Hospital, York Dispensary and the Vagrant Office in 1822 in Little Shambles, for the 'suppression of mendicity' and to stem the flow into the city of those outside the law. Many York prostitutes found scant reward in their light industry city and turned for support to the Penitentiary Society, established in 1822 to rescue and rehabilitate girls (Finnegan 1979). The Refuge was set up in 1845 as a 'place of permanent refuge for such miserable young females as may seem in the spirit of true penitence' (*York Female Penitentiary Society Minutes Book 1822-1842*. Acc. 212.40). The aim was to help them reform over a two year period and to allow them escape from the brothels, many of which were clustered around the Minster, and Friargate, close to the Castlegate Meeting House, spreading south through the city. There are records of 1,400 prostitutes and brothel-keepers in the city between 1837 and 1887; of the 412 girls admitted to the Refuge between 1845 and 1887 only 142 were rehabilitated and found work in service, although many of these returned to their former ways (Wright 1995, 74, 54).

Joseph set up the York Soup Kitchen in Black Horse Passage, by day it was soup kitchen, a tavern in the evening, which provided many with their one and only meal of the day and was to run every winter from 1846. Joseph took a very hands-on approach, establishing and controlling recipes, equipment, ticketing and distribution. By 1855 he must have been considered something of a national expert on coffee when Chancellor of the Exchequer Gladstone consulted him

171

on matters relating to the sale of coffee mixed with chicory. Joseph was also involved in the establishment of the York Dispensary. York County Hospital opened in a rented house in 1740 in Monkgate. Before that, from 1614, the City Surgeon was responsible for medical care. In 1745 a purpose-built hospital opened on the same site with fifty beds: by 1750 2,417 patients had been treated. As a charitable hospital (where the financiers could choose who received treatment there) the County Hospital was not responsible for the city's sick poor; this led to the very necessary establishment of the Dispensary. The 1745 hospital building was demolished in 1851 and replaced with a new 100 bed hospital costing £11,000. In 1887 it merged with the York Eye Institution, which opened in 1875. The York Dispensary was originally in the Merchant Adventurers' Hall, moving to St Andrewgate and then, in 1828, to New Street. The next move was to Duncombe Place in 1851. Its noble mission, as recorded in *Baines' Directory* for 1823, was 'to dispense gratuitously advice, medicine and surgical assistance, to those who are unable to pay for them'. Medicines were free of charge and 600 or so children were vaccinated here 'without cost for the smallpox'. The corporation contributed £5 towards an apothecary's shop and one guinea a year for five years. After thirty or so years 42,488 patients had been seen with 28,851 cured.

The Temperance movement and Quakers were inextricably linked; in May 1850 a meeting of the Friends interested in Temperance was held at the London Yearly Meeting. Members of the provisional committee included James Backhouse and Joseph Spence of York; in August that year a further meeting was held in York to confirm this as a national organisation. York Temperance Society was formed in 1830; Joseph Rowntree was an early, and active, member. *The Yorkshire Herald* reported on the copious statistics he provided to outline the extent of the alcohol abuse problem in York (*Yorkshire Herald* November 17th 1832): 50,000 gallons of spirits were consumed annually while some streets, for example Water Lane, were awash with beer and spirit shops – four within the space of just under 100 yards Noting that there were 302 public houses and dram shops in the city in 1851 – or one for every twenty-six families – Joseph petitioned the magistrates to grant no more licences. In 1851 it had warned:

> beware the necessity of cheap beer, or "liquid food" for the support and comfort of the working man and the desirableness of affording him every facility of obtaining it ... the Beer Act has done more to demoralize our youthful population and neutralize the labours of the Sabbath School Teacher.(*York Courant* November 19th 1840)

But it was, nevertheless, optimistic 'light finds its way through the smallest crevice ... we already perceive a vast change in the public mind'. The Band of Hope was set up and educated 1200 children in temperance principles; a trip to Moreby Hall, south of York, took 800 children; 3000 copies of their magazine, *The Visitor*, were regularly distributed.

Sabbatarianism was another cause. Joseph believed that drunkenness, prostitution and gambling were all exacerbated by breaking the Sabbath (*Yorkshireman* August 30th 1851). In 1839 he tried to persuade the railway companies not to run trains on Sundays and opposed the opening of museums, galleries and concert halls on Sundays (Rowntree 1868, 265-269). York races were anathema to Joseph: they were 'detrimental to the morals and happiness of the inhabitants'. York Theatre should be stripped of its public funding and the celebrations for Queen Victoria's wedding should be curbed. In 1854 when Victoria, Albert and five of their children stopped off at York for a meal on the way to Balmoral, he complained about the expense of such a short visit: £483 13s 7d – the meal was never eaten. Victoria got wind of the disquiet and so un-amused was she that she never visited the city again in the remaining forty-seven years of her reign. The 'Visit York' website takes up the story, some of which may be apocryphal:

> She had stated that this was a private visit, to be without ceremony. But the city council laid on a military display and erected stands for spectators; the Queen's temper was not improved when some of these collapsed and there was an unseemly scuffle. When the Queen eventually went to the Royal Station Hotel for her lunch, she was shocked to be presented with the bill to pay. She got up and said she would never visit York again, and never did. Whenever the Royal Train passed through York thereafter, she always made sure the blinds were firmly pulled down! ('Visit York' 2016)

The Rowntree Shop in Pavement 1852

George Cadbury served a three year apprenticeship with Rowntrees at the Pavement shop before he joined his family firm in Bournville in 1857. He would have quickly become familiar with the regime there: the rules of the Pavement shop were uncompromising, as set out in Joseph's 1852 Memoranda of Business and Household Arrangements:

The object of the Pavement establishment is business. The young men who enter it...are expected to contribute...in making it successful...it affords a full opportunity for any painstaking, intelligent young man to obtain a good practical acquaintance with the tea and grocery trades...the place is not suitable for the indolent and wayward. (Rowntree 1852)

Not unusually for the times, hours were long: 7.00 am or 7.30 to 8.00 pm six days a week with late night opening on market days until 10.00 pm; two days holiday – Good Friday and Christmas Day. It is worth quoting more from Mr Rowntree's fearsome memorandum:

Punctuality in the time of rising etc is important in each member otherwise the thoughtless or ease-loving individual wastes the time of the others...without neglecting business much may be done...to prevent the needless extension of meal-taking...a gratuity of 26 shillings per year is allowed to the punctual. (Rowntree 1852)

Lewis Fry, son of Joseph Fry of the Bristol chocolate company also worked there for a while, before going in to law in 1854. Further details from the memorandum give more of the atmosphere and conditions there. Apprentices (including John and Joseph presumably) were allowed out until 10 pm in the summer and until 8.45 in the winter months; they had leave to attend weekday Meetings every fortnight; they could go home once a year; they each have a separate lodging room for washing; no smoking or firearms. It ends with 'it is my earnest desire that the household may in all respects maintain those habits and practices in regard to dress, language etc which distinguish the religious Society of Friends' (Rowntree 1852).

Early Days at Rowntrees 1869

The jumble of improvised buildings at Henry Rowntree's H.I. Rowntree & Co in Tanner's Moat, which would have greeted Joseph when he joined the firm, was nothing if not full of character.

Apart from the resident parrot there was a somewhat temperamental donkey obedient to one man and one man only, and a serious danger to everyone else. On its dismissal, deliveries were relegated to a hand cart. Night shift workers were sustained by cocoa and pork pies on the firm, and most communications to and from Joseph Rowntree were through a trapdoor in the floor of his Lendal Bridge-facing office. S.C. Hanks, the foreman, paid the wages each Saturday from a hat full of silver and coppers (£60 a week usually covered it); each employee would be asked 'how much time has thee got?' and duly paid his or her going rate from the contents of the hat. Mistakes were inevitably made which prompted 'What did I give thee?' (Joseph Rowntree Papers).

Girls aged about fourteen would have earned around three shillings per week, boys a shilling more; men earned eighteen shillings at most – fairly standard money for the times. The purchase of a horse and wagonette in 1874 proved injudicious – an overhead the company could ill afford: food, farriers' and veterinary bills, and tolls amounted to twelve shillings and seven pence three-farthings per week. The horse was duly sold and the wagonette mothballed. Factory production was steam driven but hampered by the use of different machines for each of the processes involved (grinding, sifting, roasting and so on) with raw materials laboriously manhandled between machines. Hours were long: Monday to Saturday, 6 am to 6pm or 2 pm on Saturdays (Joseph Rowntree Papers). Indeed, Tanner's Moat was inadequate in every way; Seebohm Rowntree said of it: 'Tanner's Moat was Hell'; coming from a man not usually given over to such language, these were strong words indeed.

Joseph Rowntree and Industrial Espionage 1872

The early days for all the English chocolate manufacturers were tough. A difficult domestic market, relatively poor-quality products and competition from France, Germany and the Netherlands all encroaching on a large scale made things very difficult; at times the future of Rowntrees, Fry and Cadbury was extremely uncertain.

It was cocoa essence, though, as pioneered by Cadbury, which eventually, to varying extents and at different times led Fry, Cadbury and Rowntree out of their respective difficulties. Before the, though, desperate situations required desperate measures: in March, April and May 1872 Joseph Rowntree embarked on a voyage of industrial espionage, taking in London, Paris, the Netherlands, Cologne, Bristol and Bournville. His unashamed strategy was to pay employees of Fry's, Taylor's, Cadbury's, Dunn and Hewitt, the Quaker Stollwerk in Cologne, and Chocolat Menier in Paris to divulge their firms' production processes and recipes (Walvin 1997, 165) .

This is an example of one of his advertisements in the *Clerkenwell News*:

To cocoa and chocolate makers. Wanted immediately, a
Foreman who thoroughly understands the manufacture of Rock
and other Cocoas, confection and other chocolates. Also several
workmen. Good hands will be liberally dealt with.

(Ledger HIR 1/2. at the Borthwick Institute has advertisements, notes,
drawings gleaned from these interviews). Flyers were also produced (250 copies
for 5s 6d) and distributed. Taylor's of London, 'the most extensive manufacturer
in Europe of cocoa and chocolate, mustard and chicory', suffered most – Joseph
hired their foreman mixer, James French, on a trial basis for 20s per week plus a
gratuity of £5 for his recipes and £1 for his fare to York; if, after three months
he wished to return to London, he would qualify for a further £1. His colleague,
Robert Pearce, was taken on for 17s per week after 'imparting all his knowledge'.
He manufactured all the Taylor's chocolate apart from the finest for such
lucrative accounts as Hans Sloanes. William Garrett was recruited because he
'had the receipt [recipe] of Unsworth's Cream Cocoas', and a register of all his
workmates. Henry Thomson, a Taylor's man for twelve years and understudy to
a superior with three times that experience, was made an offer of 30s per week
and 'a lump sum of £10 for all his receipts and knowledge'. Thomson never made
it to York – perhaps his conscience and loyalty got the better of him . (Ledger
HIR 1/2. Borthwick Institute 4-12).

Nevertheless, it seems that Joseph came away with a fairly complete picture
of Taylor's recipes, plant, customers, wages paid and their production techniques.
After subsequent visits he was privy to their costs, budgets, sales and margins;
later, a Thomas Neal furnished a detailed engineering report . (Ledger HIR 1/2.
Borthwick Institute 22). The question 'has he any special knowledge of value?'
became the standard before job interviews . (Ledger HIR 1/2. Borthwick
Institute 159; 209-211).

Similar raids took place on Compagnie Française who were in the
Bermondsey New Road and Chocolat Menier in Southwark Street. 'Research'
was carried out on other competitors which included Cadbury, Neave's Foods
for Infants and Invalids of Fordinbridge, Chocolat Lombard and Maison
Guérin-Boutron, both of Paris, Ph. Suchard of Neuchâtel and the English
Condensed Milk Company of Leadenhall Street. How far this is an abnegation
of Quaker principles and practice in business it is hard to tell – the practice of
eliciting privileged information from competitors for money may have been
more acceptable then than it is today.

John Wilhelm Rowntree – Racist?

John Wilhelm Rowntree was born on September 4th 1868 at Top House, York, the first child of Joseph Rowntree Snr. and Emma Antoinette.

In 1898 John Wilhelm travelled to the Caribbean and Mexico, New Orleans and Chicago, with his wife, Constance. His exploits were recorded, somewhat reluctantly, in his journal 'on this floating temple of indolence [*The Aratro*] good resolves melt like butter ... I was reported alive but unconscious'. Constance, an occasional surrogate journalist, confirms the otiose lifestyle: 'John has developed such a capacity for laziness ... he will just write a postscript to correct all my erroneous statements' (Allott, 1994, 56ff). Describing a mix of chocolate business and sightseeing, the Mexico diaries are fascinating, if at times somewhat disturbing: the 'copper coloured' coolies were

> comely women to look at, small and graceful, and with such a carriage ... [with]strikingly refined faces in sharp contrast to chattering wooly-pated niggers with their coarse features, obtrusive manners, and overflowing conceit. The nigger is to the white what the Banderlog were to the jungle ... they are hopelessly incompetent, incorrigibly idle, overpowering in their conceit and more effervescent than the Parisians ... They are however very picturesque and the women ... carry themselves magnificently and walk like Greek Goddesses.[18]

Allott quotes more (1994, 57-59). Copies were sent to Frank Rowntree 'with instructions for it to be read to Acomb Adult School on the Sunday following receipt'. John Wilhelm's use of the word 'nigger' may not have been quite as offensive then as it is to modern ears. It was, though, being used in a pejorative sense from around 1900; despite this, advertisers, for example, continued to use it for some time after. There is no mitigation, however, for the comparison with Banderlogs.

In Chicago racial discrimination was there for all to see; John Wilhelm's reaction on seeing race-segregated waiting rooms is tinged with irony and inconsistent with the above, to say the least:

---

[18] Banderlog monkeys feature in Kipling's *The Jungle Book*. 'Bander' is a Hindi word, a term to denote 'Langur monkeys'; 'log' means 'people'. They appear in the tale of Kaa's Hunting, where they are ostracised by the other animals on account of their garrulous stupidity; there anthem is '*We are great. We are free. We are wonderful. We are the most wonderful people in all the jungle! We all say so, and so it must be true*'. Banderlogs communicate by mimicking other animals' speech.

I suppose coloured people are never ladies and gentlemen. It is strange that, an Englishman, from a benighted country which still supports such a medieval institution as a monarchy, should find my first sentiment on the Republican and free soil of the States to be one of indignation at the insulting inequality and injustice to a coloured race who are yet, on paper, free and equal citizens with the whites. (Allot 1994, 57ff)

Joshua Rowntree and the Scarborough Riots (1900)

During 1900 in the Second Boer War, Olive (1855-1920) and Samuel Cronwright Schreiner (1863-1936) spent six months in England campaigning against British military action in the Cape. Olive had previously failed in her efforts to dissuade South Africa from war and wrote *The South African Question by an English South African* in an attempt to reveal the true situation surrounding the war to the English public. Olive had by this time made a name for herself as a feminist, pacifist, vegetarian and socialist and was the author of the successful *The Story of an African Farm* published in 1883 – a semi-autobiographical novel which addressed topical and controversial issues such as colonialism, agnosticism, existentialism, the aspirations of women, premarital sex, pregnancy outside marriage and transvestitism. In the 1890s she met Cecil Rhodes, but soon became disillusioned with him because of his support for the 'strop bill' which allowed black and coloured servants to be flogged for trivial offences; this was the subject of her satire *Trooper Peter Halket of Mashonaland*. It was the 'strop' bill, which brought her and Samuel Cronwright, a politically active farmer, together; they married in 1894. Olive Schreiner (1855-1920) also wrote on and for the victims of aspects of British Imperialism, for example Afrikaners, and other South African groups including Blacks, Jews, and Indians (see Thurman 1973).

In March 1900 Cronwright Schreiner, accompanied by the economist and pacifist John A. Hobson, was invited to talk at Scarborough Old Town Hall followed by an 'at home' at John Rowntree & Sons' cafe in Westborough by the South African Conciliation Committee. His paper was '*The Conditions for Attaining a Durable Peace in South Africa*'. It is interesting to note that at this time Scarborough Meeting comprised 132 members, twenty-seven of whom were Rowntrees; eight others were closely related (Robson 2000, 69-72)

Schreiner's cause was not helped by his Germanic-sounding name; he had innocently extended his name when he married Olive, consequently, many thought him to be a Boer. As in other towns on the tour there was much local opposition to the Schreiner cause from patriotic supporters of the British army's efforts. In Scarborough this manifested itself initially in a hostile reception

178

committee for the Schreiner train at the station (mistaking Frank Rowntree, who happened to be on the same train, for Schreiner). Later, tomatoes and then stones were thrown at the windows of the Rowntree cafe. *The Scarborough Mercury* reported that 'the crashing of glass heralded several hours of smashing and wrecking'. (*Scarborough Mercury*, 16th March, 1900. See also Rowntree 1898-1902, 3,15 for a report on events that night). With great reluctance the meetings were abandoned on the advice of the Chief Constable and the thirty-five or so attendees made their escape. Joshua Rowntree was jostled by a 'well-dressed' young man who smashed his hat in and called him 'Judas' as he tried to flee down Huntriss Row (Rowntree 1936, 45).

His house and the houses of other Rowntrees in the town were all damaged by the angry mob: the door of John Watson Rowntree's house was smashed in and subjected to a hail of bricks – William and Mary Rowntree (ninety-three and eighty-seven respectively) were asleep inside. The rioters were still intent on ransacking the cafe – to this end stones were being sold at six for a penny – and, mission accomplished here, they moved on to wreck John Rowntree grocer's and the William Rowntree furniture shop, despite the best efforts of mounted police to restrain them. At about 1.30 am the mob was finally dispersed by the army which had arrived ready to read the Riot Act, but only after several rowdy renditions of Soldiers of the Queen from the rioters.

Joshua, however, was not deterred in his pursuit of the true situation and left for South Africa on December 3rd that year on a fact-finding mission with Isabella. They took in the squalid, hideous conditions in the concentration camps (or 'camps of refuge' as the Conservative Government preferred to call them), noted the suppression of the press and observed the treason trials; the Rowntrees were, however, restricted to Natal and Cape Colony. One of the people Joshua met on the trip was an Indian barrister, a Mr M.K. Gandhi. Gandhi had formed the Natal Indian Ambulance Corps; this was made up of about 1400 men including 300 'free' Indians and 800 labourers sent by their employers who tended the sick and wounded in battle zones such as Spion Kop, Colenso and Ladysmith. Its role was to take the wounded brought by the Natal Volunteer Ambulance Corps from the battlefield to the railheads. As for the concentration camps the British built forty-five tented camps for Boer internees and sixty-four for black Africans. In 1900, of the 28,000 Boer prisoners of war, 25,630 were sent overseas leaving women and children as the vast majority of Boers in the camps. Over 26,370 women and children died, 24,000 of them children under age sixteen, or fifty every day. All in all, 93,940 Boers and 24,457 black Africans were detained (Pakenham 1979). Emily Hobhouse (1860-1926), the welfare campaigner, sailed on the same ship as the Rowntrees, taking with her supplies of clothing for the civilians as a delegate of the South African Women and Children's Distress Fund; she was able to visit a number of camps in the Orange Free State although she had expected to find only one camp – such was the misinformation reaching England. Hobhouse published a report in June 1901 graphically contradicting St John Brodrick's, the Conservative Secretary of State for War, claim that internment was 'voluntary' and that internees were 'contented and comfortable'.

Some extracts from Hobhouse's report reveal the true situation:

> In some camps, two, and even three sets of people, occupy one tent and 10, and even 12, persons are frequently herded together in tents ... I call this camp system a wholesale cruelty ... To keep these Camps going is murder to the children ... If only the English people would try to exercise a little imagination – picture the whole miserable scene. Entire villages rooted up and dumped in a strange, bare place ... The women are wonderful. They cry very little and never complain. The very magnitude of their sufferings, their indignities, loss and anxiety seems to lift them beyond tears ... only when it cuts afresh at them through their children do their feelings flash out. Some people in town still assert that the Camp is a haven of bliss. (Hobhouse 1901)

Lloyd George accused the government of 'a policy of extermination' and Campbell-Bannerman, leader of the Liberal opposition, answered his own rhetorical question 'When is a war not a war?' with 'When it is carried on by methods of barbarism in South Africa'. The result was the Fawcett Commission – unique for the time, in that it was staffed entirely by women, under the aegis of Millicent Fawcett, a leader of the women's suffrage movement but a government supporter nevertheless. Between August and December, 1901, the Commission inspected the camps, verified everything Hobhouse had said and applied a raft of measures which radically improved conditions in the Boer camps; it must be said, however that the equally squalid black African camps were largely ignored. (Lee 1985)

Seebohm Rowntree and *Poverty* (1901)

The second son and third child of Joseph and Emma Antoinette was born at Top House on July 7th 1871. His landmark, highly influential *Poverty: A Study of Town Life* was published in 1901. Seebohm's aim in researching and publishing that research was to 'throw some light upon the conditions which govern the life of the wage-earning classes in provincial towns ' (Rowntree 1901) to assess 'how much of it [poverty] was due to insufficiency of income, and how much to improvidence'. Indeed, 'the question was not what poverty was, but what were the causes of people living in a state of poverty' (Veit-Wilson 1984, 76). In doing so he also exposed housing and health conditions of the urban poor in the city of York. Not only did his work debunk once and for all the notion that the poor were responsible for their plight due to improvidence and innate fecklessness; it also laid the blame squarely at the door of inadequate wages for over half his respondents.

A further 25% were in poverty because four or more children were dependent on the wage earner(s) and 15% more due to the death of the wage earner. Here is one example of the evidence garnered for the book: A married bricklayer's labourer lived in two rooms with wife and three young children:

> the stench here is abominable. The grating of the street drain is 1½ yards from the house door, and is blocked up. There are twenty-three houses in this yard and only one water tap ... four houses join at one closet. There is one ashpit for this yard; it is full to the top, and slime running down the wall. Rent 2s3d. (Rowntree 1901, 51)

> A nurse lives in one room, from which the last three tenants have been 'carried out' (died); her ashpit and closet, shared with four other houses, adjoin the back wall; rats and other vermin are common; rent 1s 6d21. Further up the scale in Class D the average family size is 4.03 and average weekly earnings are 41s 9¼d, including children's contributions. Paltry as it may have been, whatever the children could bring in was crucial and compelled many families to withdraw their children from school at the earliest opportunity. Poverty in Class D exists only through 'wasteful expenditure' for, example, on drink and gambling. There is no doubt that the average weekly expenditure upon alcoholic drink ... is considerable. (Rowntree 1901, 73)

The Cocoa Works Magazine, or *CWM* (1902): Exploding Bananas

The Cocoa Works Magazine, or *CWM*, to give it its official name, was launched in March 1902; the last issue was in May 1986. Over those eighty-four years it provides a fascinating and detailed record of life at Rowntree. Its subtitle was *A Journal in the Interest of the Employees of Rowntree & Co Ltd, York*; its aims and scope, in up to forty pages per issue (severely reduced during the paper shortages of the two World Wars), was to provide a means of communication within the company to keep everyone informed about what was going on at all levels; *CWM* was seen as one way in which the company could make good the loss of that personal touch when Joseph Rowntree had to remove himself from his treasured daily contact with his workers.

The inaugural issue of *The Cocoa Works Magazine* in 1902 featured John Wilhelm's account of the explosion on board the Royal Mail Steamer *Para* which would have been comical were it not so tragic; he and Constance had the misfortune to be on the vessel which was bringing, amongst other cargoes, Rowntree cocoa back from Trinidad and Granada:

> there was an appalling roar … a momentary flash followed by blinding darkness. Mrs R and myself found ourselves hurled into the air … ships officers and crew behaved as Englishmen should … the captain, while in the air, shouted for the Fire Brigade.

The explosion was caused by a shipment of bananas; one of the passengers was attempting to see if, by extracting oxygen from the containers holding his bananas, deterioration of the fruit could be avoided or retarded. Bananas were increasingly popular at the time with five million bunches imported into the UK in 1904, up from two million in 1900. The result of the explosion was catastrophic, with three dead and others injured, one of whom was 'in delirium'.

New Earswick: Garden Village and Nazism, 1904

Joseph Rowntree was responsible for the planning and construction of one of Britain's first 'industrial 'garden villages. He saw the village as an escape from the poverty and overcrowding many of his workers endured daily in York. In developing New Earswick, Joseph Rowntree was influenced not only by Cadbury's Bournville, but also, and principally, by Ebenezer Howard's (1850-1928) vision of a kind of utopian city where citizens lived in harmony with nature, as described in his 1898 *Tomorrow: A Peaceful Path to Real Reform*, retitled *Garden Cities of Tomorrow in* 1902. Howard's towns were to be slum free, managed and financed by the residents who were offered a financial interest. They combined the best of town and country life. Equal opportunity, good wages, entertainment, low rents, beauty, and fresh air were the aim; we recognise all of these elements in Joseph Rowntree's New Earswick. (See Howard 1898 and Miller 2010) Joseph saw the benefits of a semi-rural lifestyle and environment as enjoyed at Fry's

Somerdale factory, at Cadbury's Bournville self-contained village and 'factory in a garden'; and he wanted the same for New Earswick. At the same time he hoped to imbue a sense of civic pride and responsibility (avoiding the 'stultifying paternalism' of Lever's Port Sunlight (Wagner 1987, 71) by empowering the residents to be actively involved in the running of the village and its amenities (Freeman 2004, 21; Waddilove 1954, 8-10). Joseph was also concerned about the schism which he saw widening between town and country life; 'the residence of town workers in the country' (New Earswick), would, at least for York, 'help to bridge the gulf between town and country interests' (Worstenholm, n.d; Rowntree 1910). The Folk Hall was thus named to evoke an air of rusticity reinforced by, amongst many other things, its 'country dances' .

Howard's humanistic ideal and progressive vision was influential in other countries too, not least in Germany where the German Garden City Association (GGCA) 'unseren Deustschen Vettern,' as the people of New Earswick welcomed them on their visit in 1909, flourished. The delegation included engineers, mayors, doctors, factory inspectors and barristers from Germany, Austria, Poland and Russia. Joseph Rowntree's speech, translated into and delivered in German, extolled not only the philosophy behind New Earswick but also the German system of pensions, invalidity support and national education.

Joshua Rowntree and the Scarborough Bombardment (1914)

Joseph Rowntree's nephew, Joshua Rowntree, was born on April 6th 1844 in Princess Street, Scarborough. He was the fourth of five children born to John Rowntree (b. 1788), a grocer, and Jane (née Priestman) who married in 1838. Joshua did much to try and forge Anglo-German relations just before World War I and, when caught in Germany at the outbreak of hostilities, owed his passage back to England to the efforts of a German who in 1912 had attended his Adult School in Scarborough.

Out of a national membership of around 20,000, 300 or so Friends, despite the party line on pacifism, had joined up by 1916, including those going into the Royal Army Medical Corps – a small but significant number which Joseph, in tune with the general consensus, believed should not be disowned but allowed to plead their individual cases at the end of hostilities.

Joshua could perhaps have been forgiven for believing that he would not see much, if any, of the conflict. However, the events of the early morning of December 16th 1914 were to prove him very mistaken. Scarborough was to be one of four north east coastal towns bombarded by the German fleet. In the space of forty minutes about 1,000 shells were first unleashed on Hartlepool and West Hartlepool from three German heavy cruisers *Blucher*, *Seydlitz* and *Moltke*, killing sixty-three civilians and nine soldiers in Hartlepool and fifty-six civilians in West Hartlepool; 400 or so civilians were injured and much housing stock was damaged or destroyed (Chrystal 2011).

The raid on the Hartlepools was followed by similar assaults on Scarborough and Whitby in which eighteen and three people were killed respectively. The Royal Navy had received advance warning of the raid from the naval intelligence unit (the 'Room 40' group) and Admiral Warrender was despatched with six battleships, four battle cruisers, four heavy cruisers, six light cruisers and eight submarines to intercept the German raiding force. Just before the attack on Hartlepool, Warrender spotted the Germans but mistook them for an insignificant raiding party. Off Scarborough the *Derfllinger* and *von der Tann* opened fire on the coastguard station and the barracks before shelling the castle and the Grand Hotel, believing it to be a gun battery. As they passed Whitby they fired fifty rounds at the signal station, town and Abbey. The attack on the east coast caused outrage in Britain: partly because the Navy failed to intercept the Germans, but also because Whitby and Scarborough, unlike Hartlepool, were undefended, open towns. Joshua at the time was living in Staintondale and was unscathed, but the shellfire was audible and those still at Rawdon Villas had to take refuge in the cellars (Clarke 2011).

This is how George Rowntree, in his *Reminiscences*, graphically described the raid:

> I looked through the window, and to my horror saw a shell strike Mr. Turner's house, "Dunollie," just below us. Then another terrific explosion, and a mass of smoke and debris rose in the air ... Then came the heaviest firing; the noise was terrific. We could hear the swish, swish of the shells as they came over us and burst on Oliver's Mount. Some burst amongst the trees; four fell in the field on our north. Mountside was struck with three shells; Queen Margaret's Hall was badly shelled; several houses below us, Netherbank, Saxifield, Shortlands, were all badly damaged. No district in Scarborough escaped. About 300 houses were struck, and the Coastguard considered that anywhere up to 500 shells were fired ... Many have left their homes; people fled from the town along the York Road and the trains were filled with rich and poor ... Two ladies left their home on the South Cliff with their long hair down their backs, and in their hurry left their false teeth on the breakfast table. One man put his Christmas Cake under his arm; a woman who did not like to leave her best silk dress for

the Germans quickly put it on (Rowntree 1936, 16 December, 1914).

Later in the war, in September 1917, a lone U-Boat shelled the town killing three people.

Rowntrees in World War I

By May 1915 750 Rowntree men had signed up, with further 'losses' due to trained fitters and turners moving into the armaments industry under the terms of the Munitions Act. Indeed, Rowntrees would have closed had not the Ministry of Works conferred reserved occupation status on those workers remaining. In a bid to grow the depleted workforce the company rescinded its policy of not hiring men aged over thirty-five. Belgian refugees were taken on, although, Hindus were rejected on the grounds that 'it would not do to employ [them] in any of the general rooms, or where there were girls'. Between April 1916 and March 1917 the number of male employees fell from 2,644 to 1,855 while the number of women fell from 3,341 to 2,655 over the same period.

At the outbreak of the war, Lawrence Rowntree (1895-1917) John Wilhelm's (1868-1905) and Connie's (1871-1928) only son, was a conscientious objector. He nevertheless served his country as a volunteer orderly and driver for ten months in the Friends' Ambulance Unit at Dunkirk and in Belgium; Lawrence was one of the first forty to be deployed in October 1914. He then returned to England and worked at the military hospital in Haxby Road (the Cocoa Block requisitioned from Rowntrees). When conscription was introduced in March 1916, Lawrence had a change of heart and first enlisted into the Royal Field Artillery as a gunner, via the Medium Machine Gun School at Coventry on 23 May 1916. (For the quandary facing York Friends and their persecution during the First World War see Rubinstein 1999.) Lawrence saw action at Ancre, the first tank battle ever, as a crew member in HMLS Crème de Menthe: all of the forty-nine tanks in the British army being deployed there in November 1916 in what was to be the final battle in the Somme offensive. Other tanks in the section were named Chablis, Chartreuse, Champagne, Curaçao, Cordon Rouge and so on. The objective of the attack was, ironically, a sugar factory. Crème de Menthe had its tail wheel blown off; Lawrence was injured and repatriated to Edinburgh where he made a full recovery. He was later commissioned into the Royal Artillery and redeployed to the Western Front in July 1917 where he fought in the Ypres salient throughout the 3rd Battle of Ypres. Four months later on November 25th 1917 Lawrence was killed in action.

Rowntrees in World War II

Normal output and service was suspended during the course of the war to aid the war effort. A prodigious amount of impromptu management and reorganisation went into converting the Haxby Road factory into what became virtually a munitions factory. The definitive record of this fascinating chapter in the wartime lives of the staff, board and management at Rowntrees can be found in *The Cocoa Works in War-time* published by the company soon after the end of hostilities; here are some of the details recorded there: 300 clerks of the Royal Army Pay Corps moved in; the Fruit Gum Department, at the behest of the Ministry Of Food, made jams and marmalade for Frank Cooper Ltd of Oxford. Part of the Almond Block extension was taken over by York firm Cooke, Troughton & Simms for the manufacture of military optical instruments. From the Cream Department came ersatz products such as National Milk Cocoa, Ryvita, Household Milk and Dried Egg. Explosives for County Industries Ltd (CIL), a company set up mainly to produce shell and mine fuses, were housed in the Smarties block. The Card Box Mill replaced its production of fancy boxes to become a main supply depot for the R.A.S.C. Northern Command. Part of the dining block became a refuge for blitzed families; a VAD hospital with 100 or so beds occupied the rest of the building. The nursery was also in there; this allowed mothers of children aged six months to five years of age to come to work. At any one time, sixty children were looked after; cots and other furniture was made by the work's joiners and the orchard behind the Dining Block became the playground. The target for CIL set by the Ministry Of Supply was 100,000 fuses per week, made mainly for shells used in twenty-five pounder guns; this was exceeded. By the end of the war CIL had also turned out four million anti-tank mine fuses. Workers in contact with explosive powder had to protect their skin and so 'make up' rooms were set up where special face powder and topical creams were made available. Girls and women were advised to drink milk rather than tea or coffee at their mid-shift break. The sixty men and 850 women who worked here were under the management of the aptly named Mr N.G. Sparkes. The fire brigade comprised twenty-three full time and eighty part time staff, complemented by 145 fire guards. The air raid siren was on the top of the Elect Cocoa Block – throughout the war it sounded 140 times in blasts that lasted for 209 hours in total. The Estates Department was busy digging for victory: between 1939 and 1945 eight tons each of tomatoes, cabbage and onions, three tons of leeks and two tons of Brussel sprouts and 13,000 heads of lettuce along with smaller quantities of other vegetables were produced.

One of the most productive departments in the factory was the Cake (Chocolate Moulding) Department, which was engaged in the production of various types of war-time chocolate. Vitaminised plain chocolate was made for army rations and for distribution by U.N.R.R.A. for the relief of starving children in Europe. Blended chocolate and vitaminised Plain York Chocolate was made for prisoner-of-war parcels; at Christmas these were sent out with special wrappers. Special chocolate 'Naps' in sealed tins were supplied to the Ministry of War Transport as emergency rations for use on ships, lifeboats and rafts. Pacific and Jungle chocolate was specially produced to withstand high temperatures for troops and sailors in tropical climates. Oatmeal Block and Fruit Bar was made for the servicemen in the Far East. U.S. Army Field Ration Vitaminised chocolate, known as ration D, was specially packed for the American forces. An Army Emergency Ration Special Chocolate that was hermetically sealed in tins was also manufactured along with special chocolate rations for use by air crews after baling out.

Summary

These short episodes from the lives of members of the Rowntree family demonstrate quite clearly that there was much more to them than the mere founders of a global confectionery empire. The extracts reveal a prodigious tenacity, determination and sense of purpose that is arguably unrivalled in British social and industrial history. Between them, as Quakers, they pioneered charitable causes, philanthropy, sound industrial relations and workers' pensions; they laid the foundations for habitable housing conditions, they promoted pacifism with dignity and they supported the downtrodden, the marginalised and the exploited. They had a hand in the development of the welfare state we know today. Along the way they made mistakes, but who could avoid this when breaking such new ground and setting such precedents? Accusations of racism and dubious business practice can justly be levelled but, while in no way seeking to mitigate or excuse such repellent behaviour, it is important to see these aberrations in the context of the day when the world was probably an even less forgiving place. The Rowntrees are a complex family and they, to varying extents, have touched , championed and are responsible for not a few of the good things we see today in our society.

Bibliography

Allott, S. 1994. *John Wilhelm Rowntree 1868-1905*, York: Sessions.

W. Bennett, 1852 [1847]. *Narrative of a Recent Journey of Six Weeks in Ireland and Society of Friends*: Central Relief Committee.

Central Relief Committee 1852. Society of Friends, *Central Relief Commitee* (Dublin 1852).

Chrystal, P. 2011. *Hartlepool Through Time*, Stroud: Amberley.

Clarke, B. 2011. *Remember Scarborough: A Result of the First Arms Race of the Twentieth Century*, Stroud: Amberley.

Cummins, N. 1846. Letter to the Duke of Wellington and a copy to *The Times*, published on 24 December.

Donnelly, J. 2002. *The Great Irish Potato Famine*, Gloucester: Sutton.

Finnegan, F. 1979. *Poverty and Prostitution: A Study of Victorian Prostitutes in York*, Cambridge: Cambridge University Press.

Finnegan, F. 1982. *Poverty and Prejudice- A Study of Irish Immigrants in York*, Cork: Cork University Press.

Hall, T. 1849. 'Report upon the Recent Epidemic Fever in Ireland,' *Quarterly Journal of Medical Science*, vol. 7. pp. 64-125.

Hobhouse, Emily. 1901. *Report of a Visit to the Camps of Women and Children in the Cape and Orange River Colonies*, delivered to the British government in June.

Howard, E. 1898. *To-morrow: A Peaceful Path to Real Reform*, London: Sonnerschein.

Kennedy, L. , Ell, P.S., Crawford, E.M., and Clarkson, L.A., 1999. *Mapping The Great Irish Famine*, Dublin: Four Courts Press.

Lee, E. 1985. *To the Bitter End: A Photographic History of the Boer War, 1899–1902.* New York: Viking, 1985.

Miller, M. 2010. *English Garden Cities – An Introduction*, Swindon: English Heritage.

Pakenham, T. 1979. *The Boer War*, New York: Random House.

Robson, M. 2000. 'The Rowntree Family and the Schreiner Riots', *Journal of the Friends' Historical Society* vol, 59 (1), pp. 67-82

Rowntree, B.S. 1936 [1901, 1911] *Poverty: A Study of Town Life*, London: Macmillan.

Rowntree, B.S. 1910. *Land and Labour – Lessons from Belgium*, London: Macmillan.

Rowntree, G. 1936. *The Reminiscences of George Rowntree*, privately published.

Rowntree, John W: *Present Day Papers, 1898-1902*

Joseph Rowntree, 1852. *Memoranda of Business and Household Arrangements*, York.

Rowntree & co. 1925. 'Joseph Rowntree', *CWM* pp. 3-30

Rubinstein, D. 1999. *York Friends and the Great War*, York: Borthwick Institute.

Thurman, H. 1973. *A Track to the Water's Edge: The Olive Schreiner Reader*, New York: Harper and Row.

Veit-Wilson, J.H. 1984. 'Seebohm Rowntree' in Barker, P (ed): *Founders of the Welfare State*, London: Heinemann, pp.75-82

Waddilove, L.E. 1954. *One Man's Vision – The Story of the Joseph Rowntree Village Trust*, London: Allen and Unwin.

Wagner, G. 1987, *The Chocolate Conscience*, London: Chatto and Windus.

Walvin, J. 1997. *The Quakers: Money & Morals*, London: John Murray.

Worstenholm, L: *Joseph Rowntree – A Typescript Memoir*

Wright, S. 1995. *Friends in York*, Keele: Keele University Press.

Visit York! 2016. www.visityork.org , accessed 30 October 2016.

7 | Colonizer William Penn and Engineer Herbert Hoover: How their Businesses Affected their Philanthropy and Statesmanship

By Stephen W. Angell

Introduction

This chapter compares and contrasts two iconic Quaker American statesmen and politicians, William Penn (1644-1718) and Herbert Hoover (1874-1964), whose humanitarian and political activities were greatly affected by and, to some extent, presupposed broad business interests, oriented toward more personal, even selfish, goals.

The treatment of both men is necessarily selective and illustrative, even suggestive. No attempt is made toward comprehensiveness. We should note from the start that Penn and Hoover lived in two very different eras, obviously complicating the task of comparison.

The claim here is not that both men were successful businessmen. Hoover arguably was. Penn's record as a businessman is more mixed: He underwent bankruptcy in 1707 and was jailed for a time for debt, but handed on his proprietorship to his non-Quaker sons, who were able to make more business success from it. Instead, the question to be pursued is an integrative one. I explore how each man combined his business interests with his humanitarianism, philanthropy, and activity as a politician and a statesman.

Penn had humanitarian goals in humane treatment of Native Americans and concern for the peace of Europe. But he also bought land from the Native Americans and widely advertised on the European Continent to sell land in Pennsylvania (and was successful in the latter objective with many Germans). How did his actions enhance or interfere with one another?

Hoover was a successful engineer, becoming a millionaire by the age of 31. He made his name in post-World-War I humanitarian relief; among other things, he was influential in paving the way for the American Friends Service Committee, and eventually AFSC would share a Nobel Prize in 1947. He was also the only sitting U.S. Secretary of Commerce ever to win the office of U.S. President. Again, how did these actions enhance, interact, or interfere with one another?

My hope is to penetrate beyond the iconic images to get at what really made these two Quaker businessmen-philanthropists- politicians to tick.

William Penn, Colonizer

Inasmuch as colonizing was a family business, Penn was a colonizer before he became a Quaker. His father, the admiral, made a notable trip of conquest to the Caribbean during the interregnum, failing to bring the island of Hispaniola under English rule, but wresting Jamaica from the Spanish. (Peare 1956, 21) But the focus of the family activity of colonizing was focused on the Old World, not the New. From various sources (his mother's family's estate, Cromwellian grants), Admiral Penn amassed a large estate in Ireland. In fact, the young William Penn was tending to their Irish lands when he experienced Quaker convincement in 1667. (Peare 1956, 52-58) Nor did Quaker convincement terminate his connection with the family business interest in Ireland; he was concerned extensively with those matters for some years afterward. Thus, the story of William Penn as a colonizer should begin in Ireland.

Immediately prior to traveling to Ireland in October of 1669 to tend to his family's estates, Penn hired Philip Ford, a highly regarded but only moderately successful merchant, to assist him with his personal affairs, promising to pay him forty pounds per year. (Peare 1956, 91) For better or for worse, this relationship between Penn and Ford, and Ford's heirs, would endure for the next four decades. It was expected that Ford would attend well to the many small details for which Penn, a big picture man, had little patience.

In Ireland, Penn had many goals. First, he wanted to free Quakers from the prisons. This took much effort, and contacts with all manner of English and Irish officials, but eventually he had a sufficient record of accomplishment that he felt free to come home to England. On the 6th of June, the Irish chancellor promised to release Friends "by order of Councill," and nine days later the remaining Friends in prison were indeed released.

He also sought to collect rents that were due to his father and to arrange new leases of the lands, mostly along the south shore of Ireland from Baltimore to Imokilly. These business arrangements were made mostly with other English colonizers, not with native Irish. All of his father's business was also concluded by the 6th of June. Penn's Irish sojourn would conclude early in August; this visit to Ireland thus had lasted almost ten months. (Peare 1956, 94-104)

Penn attended Friends' meeting in Ireland often, and demonstrably to his satisfaction: during his time in Ireland, he had a "precious meeting" (Nov. 28); "a large & blessed meeting" (Dec. 26); "a large convincing meeting" (Feb. 13); "a precious meeting as I was ever in" (Feb. 27); "an exceeding great meeting … & several reached" (Mar. 6). There was danger ever-present, however. On May 15, "we had a good meeting, [but] we were disturb'd." Several Friends were apprehended, but they missed taking Penn into custody, even though he had spoken twice at the meeting. (PWP, I, 109, 112, 117, 119, 120)

The native Irish inhabitants lurk mostly in the background of his travel journal. Penn has numerous disputes with Catholic priests, and he wrote an anti-Catholic tract (*A seasonable caveat against popery*, published in 1670) during his months in Ireland. Penn showed little or no evidence of any positive views toward the native Irish. Passing through Cashel on his way from Cork to Dublin on October 29, Penn "passed through [the] holy Cross (so call'd) from a superstitious conceit that a peece of [Christ's] cross was brought thither from Jerusalem." Later they passed by Thurles, the site of a tenth century battle where "the English were murder'd by the Fitz.Pat," with "fitz.pat" being Penn's obscure but evidently derogatory reference to the native Irish and their ancestors. (PWP, I, 105)

In Ireland, his humanitarian impulses were directed mostly to Quakers suffering imprisonment, Quakers who were his fellow English. As directed to the Native Irish, however, there is no equivalent of the friendly address that he would later use toward the Native Americans. Colonization implies a simultaneous mingling and separation between the colonizers and the colonized. His Irish estates appear to be no exception here. Since the benefits of colonization, as sketched out briefly here, accrue entirely to the colonizers, it would follow that the people subject to colonization from outside (the Native Irish, in this instance) would be suffering from oppression. One could be forgiven for not immediately grasping this fact in a first reading of Penn's Irish Journal, however, since the Native Irish play only a very small role in Penn's narration of his business affairs. In other words, they are almost invisible in his journal.

In late June or early July of 1673, William and his first wife Gulielma Penn had the opportunity to hear a first-hand report from George Fox after his return from North America. (Peare 1956, 157) This would likely have been William's first opportunity to hear about the Delaware River valley that would loom so large in his later life. Fox had passed through what would later become New Jersey, and he described it as a great wilderness. He had visited with Native Americans in that region, but Fox apparently encountered none of the very few whites, mostly Dutch and Swedes, then resident in the Middle Atlantic region south of New York. Penn provides no written record of this meeting, but some important events in Penn's life relating to this distant part of the world closely follow upon his meeting with Fox on this occasion.

William Penn's first direct involvement in the North American colonizing enterprise occurred in 1675, when he was called in to arbitrate a dispute between two Quakers, Edward Byllynge and John Fenwick, who together had set up the colony of West New Jersey. Byllynge was broke, and Fenwick had given him the money to buy West New Jersey from royal favorite Sir John Berkeley. Penn worked out an agreement between the two whereby Byllynge would grant one-tenth of the shares in West New Jersey Colonization to Fenwick, and additionally pay him 400 pounds. In the context of the arbitration process, Penn intimated to Fenwick his doubts about the profitability of colonization, at least in the short run: "And make the best of wt thou hast, thy great Grand children may be in the other world before wt Land thou hast allotted will be employed." (Penn to Fenwick, 13 Feb. 1675; PWP, I, 386) Penn, along with two other Quakers, was appointed a trustee over the project overseen by the quarreling Fenwick and Byllynge, resigning his trusteeship only in 1681, as the new colonization project of Pennsylvania loomed ahead.

Penn was one of 152 signers of, and may have had some role in drafting, the West New Jersey Concessions and Agreements, finalized in the summer of 1676. (PWP, I, 387-408) The editors of Penn's papers call these Concessions "one of the most innovative political documents of the seventeenth century." (PWP, I, 387) As was the case with Penn's Irish estates, and would also be the case with Pennsylvania, the West New Jersey proprietors were given the prerogative of collecting quitrents from their land purchasers, even those who still lived in the British Isles, not having yet moved to West New Jersey. Several of the most high profile provisions match Penn's strong concerns and would also feature prominently in the 'Frame of Government' for Pennsylvania. Chapter 16 established freedom of conscience on religious matters for inhabitants of West New Jersey. Nobody within the province "shall be any waies upon any pretence whatsoever called in question or in the least punished or hurt either in Person Estate or Priviledge for the sake of his opinion Judgment faith or worship towards God in matters of Religion." Chapter 17 established trial by a jury of "twelve good and Lawfull men," without which no inhabitant "shall be deprived or condemned of Life limb Liberty estate Property." Native Americans featured in Chapter 25; whenever an English inhabitant accused "Indian Natives," or vice versa, the Concessions called for a trial by jury, in which the jury is to be composed of "six of the neighbourhood and six of the said Indian Natives." This same provision would be featured in Penn's letter to the Indians of Pennsylvania in 1681.

Penn was involved in the promotion of West New Jersey, advising prospective settlers that they "soberly and conscientiously endeavor to obtain their good wills [and] the unity of Friends where they live." (Pomfret 1956, 102) West New Jersey was a weak colony, with even its right of self-governance disputed by a powerful neighbor, New York Governor Edmund Andros, but Penn was able to intervene in places of power in order to "secure confirmation of both soil and government." (Pomfret 1956, 108; PWP, II, 23-24) In 1679 Penn wrote *The Case of New Jersey Stated* to argue for the province's right to its own government. (Geiter 2000, 106) Penn was also able to get Robert Barclay, a favorite of the Duke of York, to intercede with him so that the West New Jersey government would be confirmed in its ability to collect customs and duties. The anti-Catholic hysteria of the Popish plot, in which Penn was a sometime believer, complicated these endeavors, as the Catholic Duke of York had to leave England for his own safety for months on end. (Pomfret 1956, 111-112) Penn would not cease involvement in New Jersey's affairs until 1702, when the Crown's governance superseded the province's Charter. (Geiter 2000, 106)

By my accounting, Pennsylvania was to be Penn's third colonizing venture, though it was the first that he designed from its very inception as an English province. (There were a few hundred Dutch, Swedes, and Finns on the west side of the Delaware River prior to the grant of that land by Charles II to Penn, but no English.) The editors of the Penn Papers have pointed to cogent reasons for him to pursue this additional colonizing venture in 1680. English politics were in a state of paralysis, with religious toleration not on the horizon. A North American colony would be a place where Quakers could escape the rampant abuse and slanders directed against them, including those directed against Penn himself. Intra-Quaker politics were in a dismal state as well, as George Fox and his allies struggled with resilient separatists John Story, William Rogers, and John Wilkinson. Penn needed more income, and he thought another colonizing venture would provide that for him. And Penn thought that he could do a better job in promotion and marketing than his colonizing predecessors had done. He probably had a more extensive sales network than any other present or prospective colonizer. Most of his contacts were in the British Isles, but Penn had also made two ministerial trips to Holland and Germany, most recently in 1677 in the company of Fox, George Keith, and Robert Barclay, so Penn possessed contacts there that he could draw on.[19] Penn's personal contacts with

---

[19] Penn made ministerial trips to Germany in 1671 and 1677-8, prior to the founding of Pennsylvania, and in 1686, after the founding.

the heir to the throne, James, the Duke of York, and Charles II were strong enough so that he could overcome all of the substantial obstacles that would be thrown in the way of this new North American colonizing venture. The business, political, and religious aims of this new effort came together and merged and mixed together. (PWP, II, 21-22)

This treatment of the founding of Pennsylvania will concentrate on Penn as a businessman, including his use of marketing and promotion. I have written about the idealism of the founding of Pennsylvania elsewhere (Angell 2006), and in this context, it is to be noted that many of the idealistic aspects of Pennsylvania's founding were prefigured in his earlier, more modest involvement in the colonizing of New Jersey. Pennsylvania's Frame of Government would provide religious toleration and trial by jury, just as the New Jersey Concessions had. Penn's proposal in his 1681 letter to the King of the Indians for disputes between the English colonizers and the Native Americans to be settled by councils composed of equal numbers of each people also were prefigured in the New Jersey Concessions.

Again, the editors of the Penn Papers offer a useful orientation to this task:

> Founding a successful proprietary colony in late seventeenth-century America was hard work. A proprietor had to be an aggressive, pragmatic businessman who could publicize his colony widely; offer land, trading rights, and powers of government to a broad variety of settlers on attractive terms; and compete effectively with other proprietors how had the same objective – making their colonies pay. ... WP's land sales ... proceeded well. Between July and October 1681, he sold over 300,000 acres of land to nearly 300 investors from England, Wales, and Ireland. (PWP, II, 81-82)

And Penn wasn't done. He authored at least five different promotional tracts pitching Pennsylvania, at various lengths, to different audiences. The most effective (and widely read, even to this day) of these promotional tracts was Penn's letter to the "Free Society of Traders," a corporation that Penn spearheaded that sought to encourage industry and commerce in Pennsylvania. (PWP, II, 246-7) (The very founding and existence of this corporation underlines Penn's business-like interest in his province; and its fairly rapid failure shows the weakness of using a North American colony to improve one's bottom line.) Penn delivered a highly favorable assessment of the soil, vegetation, animals, and navigation, and provided also a lengthy description of the Native Americans (who he portrayed as a hospitable, "strong, & clever" people) and a briefer description of the Dutch and Swedes who preceded the Quakers to what would become Pennsylvania. The published version of the letter described the promises that the English and Indians made to each other to "live in Love, as long as the Sun gave light." Indeed, his description of the Native Americans is probably the aspect of the letter that most interests contemporary readers of it. But that was not how the letter concluded, and the conclusion of the letter pointed to Penn's varied commercial interests that he shared with the Free Society of Traders: "You are already informed what is fit for you further to do, whatever tends to the Promotion of Wine, and to the Manufacture of Linnen in these parts, I cannot but wish you to promote it ... I would advise you to send for some Thousands of Plants out of France ... I ... assure you, that I am heartily inclined to advance your just interest." (PWP, II, 442-460; quotations on pages 448, 459, 460)

While the First Purchasers were all from the British Isles, the later purchasers came from a variety of European backgrounds. Penn was well aware that the willingness of continental Europeans to move to his province could substantially aid his venture. In 1686, Penn noted that the Carolinians were urging French wine-growers to move to Carolina, and he sought ways to counter their moves and to encourage the French to move to Pennsylvania instead. Presumably the desired settlers were Huguenots, French Protestants, fleeing the repressive atmosphere in France following the 1685 revocation of the 1598 Edict of Nantes which had granted religious toleration. (PWP, III, 119-121)

However, from the beginning and well into the eighteenth century after Penn's death, the majority of the continental Europeans to migrate to America were Dutch and Germans. That this was an important aim of Penn's can be discerned from his promotional literature. Four of his promotional tracts were translated into Dutch or German, or both. According to Edwin Bronner's thorough accounting of Penn's publishing output, Penn's six promotional tracts went through 25 printings by 1690. Of these 25 printings, 17 were in English. As to the other 8, four of Penn's tracts were printed in Dutch translation, one twice, for a total of 5 printings; two of Penn's tracts were printed in German translation, one twice, for a total of 3 printings. (PWP, V, 263-276, 298-307, 320-323, 367-369) Some of Penn's writings were translated into Dutch and German in handwritten copies. (Hull 1935, 310) Penn thus undertook very concrete measures to encourage Dutch and German migration to Pennsylvania. It is not the case that Penn only had his promotional tracts translated into Dutch and German. In the decade before the founding of Pennsylvania (i.e., the 1670s), Penn had at least ten of his writings translated into those two languages. (Hull 1935, 308)

Ultimately, Pennsylvania would be heavily peopled by Germans from the Rhine river valley and other areas, beginning about 1708. While the beginnings of this migration occurred while Penn was still alive, a more immediate effect on Penn's business model took place earlier, with a migration of mostly Dutch people, beginning in the 1680s. These Dutch folk founded Germantown, now a part of Philadelphia, but then a separate settlement. (Klein and Hoogenboom 1973: 39-40)

Actually, Penn's Dutch and German translations both had an early, concrete response. In "the notorious case of the Frankford company" (in Penn's words), German investors from Frankfurt reserved 15,000 acres for migration in the 1683. But they never acted upon their promise to send over migrants, so by 1700 Penn and the Pennsylvanians had given up on them. (PWP, II, 490; IV, 688) The one German who did settle in Pennsylvania was Francis Daniel Pastorius, a lover of Penn's and James Nayler's writings, who had acted as agent for the Frankfort Company.

But Dutch settlers from Krefeld, did settle in Germantown, beginning in 1683. The settlers from Kriegsheim, from the vicinity of Worms in southwest Germany, arrived in Pennsylvania two years later. (Hull 1935, 211, 291) Pastorius was of assistance to these parties, too.

Krefeld is in the border area between Holland and Germany. In the seventeenth century, it was governed by the Dutch Protestant Prince of Orange; today, it is part of Germany. The migrants from Krefeld and Kriegsheim had both Mennonite and Quaker ties. Quaker William Ames, an English Baptist who preached extensively to Mennonites on the continent, had brought Quakerism to Krefeld and Kriegsheim in 1657. (Hull 1935, 191, 262) Penn visited Kriegsheim in 1677, and while he did not then visit Krefeld, he stopped at Duisberg, within twenty miles of Krefeld. (Hull 1935, 194, 280) Quakers in both Krefeld and Kriegsheim experienced religious persecution. In 1677, Penn wrote to the Prince in Mannheim on behalf of the Quakers in Kriegsheim. He also lodged a written appeal with the Krefeld authorities on behalf of toleration for Quakers in 1680. (Hull 1935, 202, 281)

A seventeenth-century Puritan writer, William Gouge, noted that one difference between Puritans and Anabaptists was that Puritans thought that the freedom commanded by Christ was a spiritual one, whereas the Anabaptists thought that Christ intended that all people enjoy physical and spiritual freedom. Thus, according to Gouge, Puritans were willing to countenance servitude, whereas Anabaptists were not. (Gouge 1622, 601-3) Along these lines of analysis, the English Quakers acted like Puritans, and when a slave ship dropped anchor at Philadelphia in December 1684, they eagerly bought up all the slaves that were for sale. (PWP, II, 608) Penn himself would hold slaves. (PWP, IV, 113-4, 219-20) On this matter, at least, the Krefeld Quakers, now resident at Germantown, acted like Anabaptists, writing and presenting the first antislavery petition in North America, a petition on which Philadelphia Yearly Meeting would decline to act.

The quiet tabling of the Germantown Quaker petition inaugurated a notable struggle in business ethics during Penn's absence, as to whether (using Gouge's categories) the Anabaptist or Puritan vision of Christian freedom would be the one applied in Pennsylvania. It would not be until seventy years later that a group of Quaker reformers, led by Anthony Benezet and John Woolman, would vindicate the Anabaptist ideal of Christian freedom over against the Puritan one, and thus expand the vision beyond Penn of fair and humane dealings with one's fellow human beings. A struggle between Penn and Penn's heirs, and the Dutch and German settlers that Penn worked so assiduously to attract to Pennsylvania, was necessary, before this highly desirable enhancement of Quaker views of business ethics could be brought about.

There is much more about Penn's business model and business ethics that could be explored, for which space here does not permit full exploration. For example, there are divergent scholarly views of Penn's land dealings with the Indians. Some would ascribe the deterioration between the Native Americans and the Pennsylvanians to Penn's sons, and holdover officials from Penn's lifetime such as James Logan, while Penn's record on this matter is seen as a praiseworthy one. Other scholars see Penn's dealings, too, as deriving from the same insatiable desire by Europeans for more Native American lands, and hence sketch out more of a continuum between Penn and his sons in regard to Native American land sales. This aspect of business ethics is adequately developed elsewhere. (Angell 2006; Jennings 1986; Pencak and Richter 2004) One might also explore areas of overlap and conflict between Penn's business model and his theological and ethical writings, the bulk of his output. I have explored connections between his theological work and his practical work in the area of religious toleration elsewhere. (Angell 1992; Angell 2012).

Penn's earlier wise advice to John Fenwick that it would take a long time for the lands in New Jersey could be profitably employed also applied, to Penn's sorrow, to his lands in Pennsylvania. Pennsylvania would not become a financial success in Penn's lifetime, quite the opposite. Edwin Bronner summarizes the situation well: "The people of Pennsylvania continued to think of Penn as a wealthy man after his fortune changed, and used every means possible to escape paying their quitrents and to prevent being taxed. They rejected Penn's requests for loans. ... His expenses continued unabated." (Bronner 1962, 70-71) The demand for quitrents, a carryover from colonizing ventures in Ireland and West New Jersey, turned out to be a highly inadequate source of income for Penn, leading to financial disaster. Penn underwent bankruptcy in 1707 and 1708, disputing debts that his erstwhile steward Philip Ford claimed to be owed to him, and an insolvent Penn even spent time in prison for bankruptcy in 1708. (Peare 1956, 396-404) Penn commenced proceedings to sell Pennsylvania to the Crown; this sale had not been consummated by the time of an incapacitating stroke in 1712, (Peare 1956, 412) to the eventual good fortune of his sons, who were able to amass a profit from their ethically murkier second-generation colonizing ventures.

Herbert Hoover, Engineer

Herbert Hoover, native of West Branch, Iowa, was an orphan by age nine. Two years after his father Jesse had died of a fever, his mother (and recorded Quaker minister) Hulda caught pneumonia while walking back from a ministerial engagement among Quakers and died. The eight-year-old boy was sent to live with his uncle Henry Minthorn in Newberg, Oregon. There he completed his secondary education at Pacific Academy (a forerunner of the present-day George Fox University). He subsequently gained a geology degree from Stanford University (he was a member of its first graduating class), where he met his future wife, Lou Henry. During the two decades after his graduation, he rapidly rose through the ranks of mining companies, eventually accumulating a large fortune with his work reclaiming mines in Australia and China. During this time, he came to define himself as an "Engineer," solidifying his reputation in numerous articles in scholarly journals and his 1909 book, *Principles of Mining*. (Nash 1983, 476-8) At the turn of the twentieth century, "engineer" was a burgeoning profession in the U.S., growing from 7000 practitioners in 1872 to 135,000 by the 1920s. (Gabor 2000, 9) Hoover was following a very fashionable trend.

What Hoover meant by "engineering" in 1909 affected all of the mining company's operations:

> While some of Hoover's book was devoted to technical and mechanical aspects of mining, the bulk of it concentrated on his principal interest, valuation, administration, and finance. Suffusing the text was Hoover's recognition that mining, after all, was a business, that all mines were mortal, that the mining engineer's ultimate objective was to make an investment pay. Suffusing it, too, was a brisk Hooverian emphasis on efficiency and simplicity. 'The essential facts governing the value of a

mine,' he declared at one point, 'can be expressed on one sheet of paper.' (Nash 1983, 478)

Hoover was influenced by the efficiency and scientific management emphasis of his older engineering contemporary, Frederick Winslow Taylor, (Nash 1983, 488) another turn-of-the-century icon who had been raised as a Quaker. (Nelson 2000) For ordinary laborers, Hoover preferred contract or piecework over wages, because "contract work honorably carried out puts a premium upon individual effort, and thus makes for efficiency." (Nash 1983, 488) The fact that Hoover's concept of engineering focused on financial as well as technical aspects of the mining business opened him up later on to political attacks (Mouat and Phimister 2008).[20] Hoover vigorously countered these attacks, (Rappleye 2016, 298) even to the extent of authorizing at least one Watergate-style burglary on a journalist, as a private diary from a subordinate that became available decades later would show. (Rappleye 2016, 154-157) But as his fateful 1932 re-election effort loomed ahead, he would turn out to have far more important threats to his political future than a few books re-examining his mining career from three decades earlier.

One scholar suggests that there is no way to get to the bottom of Hoover's work for the mining companies in Australia and China:

> It is unlikely that the precise nature of Hoover's activities in China will ever be sorted out. Hoover believed that the Chinese with whom he was dealing were corrupt and incompetent, and he was quite possibly right. The Chinese thought Hoover was a swindler, and he was certainly capable of sharp dealing. In Australia, he had advocated lying about monthly output in order to mislead investors. British Foreign Office representatives concluded that the dispute between the Westerners ... and the Chinese was 'a case of rogues falling out' after behavior that was

---

[20] One focus of these political attacks on Hoover was his involvement in a takeover of a Chinese coal company by European investors that had taken place in the immediate aftermath of the Boxer Rebellion in 1900. A Chinese official recalled that "Hoover [and his London bosses] knew well the value of these mines, and at that time [1900] had already begun to cast longing eyes on them. Hoover took advantage of the Boxer trouble to carry out his designs." Mouat and Phimister write that "in effect, the previous owners were defrauded of their property. None of the principals concerned [including Hoover] ... ever satisfactorily explained the parts they played in all of this. Where individual testimony survives, it is entirely self-serving." They assert that recent research shows that "in Australia, China, Nicaragua, and Nigeria, Hoover behaved pretty much as" his critics in the 1930s claimed that he had. (2008, 561-3)

'very shady on both sides' ... However questionable some of his actions may have been, Hoover proved invaluable to his employers. By skillful administration and an infusion of capital, he turned the immense Kaiping coal deposits into a flourishing enterprise. He was duly rewarded. ... A man knowledgeable about the Australian gold fields said of Hoover that there was 'no cleverer engineer in the two hemispheres.' (Leuchtenberg 2009, 15-16)

The electoral process in the United States has generally not been kind to presidential candidates who run primarily on their backgrounds in business, and it is also true that presidential candidates for whom their business credentials are among their most important qualifications have not fared well in office, even if they survive the campaign gamut.[21]

From 1908 to 1914, Hoover was in business for himself as a "mine doctor," which meant that he "turned sick operations into healthy ones for a fee based on a percentage of increased profits from the reorganized and revitalized firms." In his *Memoirs*, he sometimes would "exaggerate his accomplishments as a managerial doctor and minimize his less successful efforts." By 1914, he had accumulated a fortune of four million dollars. (Hoff Wilson 1975, 16-17)

It was also the case that Hoover was moved by the Progressive sentiment of the early twentieth century and that he evolved toward viewing labor unions more favorably as he grew older. By the 1910s and 1920s, Hoover would specifically endorse "the brand of progressivism that stressed cooperative economic organization, self-regulation by business, and voluntary activity through American society." (Hoff 2000)

In 1914, Hoover volunteered without pay to organize food aid for occupied Belgium. It has been said that Hoover's efforts resulted in millions of lives being saved. (Clements 2010, xiii; Leuchtenberg 2009, 58) Between 1914 and 1917

> Hoover's London-based organization, in collaboration with the Belgians' own Comité National, acquired, transported, and

---

[21] The most recent President whose advanced degree was an M.B.A. was George W. Bush. Both the younger Bush and Hoover are generally ranked in the bottom quartile of American presidents. For example, an NBC News poll of 65 historians in 2009 ranked Hoover 34th and G. W. Bush 36th best of the 42 persons who held the office of U.S. president prior to 2009. http://www.nbcnews.com/id/29216774/#.VzygBOTIK2U

distributed over 2,500,000 tons of foodstuffs to more than 9,000,000 helpless people in Belgium and German-occupied France. An emergency relief effort directed by an American engineer evolved into a gigantic humanitarian undertaking without precedent in history. (Nash 1996, 4)

During the period that the U.S. was an active combatant in World War I, Hoover was the head of the U.S. Food Administration (or 'food czar'), charged that there would be enough food to ensure that the Allies would win the war. According to Hoover, if Americans observed "meatless" days and adopted the "doctrine of the clean plate," it would help to conserve enough food to provision the Allies (Nash 1996, 153, 229, 256). At the peace conference that convened in Paris in 1919, the Quaker Hoover was one who sought to procure a generous peace; instead, a punitive peace requiring the defeated Axis powers to pay reparations to the Allies was promulgated. Hoover

> … was "the only man," said John Maynard Keynes, "who emerged from the ordeal of Paris with an enhanced reputation." Keynes believed that if Hoover's realism, his "knowledge, magnanimity, and disinterestedness," had found wider play in the councils of Paris, the world would have had "the Good Peace." (Kennedy 1999, 9)

Following the armistice in 1918, Hoover again worked tirelessly to provide humanitarian assistance for much of the world. In this he had assistance from the newly formed American Friends Service Committee. While the AFSC did much fundraising for feeding German children, Hoover also channeled other funds toward the AFSC. For political reasons, Hoover could not publicly advocate feeding German children, so the willingness of the AFSC to take the lead on this issue was useful to Hoover (as well as helpful to the AFSC's own reputation, when its postwar feeding programs played a large part in the award of the Nobel Peace Prize to Friends in 1947). The AFSC was only one of several humanitarian assistance programs with which Herbert and Lou Henry Hoover had a close connection. He also worked closely with the Red Cross and a variety of organizations assisting children in need. His own straitened circumstances as a child were never far from his mind. (Clements 2010, 83-84) Overall, John Maynard Keynes further noted that Hoover often acted "in the teeth of European obstruction" and that his humanitarian work "not only saved an immense amount of human suffering, but averted a widespread breakdown of the European system." (Clements 2010, 25)

Hoover was not oblivious to the many businesslike aspects of humanitarian relief, as his program kept the needs of American farmers in mind, supported the expansion of capitalism in Europe so that American trade and investment would be benefited, worked to undermine the spread of Communism, and required recipients eventually to pay for what they received.

> By putting his program [of humanitarian assistance to postwar Europe] on a businesslike basis and requiring recipients to pay for what they received, he made it acceptable to Americans. And indeed, he was correct in believing that although they did not like it, the Europeans could eventually pay for what they received (although most did not do so). (Clements 2010, 250)

Hoover enhanced his career as a member of the cabinet for Republican Presidents Harding and Coolidge between 1921 and 1929. His title was Secretary of Commerce, but it was often observed that the hyperactive Hoover was "undersecretary of all other departments." (Leuchtenberg 2009: 63; Ding Darling, "The Traffic Problem in Washington," April 1927 cartoon, reprinted in Clements 2010, 264) With his "titanic intellect," he seemed to possess "knowledge in all areas." (Hoff Wilson 1975, 23) Hoover continued with his customary concerns for child welfare. He also continued to be the "Master of Emergencies," earning mostly positive reviews for his work in countering the unemployment problem caused by the recession of 1921, and the widespread suffering caused by the floods in the Mississippi River basin in 1927. (Leuchtenberg 2009, 68-69)

Dealing with unemployment in 1921 was hampered by the fact that the government had few statistics on labor and employment nationwide, so Hoover was instrumental in beginning the collection of such statistics. As an engineer, he knew that he needed data in order to address the unemployment situation appropriately. He sponsored studies that provided valuable data, although he was too busy to read the reports as thoroughly as he needed to. Hoover called an Unemployment Conference that met in September 1921 and attempted to galvanize immediate voluntary efforts by business leaders to address the issues of unemployment. Hoover believed in state and local public works spending to jolt the economy when in recession. He did not procure any legislation to deal with the problem, nor did he define a federal responsibility for the national problem of unemployment. He seriously overestimated the effectiveness of his efforts when the nation emerged from the 1921 recession, and, in retrospect, this "mistaken assumption would have serious consequences during his presidency." (Clements 2010, 131-147; quotation on 147; Leuchtenberg 2009, 62)

Hoover was elected President by a landslide in 1928, when the incumbent Calvin Coolidge chose not to run for re-election. Hoover united the Conservative and the Progressive wings of the Republican Party behind his candidacy, and he was even able to garner electoral votes from the hitherto "solid South" held by the Democrats. To do so, Hoover had to choose whether to work with the "black and tan" delegations among the Southern Republicans – black-and-tans were party organizations composed mostly of African-Americans, and "tan" was slang for whites who worked with African-Americans – or with the "lily white" delegations. Hoover's stance during the campaign was intentionally ambiguous as he sided sometimes with one Southern Republican faction, and sometimes with the other. He denied that he opposed Jim Crow, and he ignored appeals to denounce the Ku Klux Klan. Hoover never denounced lynching. During the 1928 election campaign, the Democrats, with their strong Southern segregationist cohort, were worse on these issues.

As President, he sided with the "lily white" Republicans, trying to ease the black-and-tans out of party leadership positions, on the pretext of cracking down on corruption. As a result, when in 1930 he nominated Judge John Parker, a North Carolinian lily-white nominee, for the Supreme Court, a coalition of Democrats and progressive Republicans narrowly defeated the nomination by a 49-47 vote. Walter White of the NAACP decried this nomination from Hoover, "the man in the lily-White House."[22] (Leuchtenberg 2009, 75, 99; Rappleye 2016, 25, 131, 144-5, 148)

Sometimes Hoover manifested a progressive approach to race relations. He refused to sign a restrictive covenant when buying his Washington, D. C. home; he strongly supported the Urban League; he increased funding for Howard University, a historically black university in Washington, D.C.; and, disregarding intense protests from Southern whites, he invited Representative Oscar DePriest from Chicago to visit the White House for tea, the first time an African American had visited the White House for a social occasion in almost thirty years. (Leuchtenberg 2009, 89)

---

[22] In opposition to the Parker nomination, White cited a 1920 Parker speech in which he had stated, "The negro as a class does not desire to enter politics. The Republican Party of North Carolina does not desire him to do so. We recognize the fact that he has not yet entered the stage of development when he can share the burdens and responsibilities of government." Rappleye 2016, 143-4.

One observer, Anne O'Hare McCormick, noted the national elation when Herbert Hoover was inaugurated as President on March 4, 1929:

> We were in a mood for magic. . . . The whole country was a vast, expectant gallery. . . We had summoned a great engineer to solve our problems for us; now we sat back comfortably and confidently to watch the problem being solved. The modern technical mind was for the first time at the head of government. . . . Almost with the air of giving genius its chance we waited for the performance to begin. (Kennedy 1999, 43)

The next four years did not work out at all well. It was not all Hoover's fault. Historians, with the benefit of decades of hindsight, have come to differing conclusions about his administration. Some have viewed Hoover sympathetically; for example, Joan Hoff's book on Hoover is subtitled "Forgotten Progressive," pointing out how it was sometimes the case that Hoover's actions, such as the enactment of the Reconstruction Finance Corporation (RFC), actually paved the way for the New Deal of Franklin Delano Roosevelt. "The ill-fated Hoover administration became the first in American history to use the power of the federal government to intervene directly in the economy in time of peace." (Hoff Wilson 1975, 156)

Charles Rappleye's 2016 work, *Herbert Hoover in the White House: The Ordeal of the Presidency*, gives perhaps the most detailed account yet of Hoover's four years as President, and he draws a grimmer, unsparing portrait, although also a nuanced one:

> Hoover was not the mild Quaker soul that his friends like to portray, simply unfortunate to have entered the White House at such an unpropitious moment. . . . Hoover was a kindly enough man in person and to his friends, but in the capacity of his office he was surly, easily frustrated, and sometimes vindictive. He regarded his enemies and often his friends with suspicion, allowed few to get close to him and proved inconstant in his alliances. A look inside his White House sanctum found him seething with anger; his advisors counseled that he use fear as a weapon and Hoover embraced it, winning some legislative battles but losing the war for hearts and minds. (xvi)

Rappleye attributes his poor conduct in office to his lack of experience in elective office. Despite his extensive and admirable public service prior to the Presidency, the office of U.S. President was the first elective office that Hoover ever held. Hoover was a shy, private person. He communicated poorly with the media and with the Congress. Hoover often bristled with forbidding defenses; according to George Creel, "Writing about Herbert Hoover is like trying to describe the interior of a citadel where every drawbridge is up and every portcullis is down." (Leuchtenberg 2009, xi)

Hoover had a philosophic mind, and his key concepts were cooperation and voluntarism. He saw only a limited role for the federal government in emergencies (despite the fact that the bulk of his earlier relief efforts were funded by the federal government). After the market crash in October, 1929, Hoover called industry titans to the White House to encourage them not to engage in layoffs. Their response, in the short term, was a positive one. Carmaker Henry Ford even committed to "raising his industry-leading daily wage from $5 to $7." The next day he met with labor leaders, asking them to ensure labor peace, and they also cooperated with the president. (Rappleye 2016, 111) Hoover wanted more public works projects at the federal and state level to stimulate employment. But he did not make a public speech about the economy at this time, and to the American people, he seemed remote. He "might have the diagnosis, but he didn't have the bedside manner." (Rappleye 2016, 115) This would be a huge, enduring problem for him.

It took some time to realize how grave the crisis was. By 1930, in addition to the industrial crisis, vast crises in the spheres of agriculture and banking converged on the United States and the beleaguered Hoover. Layoffs increased dramatically. Hoover performed poorly in communicating with Congress over tariff legislation, and the result was the infamous Smoot-Hawley tariff bill in late 1930, setting tariffs at their highest rate ever and sparking an international trade war at the worst possible time. He took little interest in the messy minutiae of governance. (Rappleye 2016, 151) At their best, Quakers exhibit great skills in conflict resolution; Hoover showed such skills during and in the immediate aftermath of World War I. At their worst, Quakers indulge in conflict avoidance. Too often Hoover's activity as president seemed to verge on conflict avoidance.

To skip ahead to 1932, some of the best and the worst of Hoover's political skills were exhibited in dealing with the World War I veterans who converged on the District of Columbia in May, 1932 to demand early payment of their war bonuses, and who camped out in public spaces. After both houses of Congress turned down their request, the bonus marchers showed no disposition to leave. Hoover exhibited great patience, for a while. Hoover counseled restraint and defused potential confrontations that would lead to greater violence. (He, however, refused to have this known in the press.) By the end of July, however, federal officials monitoring twenty-five encampments in the nation's capital had had enough. Hoover reluctantly played a role in planning eviction of the veterans. On July 27, the capital police had a violent encounter with some of the protesters, with two protesters dead or dying, and three police seriously injured. The pacifistically-inclined Hoover called in General Douglas MacArthur and gave him orders to clear only the area of the nation's capital where violence had occurred. This was the first time in nearly four years in office that Hoover had exercised his powers as commander-in-chief to call the armed forces into action. (Rappleye 2016, 370-374)

MacArthur, however, exceeded Hoover's orders (no surprise to anyone knowledgeable about the General's later career), and with great dispatch moved to evict all of the bonus marchers from the capital. Hoover sent a direct order to MacArthur to cease his operations, but MacArthur ignored Hoover's order. (Rappleye 2016, 374-376) This was clearly a case of the use of excessive force, yet still the newspapers initially backed Hoover's handling of the situation. But then Hoover made mistakes. MacArthur proffered his resignation, but Hoover refused to accept it, seeming to engage in "indulgence of the insubordinate" general. Hoover belatedly blamed the confrontation on "communists and persons with criminal records," announcing that "a challenge to the authority of the United States Government has been met swiftly and firmly." (Rappleye 2016, 379) (Hoover had never commented on the political affiliations of the marchers to that point.) Thus he retroactively – in public at least – and loudly embraced all of MacArthur's actions, even those that had been the result of insubordination. Hoover's longstanding patience and toleration toward the marchers had now been replaced by belligerent vengefulness. And public and Congressional opinion swung more solidly against him. (Rappleye 2016, 377-382)

American politics were thoroughly redefined by the events of 1932 and 1933, and would remain so for decades thereafter. In the long transition from the administration of Herbert Hoover to the one of Franklin Delano Roosevelt, the nation's banking system ground to a halt in the hundred days before Roosevelt's inauguration on March 4, but resumed reasonable functioning in the hundred days afterward. This is one of those remarkably clear parts of the historical record where the quality of presidential leadership was the main variable, and what happened in 1933 is convincing evidence for why Roosevelt is generally regarded by American historians as a great president, and Hoover as a failed president.

Conclusion

We have looked at two Quaker businessmen and politicians in two very different eras. Both Hoover and Penn shared thus shared three commitments, to Quakerism, to business, and to politics. None of these three areas of human endeavor fits easily with the other two. The messy truth is that many of Penn's and Hoover's actions exhibited multiple motivations. In regard to the business endeavors undertaken by each man, they had to consider both their personal well-being, and that of their families; the actions of business competitors; and the well-being of a broader society. At some point, each man strongly focused on the whole world's well-being. Both were strongly interested in peace building and conflict resolution, as one might expect given their Quaker affiliation, and often took concrete steps to further the peace.

Each was aloof and removed, to a large degree, from the Americans, including the Quaker Americans, for whom they had governance responsibilities, at the time of their maximum governance responsibility. For Penn, of course, the remove was, much of the time and in large part, a physical one. Yet the governors that he sent in his place did not always govern capably or acceptably. (Bronner 1962) For Hoover, the Presidency of the United States presented larger burdens than he had known before, burdens which he did not always shoulder with grace; nor did he display the communication skills to explain how he was discharging his responsibilities. (Rappleye 2016)

Hoover laid aside engineering for personal gain in 1914, having earned enough to devote himself to public service. After 1914, he still saw himself as an engineer, but an engineer who was utilizing his skills for the good of a broader society. Penn's colonizing activities pervaded his life even more than Hoover's engineering did his. He could never lay aside a concern for his personal fortune, but it is also true that Penn never fully garnered the financial security that Hoover had. The portraits drawn of Penn overly emphasize his idealism over against the finances that he sometimes disdained to notice but ultimately drastically constrained his life activities.

Yet neither man was, or even could be, a pure idealist or consistent saint. They both sought the Light of Christ, and arguably sometimes found the way forward accordingly, but also sometimes fell short. Pride factored into their decisions, and each then showed fallibility, all-too-human qualities in confronting their most significant challenges, and then, afterwards, defending their chosen actions. In confronting persons of different ethnicities who co-existed in their societies, both Penn and Hoover sometimes acknowledged the full humanity of all, but they also showed inconsistency in their responses.

Both men had significant successes, and also significant failures. While it would be understandable simply to want to celebrate their successes, we should not overlook the degree to which we as students of history can learn from failures. Indeed, the case has been made in this essay that the failures of notable personages like Penn and Hoover can and should lead to an expansion of ethical vision in succeeding generations. Thus, the learning from such case studies, both in terms of what to emulate and what needs to be done differently, will be very rich.

Bibliography

Penn

Angell, Stephen W. 1992. "William Penn, Moderate Puritan." In *The Lamb's War: Quaker Essays to Honor Hugh Barbour*, ed. by Michael Birkel and John Newman. Richmond, IN: Earlham College Press. Pp. 76-90.

Angell, Stephen W. 2006. "E Pluribus Unum? Quaker Approaches to Plurality and Unity (1682-1764)," *Quaker Religious Thought* 106/107: 55-67.

Angell, Stephen W. 2012. "William Penn's Debts to John Owen and Moses Amyraut on Questions of Truth, Grace, and Religious Toleration," *Quaker Studies* 16: 157-173.

Bronner, Edwin B. 1962. *William Penn's "Holy Experiment": The Founding of Pennsylvania, 1681-1701*. New York: Columbia University Press.

Bronner, Edwin B. and David Fraser. 1986. *William Penn's Published Writings, 1660-1726: An Interpretive Bibliography*. Papers of William Penn, Volume V. Philadelphia, PA: University of Pennsylvania Press.

Bruns, Roger. 1983. *Am I Not a Man and a Brother: The Antislavery Crusade of Revolutionary America, 1688-1788*. New York, NY: Chelsea House.

Dunn, Mary Maples et al. 1981-1988. *The Papers of William Penn*. Five Volumes. Philadelphia, PA: University of Pennsylvania Press. (Abbreviated in text as PWP.)

Geiter, Mary K. 2000. *William Penn*. Harlow, England: Pearson Education Limited.

Gouge, William. 1662. *Of Domesticall Duties*. London.

Hull, William I. 1935. *William Penn and the Dutch Quaker Migration to Pennsylvania*. Swarthmore College Monographs on Quaker History, Number Two. Philadelphia, PA: Patterson and White.

Jennings, Francis. 1986. "Brother Miquon: Good Lord!" In Richard S. Dunn and Mary M. Dunn, *The World of William Penn*. Philadelphia, PA: University of Pennsylvania Press. Pp. 195-214.

Klein, Philip S. and Ari Hoogenboom. 1973. *A History of Pennsylvania*. New York: McGraw-Hill Book Company.

Peare, Catherine O. 1956. *William Penn: A Biography*. Philadelphia: J. B. Lippincott Company, 1956.

Pencak, William A. and Daniel K. Richter. 2004. *Friends and Indians in Penn's Woods: Indians, Colonists, and the Racial Construction of Pennsylvania*. University Park, PA: Pennsylvania State University Press.

Penn, William. 1670. *A Seasonable Caveat against Popery*. N.p.

Pomfret, John E. 1956. *The Province of West New Jersey, 1609-1702: A History of the Origins of an American Colony*. Princeton, NJ: Princeton University Press.

Hoover

Clements, Kendrick A. 2010. *The Life of Herbert Hoover: Imperfect Visionary, 1918-1928*. New York, NY: Palgrave Macmillan.

Gabor, Andrea. 2000. *The Capitalist Philosophers*. New York, NY: Random House.

Hoff, Joan. 2000. "Herbert Clark Hoover." *American National Biography Online*.

Hoff Wilson, Joan. 1975. *Herbert Hoover: Forgotten Progressive*. Boston, MA: Little, Brown, and Company.

Kennedy, David M. 1999. *Freedom from Fear: The American People in Depression and War, 1929-1945*. New York, NY: Oxford University Press.

Leuchtenberg, William E. 2009. *Herbert Hoover*. New York, NY: Henry Holt.

Mouat, Jeremy and Ian Phimister. 2008. "The Engineering of Herbert Hoover." *Pacific Historical Review* 77: 553-584.

Nash, George H. 1983. *Herbert Hoover: The Engineer*. New York, NY: W. W. Norton.

Nash, George H. 1988. *The Life of Herbert Hoover: The Humanitarian, 1914-1917*. New York, NY: W.W. Norton.

Nash, George H. 1996. *The Life of Herbert Hoover: Master of Emergencies, 1917-1918*. New York, NY: W.W. Norton.

NBC News. 2009. "List of Presidential Rankings: Historians Rank the 42 Men Who Have Held the Office," Feb. 16. http://www.nbcnews.com/id/29216774/#.V1iwA6LIK2V

Nelson, Daniel. 2000. "Frederick Winslow Taylor." *American National Biography Online*.

Rappleye, Charles. 2016. *Herbert Hoover in the White House: The Ordeal of the Presidency*. New York, NY: Simon & Schuster.

PART IV
Shifting Patterns

8| The Birmingham Quaker Business Community, 1800-1900

By Nicola Sleapwood

Over the course of the nineteenth century Birmingham became a centre for Quaker business families and their businesses. Birmingham's Quaker business community was focused around Bull Street and its meeting, and bolstered by intermarriage between key business families. This chapter considers this community and its businesses over the course of the nineteenth century. I argue that by the end of the century the dispersal of the community, the draw of public office, and changes in company law began to undermine the strength of the business community. However, in many ways, such as in terms of intermarriage providing support, it remained strong. The chapter's inspiration was William Adlington Cadbury's (1867-1957) biography of Birmingham Quakers *Bull Street Friends I Have Known*, which was completed in 1956.

After an overview of Birmingham's industrial heritage, the chapter looks briefly at the history of Quakers in Birmingham from 1660-1800, highlighting discipline and regulation around business.

The main body of the chapter then opens with two case studies of Quaker manufacturing families and businesses. The first begins by using the Gibbins family's business story as a prism through which to give an overview of business life generally in the earlier part of the nineteenth century. It highlights Quaker connections and considers the Society's approach to business, business expansion, and failure. The second case study focuses on the story of Albright and Wilson, a chemical manufacturing firm, as an example for the later nineteenth century, illustrating how businesses developed and changed hands between Quakers.

There are then three sections that show the diversity of Quaker businesses in Birmingham, demonstrating the centrality of Bull Street nearer the beginning of the century, and highlighting the changing nature of Quaker business developments.

Finally, there are four more thematic sections. The first focuses on intermarriage, showing how it remained strong throughout the century. Another section on Quaker involvement in civic life suggests that as this increased it could have been detrimental to businesses.

The final thematic sections are on the impact of the gradual geographic dispersal of the business community away from the town centre and across new Quaker meetings, and the impact of legal changes in company law upon the Quaker business community.

Birmingham's industrial heritage

Birmingham began its industrial life as a city renowned for its freedom, both in terms of religion and business. In the first volume to *A History of the Corporation of Birmingham*, John Thackray Bunce describes how for centuries from the medieval period Birmingham had only a manorial court (Bunce 1878, 2-4), until in 1769 came the first Street Commissioners. These were a form of early government added to over the years before Birmingham gained formal and more elaborate local government with its incorporation in 1838 (Bunce, 1878, 75-90; Hopkins 1989, 97). Two Quakers held positions among the Street Commissioners, Samuel Galton, Quaker gun-maker, from 1769, and later in 1801 Richard Tapper Cadbury, linen draper and silk mercer (Hopkins 1989, 97; Bunce 1878, 85). Birmingham's lack of formalised government, along with its status as a non-conformist stronghold from the civil war, meant that from the seventeenth through to the early nineteenth century it welcomed those such as Quakers who could not easily have started business in some other towns and cities (Carnevali 2004, 538; Rowntree 1936, 10).

However, Eric Hopkins and Malcolm Dick express a note of caution in accepting this reading of Birmingham's industrial growth more generally, Hopkins observing that 'other industrial towns such as Wolverhampton had similar advantages, yet failed to develop so rapidly', and Dick adding Coventry to this example (Hopkins 1989, 5; Dick 2016). Birmingham's perceived draw for Quakers seems to have lasted beyond incorporation, as in his introduction to *Bull Street Friends I Have Known* William Adlington Cadbury notes that 'In the first half of the nineteenth century many Friends from other parts of England came to Birmingham to start business' (Cadbury 1953).

It was not only Friends who were coming to Birmingham, between 1750 and 1841 its population grew from 23,688 to 182,922 (Hopkins 1989, 118-119). By 1914 the population had more than doubled since 1851 (Hopkins 2002, 120).

Much of Birmingham's industry grew out of the metal trade, for which it was well positioned geographically and well known by the mid-eighteenth century (Hopkins 1989, 3). The city had a reputation for having industrialised by means of many small workshops rather than large factories (Carnevali 2004, 538; Behagg 1986, 375), though Hopkins notes that by 1914 this had begun to change and there were six big firms in the city (of more than one thousand employees), the biggest of which was Cadbury's, with 6000 employees (Hopkins, 2002, 118). By the 1840s, in addition to industry, the services sector in Birmingham had grown considerably, with retailers concentrated around New Street, the High Street, Bull Street and the Bull Ring (Hopkins 1989, 79).

1660-1800, close-knit business communities emerging around Bull Street

Quakers came to Birmingham early in its and their history. In the 1660s they bought land to build their first meeting house, in what was then Colmore Lane for the first Birmingham meeting, and in the 1700s they bought land from a Friend and built a meeting house in Bull Street (Butler 1999, 617). Astonishingly, given the significant number of Quakers in Birmingham by the nineteenth century, Birmingham Preparative Meeting in Bull Street remained the only Quaker meeting in Birmingham until the 1870s. This gave Quaker business people a very regular opportunity to meet, work together and discuss business ideas, as well as to socialise.

There were three fairly prominent Quaker business families who attended this meeting in Birmingham by the eighteenth century. The Lloyds had opened Birmingham's first bank Taylors and Lloyd with the Taylor family in 1765 to support their industrial enterprises, both families having been in the metal trade previously (Lloyd 1975, 162-166). The Gibbins were also in banking as well as in metal work, and the Galtons were gun-makers. These Quakers lived at the time of the Lunar Society, a visionary group of men involved in industry and development as well as politics, and one of them, Samuel Galton junior, was a member of this group, which sometimes met for dinners at the Handsworth home of Matthew Boulton, a well-known local manufacturer. Perhaps this is a signifier of the comparatively high social esteem in which Quakers were held (Hopkins 1989, 137). Joseph Gibbins (1756-1811) also had contact with Matthew Boulton. He would have known Samuel Galton through Birmingham Meeting in Bull Street. In fact, having been a button maker thus far, in 1793 Joseph Gibbins entered business with Matthew Boulton, taking on the general management of the Rose Copper Company in Swansea, which manufactured coinage, and was highly successful (Rowntree 1936, 13; Milligan 2007, 198).

In 1790 the Quaker Yearly Meeting issued an epistle directing that Friends who manufactured or sold weapons and, given the opportunity, did not cease their activities should be disowned. Because of this we can be sure that Samuel Galton junior and Joseph Gibbins knew one another; between March and July 1795 Joseph Gibbins, along with Sampson Lloyd and one other Friend, James Baker, visited the Galtons several times on behalf of the meeting to exhort them to cease their manufacture of guns. Whilst Samuel Galton senior withdrew from the business and agreed to make no more profit from it, Samuel Galton junior defended his position and stood his ground firmly over the coming years until, in August 1796, he was disowned by Warwickshire Monthly Meeting (Woodward 2015). It is telling that the meeting nominated two other highly respected businessmen to approach the Galtons, Sampson and Gibbins, it was presumably thought, would inspire obedience in Samuel Galton junior. As we have seen, this was to no avail. However it provides early evidence of Bull Street Meeting's business community's closeness, interactions and self-regulation.

Nineteenth century case studies, The Gibbins family and Albright and Wilson

The Gibbins Family

The Gibbins' business network had been expanding over the course of the first decades of the nineteenth century, though they seem to have been temporarily stalled by the death of Joseph Gibbins senior in 1811. Joseph Gibbins junior (1787-1870) took over his father's interests, becoming a partner in at least three separate banking endeavours established between 1802 and 1809, linked to and enabled by the metal business in Swansea (Hopkins 1989, 76; Gibbins 1911, 13; Milligan 2007, 198).

By 1806 Brueton Gibbins, another son of Martha and Joseph, had taken on ownership of a glass works in Aston (Gibbins 1911, 21), demonstrating that an adeptness to business life was common in this large Quaker family, as in others such as the Cadburys. His younger brother William had joined him in a partnership by 1818 (Gibbins 1911, 66; Wrightson 1818). This business lasted until at least 1835, since it can be found in another trade directory for that year (Wrightson and Webb 1835).

*View of Aston Flint Glass Works,
belonging to Brueton & William Gibbins*

*Interior View of Aston Flint Glass Works,
belonging to Brueton & William Gibbins.*

Image 1 and 2: Images of Glass Works, Retrieved from:
http://www.drwilliams.org/iDoc/gibbins/chapt12.htm

In 1821 Martha and Joseph Gibbins' daughter Martha had married Joseph Ashby Gillett, thereby joining these two Quaker banking families (Gibbins 1911). What is more, with the marriage came for Joseph a loan of £5000 from the Gibbins, with which he bought a partnership in Whitehead's bank at Shipston on Stour (Milligan 2007, 204). This is a clear demonstration of the importance of intermarriage in the Quaker business world in the early nineteenth century, marriage often brought money, which was vital to advancing or beginning business endeavours.

By the mid-1820s and the depression these years brought, the banking business Joseph Gibbins shared with the Goode and Smith families, was in trouble (Hopkins 1989, 76). This business seems to have been started in 1802. In 1804 Joseph Gibbins senior had begun another banking business with Samuel Galton junior and his son (Gibbins 1911, 13). It is curious and perhaps striking that Joseph entered business with the disowned man he had been sent to rebuke – the cultural links, and business interests seem to have been more important to Joseph Gibbins than the possibility of rebuke from the Society of Friends. This bank, though, seems to have been experiencing difficulties too. Joseph Gibbins junior's mother Martha reflects on the troubling situation regarding the banks, which ultimately led to bankruptcy, in a letter to her son William in March 1826:

> Many and great have been the changes and trials of some since my last letter to thee. Little did I ever expect to see the commercial atmosphere so shaken; panic, consternation, and confusion spread around with unabating fury for a time; it seemed as if a terrible scourge had come to the rich and to the great, to the buyers and to the sellers, and as an awful visitation to induce them to fix their hearts upon something better than worldly treasures, to check their desires for the accumulation of great wealth. (Gibbins 1911, 181-182)

Clearly Martha had some qualms about the compatibility of wealth and godliness and was not afraid to express these in writing to other members of the family. The banking business of Gibbins, Smith and Goode seems to have gone bankrupt sometime around the writing of this letter. It seems highly likely that the banking interest with the Galtons went the same way, given the quote below about banks plural, though Hopkins does not refer to Gibbins' involvement in that firm (Hopkins 1989, 76). However, in her comments on the situation Emma Gibbins, daughter of Emma J. and Thomas, seeks to explain that:

It is said that none of the Banks with which the Gibbins Brothers and J. A. Gillett were connected would have closed their doors if it had been possible to convey cash by a more rapid means of transit than by driving. To get money transferred from Swansea to Birmingham, Banbury, or Gloucester was not then a matter of a few hours. The Banks were all financially sound, and their doors reopened after two or three days (Gibbins 1911, 184).

The family and business dealt with this situation by publishing a statement of the business accounts in a Birmingham newspaper, demonstrating a surplus, and adding to the disclosure the value of their combined personal wealth with which the business partnership could be secured (Gibbins 1911, 184-185). This seems to have been designed to reassure the public and to restore trust, which was still hugely important in business partnerships of this period. Trust would have been all the more important in Quaker businesses, and this also fits with the Quaker commitment to truth and integrity. In August 1826, however, Martha Gibbins wrote again of her concern about her son's desire for wealth in a letter to her daughter, Anne (Gibbins 1911, 187).

However, had Martha hoped that her son would cease his involvement in banking she would have been disappointed to learn that, after her death in 1827, in 1829 Joseph Gibbins junior became managing director of the Birmingham Banking Company, which had grown out of another of his banking enterprises.

Around 1835 the Gibbins family began to set up the Birmingham Battery and Metal business, in Digbeth, an area in Deritend, an industrial area on the eastern edge of the town centre, along with several other businessmen. The business's location is indicated with a circle on the map of Birmingham below. The term 'battery' refers to the process of hammering metal into shape from sheets, for items such as pans, rather than to our understanding of it today (Rowntree 1936, 32).

There were thirteen proprietors in total, at least two of them being Gibbins men (Rowntree 1936, 19). Thomas Gibbins (1796-1863), became the managing partner of the Birmingham Battery and Metal business when it was formally established in 1836.

Richard Tapper Cadbury's daughter Emma Joel (1811-1905) married Thomas Gibbins in 1837, becoming Emma J. Gibbins, whose daughter's collected letters of her family and others are so illustrative. In 1837 Thomas Gibbins moved into Digbeth House, to be joined by his wife in September when they married.

DIGBETH HOUSE.
From a Water-colour Drawing by Paul Braddon, 1880.

Image 3: Image of Digbeth House – Digbeth House by Paul Braddon, included in 'The Birmingham Battery and Metal Company' 1936, located at the Cadbury Research Library, University of Birmingham, reference, HD 9506.G74B53

This drawing demonstrates the proximity of the works to the house, and what with the building's location in Digbeth, near to the Bull Ring, this brought its dangers since in 1839, for example, there was both a fire in the works and considerable rioting (Gibbins 1911, 265).

The account of Emma and Thomas's children about daily life in the house and the business in the collected letters and memories, is full of detail,

> Our father was an early riser, and as the Works were attached to the house he used frequently to be in the office soon after 6 o'clock, and then came in later for breakfast. In all the ups and downs of the early years of her married life it brought comfort to the young wife to be able at any moment to go to her strong, helpful husband for counsel and sympathy. From time to time the proprietors of the Battery Works met to hold their business meetings, and it was usual for them to dine in Digbeth House on these occasions. The dinners were a very formidable affair to

the young housekeeper, who was unaccustomed to any entertaining outside the simple hospitality of Friends, whereas her husband, besides being fifteen years her senior, had lived abroad, and mixed in general society. One difficulty was that our mother had become a strict abstainer, and objected to have wine on the table, while her husband and his family did not hold the same views. However, in this, as in other matters, he respected her scruples, and no wine was provided. The guests proved themselves true gentlemen by their kindness and courtesy, and plainly showed their gratitude for the trouble taken for their comfort.

For many years after their marriage it was necessary for our parents to exercise great economy. The business had to be worked up, and the children, as they came one after another, increased expenses (Gibbins 1911, 264).

Alongside the picture, then, this account confirms an image of Quaker family businesses often being run from or near to the home during the first half of the nineteenth century. The image and account confirm the idea that in the era of the partnership in business the main partner, their family life, and their business were not clearly delineated.

However, in 1845, almost as soon as it became legally possible through the Joint-Stock Companies Act 1845, the Birmingham Battery & Metal business became a joint-stock company (Rowntree 1936, 48), and changed its name to the Birmingham Battery and Metal Company. This created share-holders rather than solely partners, and was generally a process which allowed a greater number of investors to gain part-ownership, without being so directly involved with the business. From this time more of the shares were being bought by the company and the Gibbins family (Rowntree 1936, 48). So in this instance joint-stock status was used to reinforce the control of the Gibbins family over the firm with its thirteen original proprietors.

Thomas Gibbins remained manager of the Birmingham Battery and Metal Company until 1851, when he sought to retire and proposed that his nephew, George Barrow (1824-1899) take over as manager (Rowntree 1936, 49; Milligan, 2007, 35). After a period on trial George Barrow managed the business until 1864, when William Gibbins took over (Rowntree 1936, 49).

Emma Joel Gibbins attended the first statutory meeting of the Birmingham Battery and Metal Company Ltd in 1897, long after the death of her husband, and along only with her sons Thomas Gibbins and Richard Cadbury Gibbins, George Barrow, another two family members and the secretary, (Rowntree 1936,

57). To have done so she must have been an engaged, respected woman, as it was very rare for women to attend smaller business meetings in Quaker businesses at this time. With dinners being held at homes earlier in the century, it is imaginable that other women like Emma may have had some indirect involvement or influence through home life, but she largely stands alone by attending this meeting.

The story of the Gibbins family in the earlier nineteenth century highlights the number of new businesses being established at this time. It shows that Quaker morals around business interests were not straight forward, and that they could divide families. It also demonstrates the closeness of family, home and business, as was typical in the earlier nineteenth century, as well as noting the impact of the beginnings of legal changes, which would be taken up by more Quaker businesses as the century progressed.

Albright and Wilson

In 1840, having briefly been an assistant at Southalls on Bull Street when much younger, Arthur Albright (1811-1900) moved to Birmingham and joined J & E Sturge in their chemical business. Here, he suggested and began the manufacture of phosphorus, mostly for use in matches (Milligan 2007, 3). He also joined Bull Street Quaker meeting, attended regularly, and served there (Cadbury 1956, 1).

Around 1848 Arthur Albright married Rachel Stacey, herself the granddaughter of a Birmingham Quaker businessman. Her father George Stacey had been a Quaker pharmaceutical chemist in Tottenham (Cadbury 1956, 53; Milligan 2007, 416). Arthur was at this point still working for J & E Sturge, and his family moved to George Road (or George Street as it seems to have been called then), Edgbaston (Threlfall 1951, 16).

Image 4: Image of Arthur Albright – from 1952 book by Threlfall published by Albright & Wilson

By this point J & E Sturge, the Quaker business Albright worked for, had a factory in Selly Oak as well as their premises on Wheeleys Road, Edgbaston, opened in the early 1840s. This was where the phosphorus manufacture Arthur primarily devoted his time to, took place (Threlfall 1951, 13). Edgbaston must therefore have been a suitable place for the Albright's home, as it was between Selly Oak and Birmingham. In the 1850 trade directory, besides this business, there are very few other industrial businesses in Selly Oak; the majority of those listed are in areas such as gardening, farming, butchery, or else listings are residential (W. Kelly & Co 1850). And Threllfall suggests that it was only the second factory in the parish (1951, 13).

Around 1850 the Sturges and Arthur Albright began the process of buying some land in Oldbury, to the north-west of Birmingham, and moving phosphorus production there (Threlfall 1951, 32-33). This move was driven by proximity to another key chemical business. By 1851 Arthur had learned about and instigated production of amorphous, or red phosphorus, which was safer for use in matches than white phosphorus. He had also begun to explore the market for phosphorus abroad (Threlfall 1951, 16).

By around 1855 Arthur Albright and the Sturges had parted ways in business, with Arthur retaining the Selly Oak and Oldbury works (Threlfall 1951, 16-17). And in 1856 he had formed a new partnership with John Edward Wilson, another Quaker whom he had met at his wife's sister's wedding to John Edward's brother, Robert (Threlfall 1951, 45-46; Pease, 2015b, 191-196). John Edward had probably come to Birmingham to join Arthur in business, and became very involved in Birmingham Meeting in Bull Street too, becoming an elder (Cadbury 1956, 82). Links with J & E Sturge were maintained, with Sturge's probably supplying one product for some years (Threlfall 1951, 34), though the Selly Oak site was soon abandoned.

In 1857 John Edward Wilson married another of Rachel Albright (Stacey)'s sisters, Catharine (Milligan 2007, 474). The following year when Arthur was in Germany on a business trip, he mentioned in a letter to Rachel that he had told some German matchmakers of the importance of trust in his honesty in their relationship, and that the firm had indeed then been very trusting and open (Albright 1958, cited in Threlfall 1951, 27). This was a time at which trust was very important in business relationships (Taylor 2006, 22-24), and Quakers could make the most of this as a group renowned for its honesty and integrity.

This case study illustrates an early example of the tendency for businesses and proprietors to move away from Birmingham town centre. It also highlights the importance of the Quaker community to its businesses, in 1856 Albright and Wilson, chemical manufacturers of Oldbury, was born almost entirely through

Quaker connections, from Arthur's apprenticeship at Southalls, to his employment by the Sturges, and to the many family and social links. Most of these were in turn enabled or furthered by Bull Street Meeting's position at the heart of the Birmingham Quaker world of the 1850s. By 1857 John Edward's marriage meant that the Albright and Wilson families were themselves family, linked by the sister wives of the founders.

Quaker businesses being founded in Birmingham, Bull Street and elsewhere

Bull Street

Bull Street, the location of Birmingham Quaker Meeting (indicated with a square on the map below), became a hub of Quaker business activity between around 1800 and 1850. Sometime between 1794 and 1818 Richard Tapper Cadbury established his business as a silk mercer and linen draper at number 92 Bull Street, until he retired from it in 1828, passing it to his son Benjamin Head Cadbury (Gibbins 1911, 253; Milligan 2007, 91). The Cadburys also lived in the premises on Bull Street (Gibbins 1911, 261). By 1850, however, Richard Tapper's silk mercer's business had been taken over by a partnership that was seemingly non-Quaker (Robson & Co, 1839; Kelly & Co 1850). Thomas Southall, son of another significant Quaker business family from Leominster and who had been trained as a chemist in his father's business, moved to Birmingham and established himself as a pharmaceutical chemist at number 17 Bull Street in 1820, to be joined by his brother William in 1832 when T & W. Southall's was formed (Milligan 2007, 412).

Richard Tapper's son John Cadbury established his tea and coffee shop next door to his father's at 93 Bull Street in 1824, where it remained until 1849. As is often highlighted, the chocolate business grew out of this, as John found the sale of cocoa so popular (Milligan 2007, 91). Therefore, if you were to take a walk down Bull Street between 1824 and 1828, not only would the Quaker Meeting House have been evident, but also at least three Quaker businesses. Less popular than New Street or the High Street, Bull Street was a fairly long retail street, so these businesses were by no means alone, but it does seem to have been a location favoured by Quakers. In fact the Quaker businesses, and several homes, seem to have been grouped together within a fairly small section of the street. By 1835 Josiah Pumphrey, another member of Birmingham Quaker Meeting, had opened a further business as a wax and tallow chandler near to the other Quaker businesses on Bull Street at number 81, though this was probably fleeting as it does not appear under his name in an 1839 directory (Wrightson and Webb 1835;

Robson & Co 1839). And in 1844 another Quaker, Henry Newman (1818-1908) added a booksellers to these at 14, Bull Street (Milligan 2007, 319; Kelly & Co 1850, 30).

<u>Elsewhere in Birmingham</u>
There were many Lloyds doing business of various varieties in Birmingham at this time, at least some of them Quakers, such as Samuel Lloyd II (1795-1862) who Milligan calls an ironmaster, though he is listed in the 1830 directory simply as 'nailmaker' (Wrightson and Webb 1835; West 1830, 359). Besides Samuel Lloyd, there was George Braithwaite Lloyd's (1824-1903) boiler tube manufacturing firm which was based in Gas Street in the town centre until 1857 (Lloyd 1975, 272), when he was needed at Lloyd & Co bank in the town after the death of his father, and so ceased his own business (Milligan 2007, 287).

Joseph Sturge was also prominent in Birmingham Quaker Meeting at this time. He was an anti-corn law and anti-slavery campaigner and railway director, as well as being joint owner with his brother Charles of a corn merchant's business J & C Sturge, in Broad Street between the town centre and Edgbaston to the south in 1835 (Wrightson and Webb 1835). John Sturge (1799-1840), another of Joseph's brothers (Pease 2013, 2), and a member of Bimingham Quaker Meeting, had founded a manufacturing chemist in Bewdley, Worcestershire the previous year and moved his business to Edgbaston in 1823. Edgbaston was a large area to the south of Birmingham which bordered the outskirts of the town, but became much more rural and leafy as the distance from the town increased. Wheeleys Lane or Bath Row where the business was, was on the north-eastern side of Edgbaston, near to the town centre. In 1830 John was joined in this business by his brother Edmund (1808-1893), and the business became known as that we encountered above, J & E Sturge (Wilson in Cadbury 1953, 66). It was this business Arthur Albright moved back to Birmingham to join.

The later nineteenth century, expansions and take-overs between Friends
Sometime not long after 1848, William White, a relatively new convert to the Society of Friends from Methodism, came to Birmingham on the recommendation of John Heath, a Quaker pen manufacturer and member of Birmingham Meeting (Morland 1903, 26; Milligan 2007, 468-469), with a partner Cornelius Pike who does not seem to have been a Friend. At John Heath's suggestion White and Pike bought Henry Newman's shop on Bull Street upon moving to Birmingham.

George Barrow, one time manager of the Birmingham Battery and Metal Company, had followed his brother Richard Cadbury Barrow, to Birmingham from Lancashire. Richard Cadbury had arrived around 1849, having been offered his uncle John Cadbury's tea and coffee business on Bull Street, which he oversaw alongside John's son John for five years before the Cadburys sought to transfer it wholly into Richard Cadbury Barrow's hands (Barrow 1949, 5, 23; Milligan 2007, 36). Richard Cadbury expanded the range of goods sold considerably, and the store was renamed Barrows Stores (Barrow 1949, 25). George and Richard Cadbury both joined Birmingham Quaker Meeting (Cadbury 1956, 6-7).

Around 1852 Richard Tangye, having seen an advertisement in the *British Friend* Quaker magazine, moved from Cornwall to Birmingham to work for Thomas Worsdell, a Quaker and civic and railway engineer, in Brasshouse Passage in the town centre (Waterhouse 1957; W. Kelly & Co 1850, 25). Richard was followed to Birmingham and into Worsdell's business by four of his brothers.

By 1856 Richard had left Worsdell's, setting up business with his brother Joseph (Waterhouse 1957). Soon their brothers, some of whom remained Friends, joined them, and in 1857 they set up as James Tangye and Brothers.

In 1868 J & E Sturge was bought from Edmund Sturge by Charles Dickinson Sturge and Francis Corder Clayton, two other Quakers from Birmingham Quaker Meeting (Wilson 1953 in Cadbury 1956, 66). Charles Dickinson Sturge was also a partner in J C Sturge at this time, and Francis Corder Clayton had also worked for that firm previously (Cadbury 1956, 20).

Almost simultaneously, another Birmingham business had changed hands between Quakers, Richard Cadbury Gibbins (1846-1928), one of Thomas and Emma Joel's sons, as well as working at the Birmingham Battery and Metal Company, had taken over Thomas Worsdell's business, and renamed it R. C. Gibbins & Co (R. C. Gibbins & Co 1869).

By the early to mid-1870s George Cadbury had begun to revitalise and expand his father's cocoa enterprise, and the growth continued over the remainder of the nineteenth century. William Adlington Cadbury, author of *Bull Street Friends I Have Known*, still at Birmingham Meeting, entered the chocolate firm in 1887, to become a director in 1900, and later in the twentieth century after his father George's death, chairman (Milligan 2007, 88, 91-92).

Francis Corder Clayton must have acquired sufficient wealth by 1889, for in that year, after Charles Dickinson Sturge's retirement in 1886, he sold J & E Sturge to its third set of Quaker hands, brothers Henry Lloyd and Alfred Wilson (Wilson 1953 in Cadbury 1956, 66), sons of John Edward Wilson (Pease, 2015b

543), original partner in Albright and Wilson. Henry Lloyd Wilson was also a director of Albright and Wilson until 1915 (Milligan 2007, 473-474).

Two Birmingham Quaker businesses were not immune to the economic downturn of the 1880s and 1890s, J & C Sturge suffered due to the Crimean War and other difficulties, closing down in 1882 (Cadbury 1956, 66). And William White's business, White and Pike, having been successful for decades, and in which he had been less involved towards the end, suffered too, closing down not long after 1895 (Milligan 2007, 468; Morland 1903, 34; Birmingham Preparative Meeting 1895).

Thus, in the latter part of the nineteenth century few entirely new Quaker businesses were established in Birmingham, but this was a half century during which those already set up in the town grew, and when businesses often changed hands within the still-strong Quaker community at Birmingham Meeting.

Intermarriage 1800-1900

During these years there was more dual intermarrying between the Cadburys and the Barrows, a family who rose to prominence in Birmingham later. In 1823 Sarah Cadbury married John Barrow of Lancaster, and moved to Lancaster with him. Then in 1832 Candia Barrow, John's sister, married John Cadbury, Sarah's brother, and moved to Birmingham (Gardner 2016). To further illustrate the many links between these families, John and Candia Barrow were the children of a George Barrow and an Elizabeth Pumphrey (Pease 2015a, 2), probably of the Pumphrey family who were in Birmingham around this time.

In 1824 Thomas Southall married Sarah Shorthouse, daughter of another Quaker pharmaceutical chemist in Birmingham (Milligan 2007, 412). In 1826 Thomas's brother Samuel Southall, who had remained in Leominster, married Priscilla Sturge (1797-1859), Joseph Sturge's sister, thereby uniting two significant Quaker business families (Milligan 2007, 411). Come 1841 Edmund Sturge had married Arthur Albright's sister Lydia (Cadbury 1956, 72), uniting these two families. Josiah Pumphrey's daughter Rebecca (1824-1864) married another Quaker businessman in Birmingham, George Baker (1825-1910), a blacking manufacturer (Milligan 2007, 26) in 1848. These are just some of the links that existed at this time.

Intermarriage between Birmingham Quaker business families in the second half of the century remained strong, as is demonstrated by the story of Albright and Wilson here. This continued, there were at least another three intermarriages between key Quaker business families in the 1890s, suggesting that while the rule about endogamy had been relaxed in 1859, the strength and mutual benefit accorded Quaker businesses by marriage was fairly slow to be undone. This is reinforced by Henry Lloyd Wilson's grandson, Alan Hodgkin, vividly recalling his aunt describing the closeness between the Lloyd, Albright, Wilson, Stacey and Gibbins families (1992, 18).

Together these examples serve to demonstrate the considerable degree of intermarriage between local Quaker business families, as well as some on a national scale. Intermarriage undoubtedly boosted Birmingham Quaker businesses themselves financially and in terms of knowledge exchange, and it helped to boost and to bolster the Quaker community.

Civic life and local politics, 1800-1900

In 1838 Birmingham became a corporate town under the Municipal Corporations Act 1835. This process created the town council, which was much more democratically elected than had been the Street Commissioners (Bunce, 1878). This was also the year in which the Yearly Meeting of the Society of Friends had considered the question of Quakers participating in government, and advised against it, concerned it would endanger qualities 'essential to the Christian character' (Bailey 1952, 49).

Despite this, four Quakers stood for election to the town Council at its inception. The opportunity to get involved in local politics provided by their increasing status as businessmen in the town must have been more important in their minds than the pronouncement of the quietist Religious Society of this time (Isichei 1970, 188-190). Richard Tapper Cadbury was one of these men, and unlike the other Quakers who stood for the Liberal Party, Cadbury, who described himself as not being a party man, ran as a Conservative candidate (Bailey 1952, 49-50). Two of the other three who stood we have already encountered, Joseph and Charles Sturge; Bailey argues that the Society regarded them as rebels (Bailey 1952, 50). George Goodrick, the fourth Quaker to stand for office was also a businessman, recorded in an 1858 trade directory as a 'rope and twine maker' in Edgbaston (Bailey 1952, 47-50; Dix 1858, 139). It is evident then, that whilst it was generally disapproved of, several Quaker business men felt called to stand for local office in this period.

After the relaxation of the Society of Friends' approach to political involvement over the previous few decades (Isichei 1970, 193-200), between 1866 and 1873 five more Quaker businessmen were elected to the town council, joining Charles Sturge and George Goodrick, who by this point were aldermen (Bailey 1952, 115). George Braithwaite Lloyd and George Baker, the blacking manufacturer mentioned above, were the first two to be elected, as Liberals (Bailey 1952, 117). By 1870 George Braithwaite Lloyd had become Mayor of Birmingham, following in the footsteps of Charles Sturge, who had also been elevated to this office in 1862. By 1875 George Braithwaite Lloyd was a magistrate, a member of Birmingham school board, treasurer of Birmingham Town Mission, and vice-president of Hospital Saturday Collections (White 1875, 1416). In 1871, when George Braithwaite Lloyd was made an alderman on the council, Richard Cadbury Barrow succeeded him in his seat. Richard Cadbury Barrow and George Baker were also mayors in the 1870s (Bailey 1952, 126).

Linda Jones has highlighted that businessmen were the most represented group of men on the council throughout 1860-1891, always constituting at least 55% (1983, 241). Come 1873 Joseph Chamberlain, himself from a manufacturing background, had become Mayor of Birmingham, and Jones convincingly argues that he furthered the representation of commercial managers from large-scale manufacturers in particular (Jones 1983, 243). It was in this year that William White was elected onto the council (Bailey 1952, 121). In 1878 Chamberlain recruited George Cadbury to the council too (Jones 1983, 243). He also recruited Richard Tangye (Jones 1983, 243), though by this time his Quakerism had lapsed.

In 1882 George Cadbury resigned from Birmingham Council, on the grounds that the relocation of his home and business meant that he was not able to look after his now more distant ward as thoroughly as he previously had (Bailey 1952, 128).

Charles Sturge and George Goodrick resigned in 1882, probably because of age. Richard Tangye too, but it was another Quaker we have already met, Francis Corder Clayton, owner of J & E Sturge, who took his seat (Bailey 1952, 131). Corder Clayton too went on to become mayor. Harrison and Walter Barrow had also joined the council by 1898, following in their father's footsteps.

Francis Corder Clayton, George Braithwaite Lloyd, George Baker and Richard Cadbury Barrow all acted as heads of committees while serving (Bailey 1952, 131-132), Francis chairing the finance committee from 1886-1890 (Jones 1983, 248).

As we saw above, Francis Corder Clayton had retired from business in 1889 at the age of just forty-six, and seven years after entering office. Further, William White had largely ceased his involvement in White and Pike by 1880, also seven years after entering office. Thus there may well have been a relationship between Quakers' office-holding and their businesses as their influence grew; both that the wealth they began to acquire afforded them the option financially of taking office, and that taking office led to their at least partial withdrawal from their business. This is supported in the realm of involvement in Quakerism nationally by the cases of Henry Lloyd Wilson, who would become clerk of Yearly Meeting and largely left the running of J & E Sturge to his brother and partner Alfred

Wilson, and of William Littleboy, who was sufficiently wealthy to retire from manufacturing chandeliers by his forties in the 1890s (Milligan 2007, 473, 286).

Those Quaker business men involved in local government would have had considerable influence. Indeed four were elected mayor. But involvement in public life, whilst increasing a Quaker businessman's general influence, may well have been to the detriment of Quaker influence in the business realm over the course of the nineteenth century by drawing those involved away from their businesses.

Change in the Quaker community – geographical distribution, the separation of business and home, and new preparative meetings

Up to the 1870s Birmingham Preparative Meeting and Bull Street remained at the heart of the Birmingham Quaker community and business network. For example, we hear from Morland of White and Pike's shop that, as well as being just a few doors down from T & W Southall's and opposite John Cadbury's shop, 'Over their shop was a room in which was kept the library belonging to the Birmingham Friends' Reading Society, and their office was quite a meeting-place for Members of the Society of Friends' (1903, 27). Also in Bull Street in 1857, the Meeting House at the heart of the business community was rebuilt (Butler 1999, 619-620).

And in 1856 Richard and Joseph Tangye established themselves just off the Parade in the centre of Birmingham (Waterhouse 1957). Thus in the early years of the second half of the nineteenth century Quaker businesses were still flourishing in the centre of the town, strengthening its community in doing so.

However, simultaneously, we begin to see a geographic shift of Quaker businessmen's homes from the town centre and Bull Street southwards towards Edgbaston (circled in black on the map below). This is also evidence of the growing separation between workplace and home which took place over this half century. For example, in 1850 the Gibbins family moved away from the metal business in Deritend to Edgbaston, to Highfield Road, very near to George Road, where the Albrights were living. The moves of both the Albrights and the Gibbins were probably in fact preceded by Charles and Mary Sturge, of J & C Sturge and Co, who moved to Frederick Road sometime after 1831 (Lewin 1980; Pease 2013, 13). For the Sturges, Frederick Road was fairly close to their business on Broad Street.

The movement of influential Quaker business people to Edgbaston continues in the 1860s and early 1870s, William White moved from Bull Street to Sir Harry's Road in 1869. George Cadbury too moved to George Road,

Edgbaston in 1872 after his first marriage to Mary Tylor (Milligan 2007, 88). George Road is indicated by a triangle on the map below.

A few of these business people, such as the Albrights, seem to have moved to be nearer their businesses. However it seems likely that leafier suburbs such as Edgbaston to the south of Birmingham would have been more desirable to many of these Quakers who were growing wealthier through business. Joking amongst Friends about Deritend in the town's industrial heart being 'Dirty End' in the 1830s supports this (Gibbins 1911, 261). In moving to Edgbaston their shared membership of the Society of Friends was probably a factor in their choosing to maintain the close geographical proximity to one another that many of them had previously enjoyed.

From the 1870s more Quaker business people begin to move their businesses outwards, following the early example of J & E Sturge and Co moving to Selly Oak in the 1840s. The Birmingham Battery and Metal Company largely relocated to Selly Oak in these years (Rowntree 1936, 53-54).

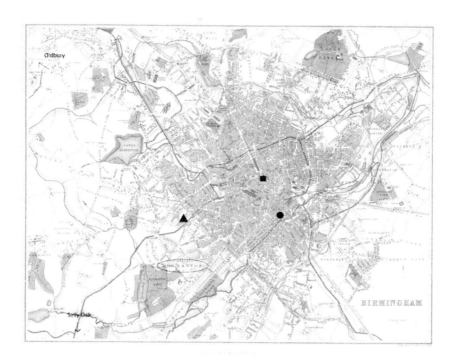

Image 5: Map of Birmingham 1866 – antiqueprints.com

Black Square: Bull Street, **Black Circle:** Birmingham Battery and Metal Co, Digbeth, before its move, **Black Triangle:** George Road, Edgbaston

This movement sheds light on the founding of the first preparative (local) Quaker meeting other than Birmingham Meeting on Bull Street in Birmingham and the surrounding area. The meeting, initially known as Bath Row, was settled in Edgbaston near to the homes of these business people sometime in 1872. It moved to George Road, Edgbaston around 1892 when the site for the meeting house was bought by Charles Dickinson Sturge, former partner in J C and J & E Sturge, and his wife Eliza Sturge (Butler 1999, 625). As I have shown, this is at the heart of the area these Quakers lived in.

In some senses, it is a surprise that another meeting in Birmingham had not been settled earlier, Birmingham had been a large meeting for years, judging by Cadbury's record of it (1956), and Butler notes overcrowding as the reason for George Road's settlement (1999, 625).

What impact did the founding of Bath Row Quaker Meeting have on the Birmingham Quaker business community of the late nineteenth century? I have shown how close the business families of the meeting seem to have been earlier in the century, which begs the question as to whether the lack of purposeful opportunity for all the business people to meet weekly damaged Quaker business prospects at the time. Certainly, relatively casual interactions about business affairs after Meeting would have been made harder by the splitting of the community in this way between Birmingham and Bath Row Meeting.

In 1879, trade and expansion having taken off further still at Cadbury's, building began on the new Cadbury's factory outside of Birmingham in Bournville, overseen closely by George Cadbury. Therefore, in 1881 George Cadbury had bought Woodbrooke, on the outskirts of Bournville and Selly Oak, as his new family home, and by 1895, Bournville Preparative Quaker Meeting had been settled (*Birmingham Preparative Meeting Minute Book* 1895-1899). So George Cadbury would probably have moved from Bath Row to Bournville Meeting around this time.

As well as the gradual outward spread of Quaker business families from the town centre by 1880, Bull Street was quite literally being divided under plans drawn up by the town council, or Corporation of Birmingham. For Corporation Street began to be built, a huge road cutting through other roads and slums in central Birmingham. Its path directly crossed the section of Bull Street discussed above, where most of the Quaker businesses were or had been.

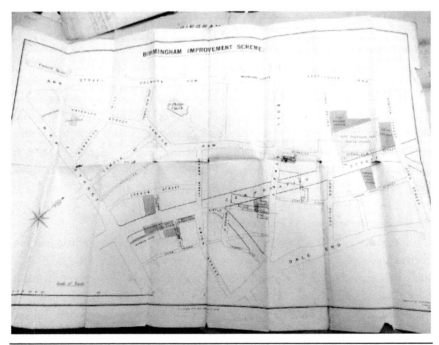

Image 6: Image of Corporation Street plan – courtesy of Sheila Barrow

Two remaining Quaker businesses were affected by this, in 1875 T and W Southall still had their chemists at 17 Bull Street (White 1875, 1556). By 1896 they were based solely on Broad Street as Southall Bros and Barclay (W. E. Peck 1896-1897, 303).

The other business which was profoundly changed by the building of Corporation Street was Barrow's Stores, which Richard Cadbury Barrow had passed on to his sons Walter, Harrison and Louis, with Harrison acting as managing director from 1894,

> the site of the Bull Street warehouse and the garden behind was sold to the Corporation by R. C. Barrow to facilitate the cutting of the new Street, and he became one of the first Corporation leaseholders in the new Corporation Street, where he built large new premises which he called Lancaster buildings (Barrow 1949, 27)

Image 7: Image of Bull Street before and after – courtesy of Sheila Barrow

Along with Bath Row and Bournville Quaker Meetings, Longbridge and Selly Oak Meetings had been settled by 1898 (*Birmingham Preparative Meeting Minute Book* 1895-1899). This further dispersed the Birmingham Quaker business community whose families had once all congregated at Birmingham Quaker Meeting on Bull Street.

A study of the minutes of Birmingham Preparative Meeting from the period 1895 to 1899 reveals that there are some Quaker businessmen who are very much still present and active at Birmingham Meeting at this time. Interestingly this includes some of those who or whose families had moved out of the centre nearer to Bath Row Meeting in Edgbaston, William Gibbins, Thomas Gibbins (probably the son of Thomas and Emma Joel, though possibly his cousin) and Charles Dickinson Sturge (despite having bought the site for Bath Row Meeting on George Road), are here. The Southalls are also active in the meeting, including Wilfred, who was clerk of the meeting in 1895, having been a director of the business that came out of T & W Southall in 1889, and who certainly lived in Edgbaston (though his business was still in the city centre; Milligan 2007, 412). The committee of accounts over this period featured several business heavyweights, from Walter and Harrison Barrow, to George Braithwaite Lloyd, John Edward Wilson, and William White (1895-1899). As I show below, many of these men were also civil heavyweights. Notably absent, however, from the minutes are George Cadbury (presumably at Bournville), any Albrights, or Henry Lloyd Wilson.

These minutes and those absent from them strongly suggest that the Birmingham Quaker business community was starting to fracture by the end of the nineteenth century. So while the general move towards Edgbaston as a place of residence may have aided the community's social closeness, it was arguably the trigger for the beginning of the separation of the community between different meetings. And the minutes demonstrate a relative lack of correlation between location of residence and meeting, indicating that while the Quakers might have lived in proximity this did not guarantee their worshipping at the same meeting. The growing number of meetings certainly seems to have reduced the opportunities for the whole of the Birmingham Quaker business community to come together.

The business environment and legal changes
As we saw briefly above, the 1844 Joint Stock Companies Act had created shareholders and increased the possible number of investors in a business. It also created the company as an entity, where previously partnerships had meant that owners were partners, usually directly running the business (Taylor 2006).

During the 1860s the Gibbins family used the Birmingham Battery and Metal Company's joint-stock status to buy out the other original proprietors, and the business became a wholly family affair (Rowntree 1936, 48). Thus the

Gibbins used a system, which often meant that businesses moved away from direct family control, to strengthen that control. However on the whole the introduction of the joint-stock company in 1844 distanced the firm from its chief owner and manager, and enabled a higher number of investors who need not be involved in the day to day running of the firm.

Then in the 1890s the business converted to limited liability status. Limited liability was made possible by further changes in company law in 1855 and 1856. It meant that shareholders would no longer be personally liable beyond the value of their shares if a business went bankrupt (Loftus 2009, 79), and it thereby arguably eroded responsibility and therefore trust (Crowther 2004, 45-46), and encouraged over-extension.

Also in the 1890s, several other Birmingham Quaker businesses converting to limited liability status, Albright & Wilson in 1892, Barrows Stores in 1894, when Harrison Barrow took over as managing director, the Birmingham Battery and Metal Company in 1897, Southall's in 1898 and Cadburys in 1900. It seems too coincidental that all these Birmingham businesses became limited liability companies within a period of seven years, so I would suggest that these businesses and their families may have been finding ways to discuss this process over this period, even if they were at different meetings by this point. There is also the possibility that the economic downturn led them to seek this new legal status.

At least one Quaker business, White and Pike, was perceived to have suffered as a consequence of conversion to a limited liability company, 'Ill-advised extensions, however, after the firm had been converted into a limited liability company, led to commercial disaster, which much saddened his last days.' (Morland 1903, 34) Morland's implicit view that limited liability at best could be a path to ruin, seems to have been chimed with the view of Quakers elsewhere. When a Quaker iron partnership faced ruin in the north-east of England in the early 1860s, the partners were only allowed to maintain their membership of the Society of Friends because they were prepared to cede their personal property in order to fulfil their liabilities (O'Donnell 2003, 81-82).

Thus the growing separation of person and firm, business and home, and responsibility and trust from practice enabled by changes in company law did not sit well with many Quakers by the end of the nineteenth century. Where in the first half of the century we saw Arthur Albright's concern for trust, these limited liability conversions in the late nineteenth century jeopardised the reputation of Quaker businesses.

Conclusion

As the Birmingham Quaker business community entered the twentieth-century, then, it had experienced considerable change over the preceding hundred years, but some things had remained similar. There was still a considerable degree of intermarriage and familial closeness, despite this not having been regulated for over forty years. And some of its business families, such as the Cadburys and the Lloyds remained successful over the century.

However, the community had shifted and dispersed considerably geographically. Whereas in the first half of the century the community had been focussed on Bull Street, this changed as the century wore on and the business community generally moved out towards Edgbaston. The significant influence of Quaker businessmen as they moved out over the century had somewhat brought its division on itself by encouraging the establishment of new meetings, and by bringing employees of larger firms into the community. This division probably had some detrimental effect on the community's interactions and mutual support.

Many new businesses came into existence, particularly in the first half of the century. However many, such as smaller ones like Josiah Pumphrey's shop on Bull Street, had come and gone. The number of firms changing hands between Quakers in the mid to late century attests to the enduring strength of their networks; I would suggest the dispersal affected mutual support on finer details, rather than exchanges such as these. What was lost was the opportunity to discuss business on a weekly basis which Birmingham Preparative Meeting on Bull Street had enabled.

Quaker businessmen had become increasingly influential in public life, as well as affluent. This meant that some chose to retire or cutback their business considerably to do this or to work within the Religious Society of Friends, which was ultimately not in the interests of business.

All the firms I have found converted to being a company from a partnership, and most then became limited liability later in the nineteenth century. Lloyds even became a public company very early, in 1865 (Lloyd 1975). By limiting responsibility and introducing the possibility of many more share-holders, this began the process of undermining some core Quaker values which had aided their business ventures, such as character, trust and integrity.

Where at the beginning of the nineteenth century partnerships and close ties had existed to bolster the Birmingham Quaker business community, while intermarriage remained strong, the Birmingham Quaker business community left the nineteenth century in a weaker position due to its dispersal across the city and meetings, the draw of public office, and changes in company law.

Bibliography

Bailey, M. H. 1952. *The Contribution of Quakers to Some Aspects of Local Government in Birmingham, 1828 to 1902*. MA. University of Birmingham.

Barrow, G. C. 1994. *The Barrow Family, Myth, Legend and some Fact*, Birmingham, for private circulation

Behagg, C. 1986. 'Myths of Cohesion, Capital and Compromise in the Historiography of Nineteenth-Century Birmingham', *Social History*, 11,3, pp. 375-384.

Birmingham Preparative Meeting Minute Book, 1895-1898. Birmingham, Archives of the Library of Birmingham.

Bunce, J. T. 1878. *A History of the Corporation of Birmingham; With a Sketch of the Earlier Government of the Town*, vol. 1. Birmingham, Cornish Brothers.

Butler, D. M. 1999. *The Quaker Meeting Houses of Britain*. Friends Historical Society.

Cadbury, W. A. 1956. *Bull Street Friends I Have Known*. SF/3/4/11/2. Birmingham, Library of Birmingham.

Carnevali, F. 2004. "'Crooks, Thieves, and Receivers', Transaction Costs in Nineteenth-Century Industrial Birmingham." *Economic History Review*, LVII, 3, pp. 533-550.

Crowther, D. 2004. "Limited liability or limited responsibility?" in Crowther, D. & Rayman-Bacchus L., eds. *Perspectives on Corporate Social Responsibility*. Aldershot, Ashgate. Chapter 3, pp 42-48.

Dick, M. 2016. personal correspondence.

Dix, W. H. 1858. *General and Commercial Directory of Birmingham*, [online] available at <http,//specialcollections.le.ac.uk/cdm/compoundobject/collection/p16445coll4/id/339979/rec/16> [accessed 7 May 2016].

Gardner, P. 2016. personal correspondence.

Gibbins, E. ed., 1911. *Records of the Gibbins Family*. Birmingham, Cornish Brothers.

Gibbins, R. C., & Co. 1869. Advert. [online] Available at <http://www.gracesguide.co.uk/Richard_C._Gibbins_and_Co> [accessed 30 April 2016].

Hodgkin, A. 1992. *Chance and Design, Reminiscences of Science in Peace and War*. Cambridge, Cambridge University Press.

Hopkins, E. 1989. *Birmingham, The First Manufacturing Town in the World 1760-1840*. London, Weidenfeld and Nicolson.

Hopkins, E. 2002, 'Industrial Change and Life at Work in Birmingham 1850-1914', *Midland History*, 27, pp.112-119.

Isichei, E. 1970, *Victorian Quakers*, Oxford, Oxford University Press.

Jones, L. J. 1983. 'Public Pursuit of Private Profit? Liberal Businessmen and Municipal Politics in Birmingham, 1865–1900', *Business History*, 25/3, p.240-259

Kelly, W. 1850, *Post Office Directory of Birmingham with Staffordshire and Worcestershire*, [online] Available at, http,//specialcollections.le.ac.uk/ cdm/compoundobject/collection/p16445coll4/id/339983/rec/3 [accessed 7 May 2016]

Lewin, S. 1980. *The Sturges of Birmingham, Gaunts Earthcott to Frederick Road* [e-book] Available at, http,//www.sturgefamily.com/Discover/THE% 20STURGES%20OF%20BIRMINGHAM.htm [accessed 15 June 2016]

Lloyd, H. 1975. *The Quaker Lloyds in the Industrial Revolution*, London, Hutchinson.

Loftus, D. 2009. Limited liability, market democracy, and the social organization of production in mid-nineteenth century Britain. In Henry, Nancy, Schmitt, Cannon eds. 2009. *Victorian Investments, New Perspectives on Finance and Culture*. Bloomington, Indiana University Press, pp. 79–97.

Milligan, E. H. 2007. *Biographical dictionary of British Quakers in commerce and industry, 1775-1920*, York, Sessions.

Morland, O. 1903. *William White, A Brother of Men*, Birmingham, Morland & Co.

O'Donnell, L. 2003, 'Deviating from the Path of Safety, the Rise and Fall of a Nineteenth Century Quaker Meeting' *Quaker Studies*, Vol. 8, Iss. 1, 68-88.

Pease, C. E. G. 2013. *The Descendants of Joseph Sturge*, [online] Available at, <http,//www.pennyghael.org.uk/Sturge.pdf> [accessed 4 May 2016].

Pease, C. E. G. 2015a. *The Descendants of James Cadbury*, [online] Available at, <http,//www.pennyghael.org.uk/Cadbury.pdf> [accessed 2 May 2016].

Pease, C. E. G. 2015b. *The Descendants of William Wilson*, [online] Available at, <http,//www.pennyghael.org.uk/WilsonWilliam.pdf> [accessed 4 May 2016].

Peck, W. E. 1896. *Trades Directory to the Manufacturers of Birmingham*, [online] Available at, http,//specialcollections.le.ac.uk/cdm/compoundobject/collection/p164 45coll4/id/339980/rec/2 [accessed 3 May 2016].

Robson, W. 1839. *Birmingham and Sheffield Directory*, [online] Available at, http,//specialcollections.le.ac.uk/cdm/compoundobject/collection/p164 45coll4/id/167166/rec/2 [accessed 7 May 2016].

Rowntree, A. 1936. *The Birmingham Battery and Metal Company*, Birmingham, for private circulation.

Taylor, J. 2006. *Creating Capitalism, Joint-Stock Enterprise in British Politics and Culture, 1800-1870*, London, Royal Historical Society.

Threlfall, R. E. 1951. *100 Years of Phosphorus Making, 1851,1951*, Oldbury, Albright and Wilson Ltd.

Waterhouse, R. E. 1957. *A Hundred Years of Engineering Craftsmanship, A short history tracing the adventurous development of Tangyes Limited, Smethwick, 1857-1957*, Smethwick, Tangyes Ltd.

West, W. 1830. *The History, Topography, and Directory of Warwickshire*, [online] Available at, http,//specialcollections.le.ac.uk/cdm/compoundobject /collection/p16445coll4/id/167168/rec/1 [accessed 7 May 2016].

White, F. 1875. *Commercial and Trades Directory of Birmingham*, vol. 2, [online] Available at, http,//specialcollections.le.ac.uk/cdm/compoundobject/ collection/p16445coll4/id/112374/rec/2 [accessed 7 May 2016]

Woodward, E. 2015. *Faith and Disunity, Samuel Galton and the Quakers.* [online] Available at, <https,//theironroom.wordpress.com/2015/03/23/faith-and-disunity-samuel-galton-and-the-quakers/> [accessed 1 May 2016].

Wrightson. 1818. *Triennial Directory of Birmingham*, [online] Available at, http,//www.genuki.org.uk/big/eng/WAR/Birmingham/bham1818-g [accessed 3 May 2016]

Wrightson and Webb. 1835. *Directory of Birmingham*, [online] Available at, http,//specialcollections.le.ac.uk/cdm/compoundobject/collection/p164 45coll4/id/218289/rec/3 [accessed 7 May 2016].

9 | Quaker Business Method: A Contemporary Decision-Making Process?

By Nicholas Burton

Introduction

Friends have a long tradition in the world of trade and business, as discussed throughout this collection. While Quaker entrepreneurs from the eighteenth and nineteenth centuries such as Abraham Darby, Joseph Rowntree and George Cadbury continue to be studied widely today, the sustained influence of Friends on contemporary responsible business practice remains largely underexplored. In a Faculty publication at George Fox University, Anderson (1995), for instance, notes that "Quakers have influenced the field of business and other professions far beyond their numbers but the facts remain largely unnoticed". While it is quite a daunting task to try to capture the dense fabric of what characterises a 'Quaker way' of responsible business practice, the *theology* and *process* by which Friends conduct *Meetings for Business* deserves renewed attention given its potential relevance as a collaborative method of decision-making in today's increasingly complex business organisations.

The term *Meeting for Business* often causes some confusion in the circles of Friends. In this Chapter, I distinguish between a 'Meeting for Business' – sometimes referred to as a 'Meeting for Worship for Business' - and a 'Business Meeting' that typically occurs in contemporary business organisations, such as board meetings, project meetings, team meetings and the like. Later in this Chapter, I argue that the *process* that underpins a Meeting for Business in the manner of Friends has the potential to be transferable in full or part to contemporary business meetings, and may perhaps rapidly improve their degree of inclusiveness and effectiveness. In other words, I hope to argue that the Quaker Business Method (QBM) - a term applied to the decision-making processes of Friends (Sheeran 1983) – has the potential to be transferable to modern management and organisational practice. In other words, I take up an optimistic position in this chapter.

QBM is perhaps the most interesting aspect of Friends' broader approach to corporate governance, characterised as a participative, transparent and non-competitive method of decision-making (Velayutham 2013). The corporate governance of the Religious Society of Friends is tightly bound to the theological roots and discipline of early Friends. The theology of Friends emerges from the belief of a 'Light within' that is available to everyone and a readiness to answer 'that of God in every one'. As Friends believe in a direct and unmediated relationship with the Spirit or God[23], it seems natural that traditional and human forms of hierarchy would be typically avoided, unlike many corporate governance models in the contemporary business world. In other words, Friends approach corporate governance as a collective in order to make decisions, whether strategic or operational, local, regional or national. Quoted in Velayutham (2013, 230-231), Roberts (1991, 1996) characterises the corporate governance of Friends as fundamentally different and distinct from the typical structure of many business organisations and highlights that hierarchical, Board-based forms of corporate governance are 'individualising', whereas the governance structures of the Society are, in contrast, 'socialising' and non-hierarchal, providing the framework for a powerful form of collectivised decision-making. With the contemporary business landscape arguably littered with examples of 'poor' decisions, what can the distinctive Quaker Business Method offer contemporary business organisations? Can collective and unitive decision-making help contemporary business organisations make 'better' decisions? Is the Quaker Business Method a hidden gem, bequeathed by early Friends, to contemporary business practice?

Spiritual roots

QBM can be considered to encompass two broad dimensions: (1) a spiritual dimension described within the theology of early Friends, and (2) a decision-making process, tried, tested and refined by Friends for over 350 years (Anderson 2006). Being distinctive, the process of decision-making may, to new-comers, seem unusual and idiosyncratic, often taking practice and participation over a long period to become accustomed to the nuances of the proceedings. Michaelis (2010, 16), for example, argues that "...the discipline of Quaker business meetings is quite subtle and it is best conveyed through experience...". However, despite its initial distinctive appearance, users of the method only

---

[23] I will use these terms interchangeably throughout this chapter

require spiritual discipline and the right attitude to participate in a Quaker Meeting for Business (Grace 2006,48). The spiritual dimension of QBM requires Friends to turn their attention to the Spirit as the source and authority in decision-making, relegating the role of human and individual authority. Friends understand that anyone present in the Meeting may experience 'leadings' of the Spirit and this has an important effect on the way that Friends make decisions together in a process of *'corporate discernment'*. The theological doctrine of early Friends is that "each person is capable of a personal, direct relationship with God" (Karkkainen 2002, 63). Quoting Grace (2000):

> … the living Christ is present to teach us Himself…Quakers believe that the Light of Christ is given in some measure to all people. This experience of the immediate presence of Christ, both personally and corporately, implies that we may be led by the Inward Teacher. Since Christ is not divided, the nearer we come to Him, the nearer we will be to one another. Thus the sense of being led into Unity with one another becomes a fundamental mark of the Divine work in the world.

As everyone has an unmediated access to the Spirit, then it follows that every participant at a Meeting for Business has the potential to contribute to the process of decision-making. By extension, every person present has the responsibility of waiting and listening to what the Spirit may say *through* him or her as part of the proceedings. Anderson (2006, 29) eloquently describes the process of silent waiting and listening as thus "This means bathing the event in prayer and coming ready to put aside the distractions of our busied lives in order to listen intently to the gentle whispers of the Holy Spirit within and among us". A Meeting for Business, therefore, is less about making an 'efficient' decision, and more to try to collectively discern the will of God. In other words, "A Quaker Meeting for Business is conducted in the context of worship, and with the same expectant waiting upon the Spirit as in the Meeting for Worship" (Grace 2000). The process of corporate discernment, therefore, has a theological dimension that helps focus those present on a collaborative and cooperative approach to decision making in contrast to the highly-competitive and confrontational forms of decision-making widely used in corporate board rooms. As Grace (2006, 48) notes, the corporate discernment process "…draws us closer to each other, closer to God, closer to the truth, and closer to a knowledge of right action in the world."

Friends enter into a Meeting for Business to "Come with heart and mind prepared' (QF&P, 2.42) as early Quakers noted, and with the expectation that a 'leading' will emerge for those present. George Fox advised "Be still and cool in thy own mind and spirit from thy own thoughts, and then thou wilt feel the principle of God to turn thy mind to the Lord God, whereby thou wilt receive this strength and power from whence life comes to allay all tempests against blusterings and storms." Fox eloquently draws attention to the importance of the right attitude and being sensitive to God's leading such that "…this attitude is possible when Friends tune their mind to God and that even if the participants may be distracted in many ways, they will be empowered to overcome whatever might cause them not to understand and follow the will of God" (Niyonzima, 2013, 13). When participants in a Meeting for Business wait in expectant silence "…with hearts and minds prepared and open, they can be gathered up by the Spirit to experience communion with God and with each other in a way that is not possible when praying or meditating alone. A time of covered worship is more than the sum of its individual participants" (Grundy 2002, 7).

The use of silence is an important characteristic of Meetings for Business, and uncommon within a wider cultural context where talk is often seen as synonymous with action (Molina-Markham 2014, 155). Meetings for Business begin and end with periods of silence, allowing those present to open their hearts and minds to God's guidance, rather than to focus on individual or selfish wishes or needs creating a powerful atmosphere for "attending, discerning, and minding the Divine Will" (Anderson 2006, 27). For Friends, "…silence can be discerned as having qualities such as: active, redemptive, nourishing, prayerful expectancy, an intensified pause and as a form of liberation (Brigham & Kavanagh 2015, 4). In addition, silence can also be used *during* the proceedings. For example, short periods of silence between contributions give time for those present to reflect on their meaning and to consider whether their own individual 'leadings' can add to the process of corporate discernment. Second, short periods of silence may also reduce the risk of a confrontational, ego-based debate. Third, should proceedings become heated, the Clerk may request a period of silent reflection to help re-focus the Meeting to concentrate on discerning a unitive way forward. Thus, silence can have a calming effect on those present. Silence at the end of the Meeting may also help to provide a reflective closure to the proceedings. In other words, Quaker business meetings are very different from more typical business meetings because silence is ever present. Law (1998, 20) describes the character and use of silence as thus:

It is not heavy and preoccupied, like the desperate hush of the exam room. Nor is it disciplinary and repressive, like the pressure that expands to fill the space of the parade ground where you hardly dare breathe. It is not the silence of the graveyard, with its imagined echoes and distant memories. Nor is it the silence you hear when you lie in the sun … It is none of these, though perhaps the last of these comes closest to it. Instead it is, as they say a 'centred' silence.

In a Meeting for Business, there is, then, a shared understanding of the role of silence and in finding the sense of the meeting. Relying on a "sense of the meeting" offers a possibility for creating and sustaining a shared sense of community in decision making that may not be possible in other contexts when voting is used (Brigham & Kavanagh 2015), a matter which I turn to next.

Unity or consensus?

Through the process of corporate discernment, the primary objective of a Meeting for Business is to reach *unity* in its decision-making (Bradney & Cownie 2000; Sheeran, 1983). As a social and collective process, decision-making via resolutions or the casting of votes is definitely *not* part of QBM. Decision-making via the casting votes may result in the perspectives of minorities being disregarded or overridden, as one 'side' claims a numerical victory, while the other 'side' is defeated. In contrast, Meetings for Business aim to arrive at a *sense of the meeting*. Niyonzima (2013, 16) highlights:

> Friends are not fundamentally opposed to democracy… Rather, the process is based on the understanding that God's followers understand that they operate within a theocracy, not a democracy. The goal when Christians gather to make decisions is to listen to God's voice: not to find what the majority can support, but find what those present understand to be God's will.

How is unitive decision-making conceptualised in the management literature? Typically, four styles of decision-making are envisaged: (1) an autocratic decision-making process in which the leader accepts responsibility for the outcome, (2) a democratic process that involves voting, (3) a collective participatory style where everyone is given the opportunity to provide input but the leader still makes the final decision, and, (4) a consensus process in which the leader understands that the group is responsible for the decision and everyone must agree (Leadership Management Development Center, 2013). However, is unity the same as consensus? Consensus is a word that is sometimes used to describe the characteristics of QBM. Yet, Friends often insist that unity and consensus is not the same thing. On the one hand, consensus is based on a notion of human reason and authority, and commonly understood as requiring mutual compromise between human beings; the decision taken must be agreeable to all present, or at least objectionable to none. Pollard (1954, 5) rejects the notion of consensus, arguing that "Quakers reject debate on account of a number of defects: its assumption that man is a wholly rational being, its disregard of the unconscious, its tendency to establish controversial speech habits as fixed attitudes, its accentuation of antagonism and differences and the desire to beat the opponent. A desire to dominate…is absent…". Anderson (2006, 30) also asserts that the term consensus has a different meaning to Friends:

> …consensus is not simply a factor of compromise, wherein some give a little in one way, and others give a little in another. Modification of one's understanding will indeed happen on the basis of one another's input, but the goal is not to sort out one's opinion by means of forcible jostling back and forth until the path of least resistance produces an outcome. Nor is it a quid pro quo exchange: "You come my way, and I'll go yours."… Such are products of creaturely activity, not submission to the Divine Will.

In contrast, unity and a 'sense of the meeting' is based on a spiritual and corporate discernment of God's will. *Quaker Faith & Practice* (2.87) describes the spirit in which Friends make decisions, well-expressed by Edward Burrough:

> Being orderly come together, proceed in the wisdom of God not in the way of the world, as a worldly assembly of men, by hot contests, by seeking to outspeak and overreach one another in discourse, as if it were controversy between party and party of men, or two sides violently striving for domination, not deciding affairs by the greater vote, or the number of men, but by hearing and determining every matter coming before you, in love, coolness, gentleness and dear unity.

Friends' belief in a fundamental difference between unity and consensus has far-reaching consequences. For example, a phrase heard in many board rooms is

247

'what does success look like? Or 'what are the critical success factors'? Here, again, Anderson (2006, 31) highlights how unitive approaches decision-making redefine how success or failure in decision-making is conceptualised:

> …this change in perspective causes us to redefine our understandings of "success". Rather than seeing success in terms of material, bottom-line matters of the conventional world, success in the Kingdom of God involves lifting our sights to the higher goals of discernment, wisdom, understanding, conviction and commitment. Where Christ's leadings are attended and discerned, that's success! Likewise, "failure" is radically redefined. Rather than evaluating outcomes on the basis of popularity or outward measures, the more central question is whether Christ's will was done and whether it was carried out in the loving spirit of his way.

The role of human leadership

The higher goals of corporate discernment subordinate human authority and leadership. Those nominated who moderate and 'clerk' the Meeting are seen as facilitators of the corporate discernment process. Often, contemporary business meetings tend to be structured around a Chairperson who manages the meeting and a Secretary who produces minutes at some future point *after* the meeting. In contrast, in a Meeting for Business these two functions are combined into the role of a Clerk (or in the USA a Clerk and Recording Clerk), who both guide the Meeting and produce minutes in real-time. The Clerk is not there to 'lead' the Meeting in the traditional sense, present motions or oversee votes, and as Pollard (1954) highlights, the role of Clerk is certainly not a vehicle for the ambitious or for those who want to dominate proceedings. Moreover, "Those who come to meeting not so much to find the Lord's will as to win acceptance of their own opinions may find their views carry little weight" (Willcuts 1984, 82). In one sense, perhaps the Clerk's role is one of stewardship, rather than leadership as "leadership is seen as provided by the spirit, by God; and this leadership comes through the clerk…Stewardship is perhaps a more accurate term than leadership to indicate the functioning of the person designated to convene and guide a particular committee" (Reis-Louis 1994, 48).

Clerks are appointed for a limited time, sometimes triennially, and the role of Clerk, and other roles, is often widely shared among the Membership of the Meeting. Grace (2006, 50) highlights that "The Clerk has no formal authority of their own and cannot speak for the Meeting. Their task is to focus and enable the discernment of the Meeting by laying business before it in an orderly way, managing the pace and discipline of the discussion, listening for the Sense of the Meeting to emerge, restating that Sense in clear language and asking for approval, and recording the business in written minutes". Cranmer (2003,187) similarly highlights that "The clerk combines the roles of convener and secretary, sharing with the elders responsibility for the 'right ordering' of the meeting. Right ordering has overtones of seemliness, dignity, and respect for tradition as well as 'doing things by the book.'"

To ensure right ordering, the Clerk will prepare an agenda, discerning whether a particular agenda item is ready for discussion or requires further shaping by a sub-committee or perhaps discussion at a Threshing Meeting. The agenda is also likely to encompass any matters of business held over from a prior Meeting where unity could not be discerned. However, despite the creation of an agenda, there is always sufficient room to remain open to new 'leadings' that may take the Meeting in a new direction, as "The sense of openness to new leadings in the group or individual must be cherished" (Vogel-Borne 1990, 9). However, Friends are often more likely to ensure any new concerns are discussed and nourished with experienced and respected Friends before raising them formally as an agenda item in a Meeting for Business. Friends will also want to come to a Meeting for Business informed about the agenda and issues, so that "...contributions will be seasoned with knowledge and perspective" (Anderson 2006, 29). However, in order to remain open to the 'leadings' of the Spirit, it is unusual for those present to pre-plan vocal ministry ahead of time, but rather to listen to God's guidance as to whether there is a 'leading' to contribute. After all, many Friends would highlight that it is impossible to corporately know the will of God prior to the Meeting. Those present, as a consequence, expect that a new way will emerge from the proceedings of the Meeting (Grace 2006).

The Clerk will open proceedings by inviting the Meeting to accept the agenda. Following this, agenda items are introduced, and the Clerk or a person present may introduce the issue or decision under consideration in a neutral manner, perhaps outlining a few options. Once a matter is 'before the meeting', the approach usually taken is to resist narrowing the options too soon (Anderson 2006). If several Friends feel they are led to contribute, the Clerk determines who may speak and in which order, and may at an appropriate moment encourage someone to speak who has relevant knowledge or an important perspective but has remained silent. Via contributions to the proceedings, a creative process ensues and each person has a responsibility to contribute and not hold back, if they have a leading to speak. In fact, Friends are encouraged by the Clerk to contribute where they can so that a 'sense of the meeting' can be more properly discerned.

The spoken contributions are considered a form of vocal ministry (as in a Meeting for Worship) in which a person shares the leadings they have experienced. Friends are advised to listen to the words of other Friends speaking, imbued as they are with the Light. Moreover, Friends are encouraged to thoroughly consider contributions before making any reply (Bradney & Cownie 2000, 73). Michaelis (2010, 16) highlights that "Contributions are normally offered without strong emotion, making space for alternative points of view. However, sometimes a passionate contribution based in personal experience can be valuable, enabling participants to grasp some new significance or perspective in their deliberation" In Meetings, contributions tend to follow a few simple rules. Friends are advised, especially in larger Meetings, to limit repetition as the Meeting is generally not interested in any numerical counting system in order to reach unity (Sheeran 1983). Furthermore, oratory, rhetoric or politically-charged contributions are seldom welcomed. Sheeran (1983, 58) also notes that the role of monitoring one's emotions plays a key role in the Meeting, and Friends often try to recognise and temper their emotions in order that contributions remain neutral and to encourage a wide participation in the corporate discernment process. Sheeran (1983, 55) helpfully uses the analogy of musical compositions to describe the process, highlighting that contributions are musical notes that, once assembled, create a musical composition that best represents the will of God.

Rather than compiling a list of pros and cons, or employing a form of numerical counting system, the Clerks are still responsible for judging the "weight" of each contribution by discerning the movement of the Spirit (Grace 2000). The Clerk may decide that some Friends have more wisdom on a particular issue than others, and should therefore carry more weight. However, weighting the contributions is not an easy process for the Clerk. For instance, Bishop (2006, 4) highlights that "Quakers often struggle to balance the idea that every voice needs to be heard with the reality that the process of weighing means every voice does not contribute equally. Good communication, clear relationships, and a shared commitment to seek God's voice above all else are all necessary for such corporate weighing to be effective". A further difficulty for the Clerk is how to weigh-up the contributions of those who remain silent, and this is often done creating a cooperative and caring atmosphere to draw those Friends into the discussion, and not to over-rely on contributions from experienced and respected Friends. Bishop (2006, 4-5) highlights the problem:

> Someone may have the reputation of speaking with spiritual weight,
> or may be asked to shoulder positional responsibilities because of

the weightiness of their words, but even words from these people must be weighed every time they are shared. The gathered community never knows when a normally Spirit-sensitive person might be having a distracted day, or be thrown off-balance by a personal issue. True spiritual weight is recognized in the moment, as the Holy Spirit confirms the truth of the words by Scripture and within the hearts of others.

Once those present have contributed, the Clerk will offer a minute that reflects the sense of the meeting. Anderson (2006, 42-43) notes that "…offering a Sense of the Meeting becomes something of a summary of where the group feels a oneness of accord on both the identification of the issues to be addressed and what might be "the mind of Christ" in addressing those issues". Following the minute, those present may then deliberate further on whether it adequately reflects the sense of the meeting, and if not, this may lead the Clerk to suggest an amendment to the minute before it is finally agreed by the Meeting. Although rare, the minute may take a few iterations to reflect the sense of the meeting. Brigham & Kavanagh (2015, 15) highlight that the process is "…axiomatic that the clerk clerks best when everyone is clerking together".

Unlike contemporary business meetings, the Clerk makes sure the Meeting understands what is being approved *at the time the decision is made*. Once agreed, Cranmer (2003) highlights that Friends often signify assent by the traditional response, 'I hope so' ('Approve' in the USA). Why do many Quaker's say 'I hope so' after a draft minute is accepted? Mace (2012, 120) writes: "I think it means to pay respect to the presence in the empty chair … it's an expression with an element of provisionality about it … I am trusting our discernment has taken us to this place, but I am recognising that we might not have". Anderson (2006, 42-43) summarises the benefits of the process in terms of participant understanding and ownership, highlighting that "Decisions that are both understood and collectively owned have a far greater chance of being carried out with missional success than do quickly made decisions that are mandated by a dominant individual or group". In other words, unitive decisions in the manner of Friends are often more likely to be implemented with good grace, imbued, as they are, with the will of God. The process of writing and agreeing minutes in real-time sits in stark contrast to the process in typical Business Meetings where minutes are often produced by the Secretary after the meeting, and then accepted as correct at the following meeting. While perhaps a quicker process, this approach can have serious drawbacks, of course. For example, the people approving the minutes at a following meeting might be different from those at the original meeting. Second, the minutes sometimes turn out be a version of what should have been said rather than what actually was. Third, the need to approve the minutes at a subsequent meeting can sometimes allow all the original issues to be raised again[24]. In Meetings for Business, however, the minutes, once approved, become authoritative. Thus, minute-writing and minute-taking are crucial to QBM and are imbued as a spiritual practice rather than simply a clerical function. Those who were not present accept the decision of the Meeting as God's will. However, the process of corporate discernment is never free of human imperfection, and 'new Light' may be found on an issue at a future date (Grace 2006). A sense of the meeting can often only be achieved by the Clerk when those participating respect and care for one another (Grace 2006). The process requires humility, and according to Grace (2006), a purity of motive. Sheeran (1983, 61) suggests that "The emphasis is on acceptance of one another, mutual respect, avoidance of the manipulative conduct which rhetorical style often hides, a sense of the partiality of one's own insights, and one's dependence on searching together with the group for better conclusions than anyone alone could have attained". However, that is to say Friends should not remain silent for the 'sake' of unity, however. If a Friend disagrees with what is being said, or have serious reservations about it, then Friends have a duty to say so. Otherwise, the Clerk can easily misread the sense of the meeting.

Some drawbacks to overcome

Despite my optimism for its potential benefits, QBM undoubtedly takes more time and patience. It is no place for forced deadlines and the pressure of time. Indeed, perhaps one of the greatest challenges in transferring the process to contemporary business organisations is the time commitment of participants to corporately discern the 'best' decision or outcome. Though the process may take a time commitment, it is entirely possible that implementation following the decision may occur more quickly as a result because time was invested up-front in discerning unity and securing commitment. As Adrian Cadbury (2003) recalled "in industrial relations…it often meant considerable time spent in debate and argument, but it also meant that decisions once arrived at could be implemented quickly and with commitment".

Friends are often asked what happens when unity is not discerned. In simple terms, should unity not be discerned, no change to the state of affairs is made, or when in doubt, wait! (Sheeran 1983). It is possible that allowing more time to

---

[24] I am grateful to Bill Waghorn for these points, drawn from an unpublished working paper on the Quaker Business Method for Quakers & Business.

reflect on the matter at hand may help unity to be discerned in the future. Gentry (1982, 234) highlight the tension at the heart of corporate discernment and unity:

> If the Inner Light is within each person but consensus is a group process, then a natural tension should be expected. The presence of natural tension or conflict is explained by suggesting that the Spirit has not as yet been sufficiently found in all members of the group. Quakers have built in several techniques to manage conflict. Uniquely, Quakers use a period of silence in which members consider their own and others' views. During this period, self-interests which may impede seeking the Inner Light are to be set aside.

Despite the use of silence and more time, it may remain difficult to achieve unity and taken as a sign that God's will has not been discerned (Grace 2006). Sheeran (1983, 66-70) identifies three different types of 'dissent' to unity: (1) 'I disagree but do not wish to stand in the way'; (2) 'please minute me as opposed'; and, (3) 'I am unable to unite with the proposal'. The first type of dissent is probably the most common, and is an act of sensitivity to the integrity of the process in order to preserve unity. Requesting a minute as being opposed to the decision is a stronger opposition to the emergent unity, while it still recognises that the objection should not stand in the way of the proceedings. As Sheeran (1983, 69) notes, "its use leaves the meeting free to proceed but also tends to make the group more reluctant…"

Refusing to unite and stand aside is the most severe form of objection. However, Grace (2006, 51) highlights that Friends should consider the validity of the corporate discernment process so that:

> When a Friend feels he or she must "stand in the way" of Unity, the Meeting and the Friend will patiently labor together in hopes of coming to a truer understanding of God's will. However, individuals do not hold a power of veto, and should be ready to recognize the validity of corporate leadings and to submit to them if conscience allows, being recorded in the minutes as standing aside.

Where a Friend is unwilling to stand aside, the Clerk will often delay the decision until a later Meeting, and Friends, such as Elders and other experienced and respected Friends, may, between Meetings, discuss the objection with the dissenting Friend. A few possible outcomes are possible. First, it may be possible that the Friend is subsequently able to reach unity as the Friends' respect for the judgements of experienced Friends may often ease the disagreement. Second, the dissention of the Friend may cause other participants of the Meeting to reflect whether they were in fact mistaken. Thirdly, it is possible that that if unity cannot be reached after sufficient discussion, the Clerk may disregard any option to block the sense of the meeting by objection. In that case, the dissenter can either to stand aside, or to have one's name recorded in opposition.

What about the common drawbacks of QBM? Like any other human process, QBM relies upon Friends' integrity towards it. Grace (2006, 52) highlights that criticisms of the process are often based on human imperfections:

> Most Friends are painfully aware of how our human nature falls short of the spiritual ideal, and of how fragile our process can seem. Corporate discernment of the will of God is a risky and imperfect proposition. In relying so extensively on the Holy Spirit, we make ourselves vulnerable to pitfalls and failures….

However, according to Grace, "Far from being a weakness, such vulnerability is central to our understanding of the power of worship (and business) "in spirit and in truth". Human imperfections can take an almost infinite number of forms, however the most common are likely to be the risk of falling into the trap of compromise, rather than discerning the will of God. For example, Sheeran (1983, 54) refers to Friends resorting to decisions that are the lowest common denominator, or the easiest path to follow that achieves unity. In contrast, Dandelion highlights that some Friends may feel alienated by the theocracy of the process and "…participants can feel marginalised or silenced by a decision taken without them or by a clear majority" (2002, 217). There are also strong social pressures to discern unity. For example, where a Friend cannot unite with a decision and 'stands in the way', social pressures may increase exponentially across time as decisions are delayed. Elders and other respected Friends may also exert a strong social influence to conform to the corporate discernment process. The Clerk is also in a unique position to influence the decision-making process. Consciously or unconsciously, the Clerk may organise the agenda, mould the proceedings or draft a minute that reflects his or her personal view of the decision at hand. Thus, Meetings for Business are by no means immune from human manipulation and it is entirely possible that what carries most weight is the personal reputation of the Friend addressing the Meeting.

Friends often emphasise the importance of the integrity of the process over the product (i.e., the decision) (Grace 2006). While this can have benefits, it can also sometimes hamstring the process itself. For example, in an edition of *The Friend*, Beeson (2015, 13) highlights that there is a strong risk that Friends see the purpose of a Meeting for Business as to discern a 'minute,' whereas the primary purpose is to address an issue. In fact, Beeson argues that QBM would be improved if it allowed more time for exploratory, discovery and deliberative phases, stressing the advantages of holding threshing meetings prior to a more formal Meeting for Business.

The Future

In these concluding remarks, I argue that QBM may be transferable as a decision-making process to many contemporary business meetings. At its heart, QBM balances the creativity and leadings of individuals with a 'testing' role of the Meeting (Michealis 2010, 17). With many contemporary businesses striving to find new ways to improve engagement and participation throughout the organisation, and ultimately to make better decisions, such a collaborative and unitive decision-making process should be of interest to practitioners, where Friends or non-Friends.

Most Friends would agree that QBM has a spiritual dimension. However, some Friends, and non-Friends alike, have clear differences in personal theology and belief. This leads us to consider whether a secular organisational context would render the processes underpinning QBM of any value? Grace (2006, 48) cautions that while Friends may frown at the idea that QBM is simply a *process or technique*, it is perhaps the dimensions of cooperation and trust that lies at the heart of QBM that can in fact make a contribution to the challenges faced by business organisations. Ultimately, QBM "…nurture(s) a culture of listening, enabling participants to achieve a shared understanding of a complex situation and of other people's positions and perspectives on it. [The] Quaker business method…is a unique process that can develop solidarity around a collective way forward" (Michaelis 2010, 17). In other words, even in secular contexts, it is entirely conceivable that QBM as a process, rather than as a spiritual practice, can be used by individuals and teams in organisations who find "…in Truth the best aspirations of man…" (Sheeran 1983, 73). Again, Sheeran (1983, 78) makes a useful observation that for many Friends who deemphasise the Christian theological roots of QBM, the process of decision-making remains strongly associated with trust and a shared desire for unity.

In an online article for Forbes, Lewis (2009) interviewed Margaret Benefiel, author of *Soul at Work: Spiritual Leadership in Organizations*, who suggests that

I think that managers can adapt certain elements and the guiding spirit of the Quaker business meeting to their purposes", including "a quiet, reflective frame of mind, mutual respect, [and] the idea that no one person has all the truth, but must listen deeply to others to gain a fuller picture of the truth. Studies show that half of management decisions fail. Quaker practices can help managers make better decisions.

Lewis also interviewed David Hurst, author of Crises *and Renewal: Meeting the Challenge of Organizational Change*, who highlights that:

I suppose that on a very small scale, if you are trying to get people who already trust each other somewhat to express real concerns or come up with different ideas, it can help to think about starting a meeting without an agenda and in silence. The pressure of silence is immense, so you can't just spring it on an unsuspecting group. They have to know it is coming and what the objective is. A complete change in physical context from the office environment might help too.

The key point is that contemporary businesses may find benefits in using at least some component parts of QBM, if not the entire process or the theology. For example, Pollard (1954, 8) suggests that:

What can be used easily in other bodies is the absence of voting, the requirement of unanimity, discussion in an atmosphere of conciliation rather than domination, the occasional use of periods of silence and the adjournment of discussion. It is more important to get the correct decision than to get a decision by a certain time.

While I may be charged with being over-optimistic as to the transferability of QBM to other face-to-face decision-making settings, the rapid emergence of remote or online decision-making practices in contemporary organisations raises particular issues for advocates of QBM. Many Friends use technology to explore Quaker practice, learn, study and participate in online Meetings for Worship. However, the use of remote technologies also raises the question of whether corporate discernment can operate in the presence of such technological advances? Michaelis (2010) observes that, perhaps ironically, there has been little corporate discernment about how technology may affect the practice of Friends. Indeed, as you would expect, there is no mention of the internet or social media in *Quaker Faith & Practice* (1994). Quaker Life (2012) has published guidance for Friends on conducting telephone conference meetings, although similar guidance would cover internet-enabled conferencing as well. The guidance states that:

> Experience shows that we can maintain the worshipping spirit of our Quaker business meetings very well over the telephone. It does require us to be alert to seeking the most appropriate ways to ensure right ordering and discernment, according to the circumstances. Teleconferencing is very effective when dealing with routine business or any matters that do not need threshing or extended consideration. Difficult matters needing lengthy discernment are clearly best handled face-to-face…. It may often be helpful for (sub-)committees to meet by teleconference. One simple factor is key to maintaining confidence in Quaker discernment by telephone conferencing: while the method has been adapted to a new medium, the principles of the Quaker business meeting remain unchanged. As in other business meetings, we need to plan properly, to agree the process for the meetings, and to allow time for all participants to learn how it works. (*Quaker Life* 2012, 4-5)

The use of conferencing technologies therefore has a number of significant benefits for Friends. For example, Quaker Life (2012, 5) highlights the benefits of holding remote meeting where it is impractical to hold face-to-face meetings such as geographic distance, and it can help reduce costs and lower carbon footprints. Adding to these benefits, it may also be helpful for groups of Friends with shared interests, regionally, nationally or internationally to conduct meetings. In addition, new technologies such as You Tube have assisted communicating the 'Quaker way' to new audiences globally, such as the videos on the practice of Friends by QuakerSpeak. In fact, Barnett (2015) highlights that "In some ways this echoes the vigorous pamphleteering of early Friends, which made use of the new communications technology of the printing press to create a new participatory culture of religious publishing".

However, despite these benefits, Sheeran (1983, 60) notes that Friends find the discipline of QBM more difficult when communication is not held face-to-face. Sheeran's study of Friends, held in the early-1980s, revealed that Friends expressed anxiety about how remote decision-making undermines the spiritual practice of Friends. In the 1980s, of course, modern remote technology was the 'phone! Today, of course, technology encompasses internet services such as Skype and video-conferencing which may change the nature of the experience and the practice again, and Friends need to be open to receive 'new Light' on communication technologies.

In a contemporary business context, the emergence of new communication technologies may put a further obstacle in front of the use of QBM. On the one hand, with many secular organisations under pressure from shareholders to maximise shareholder value and to be socially responsible in its use of fossil fuels by limiting unnecessary travel, the use of new communication technologies may only be set to increase further in the future. For many Friends, on the other hand, a Meeting for Worship or Meeting for Business is a collective and physical form of worship which requires us to place our whole physical being in the presence of God. It seems highly likely that participating in an online Meeting for Worship or Meeting for Business may be experienced as significantly different from a collective and physically-present form of worship. Barnett (2015) highlights that "Meeting together in virtual space, we can scarcely avoid presenting a persona that is only a fragment of who we are as whole people" and continues "In modern times…there is a widespread assumption that any differences between long-distance and face-to-face relationships are relatively trivial, and that text-based communication or Skype conversations are effectively equivalent to meeting in person. This seems to neglect the extent to which who we are, is not fully reflected by our written words. It is intimately bound up with our embodied presence". However, on the reverse side of the coin, online Meetings for Worship may be a useful innovation to help geographically-distant Friends incorporate the spiritual practice of Friends into their daily lives. Indeed, online Meetings for Worship can be used to develop spiritual community in international communities of Friends, Friends' special interest groups, and to supplement attendance at physically-present Meetings. Of course, different uses are numerous and varied. For example, in the U.S, where perhaps online Meetings are used more extensively, the focus can be to explore issues of interest to Friends, or as a communication tool within or across Area Meetings, such as the use of telephone conferencing across the geographically-diverse area of West Scotland.

One question that arises is whether the absence of physical presence significantly reduces the sense of spiritual and collective worship as noted by Barnett (2015), and where online Meetings for Worship can be transferred to Meetings for Business, and beyond into the business world? Different views no doubt abound. However, despite the potential drawbacks of online Meetings, the possibility of a sense of community and spiritual solidarity may still exist for some irrespective of the virtual space, time zones and geography. Perhaps simply knowing that individual Friends are gathering for a Meeting for Worship is encouraging and energising enough? Advocates of online Meetings for Worship think so. For example, Mendoza (2014) hopes that "the online presence of Friends will be what it has been offline: small, but potent…. The Spirit can lead us to a better use of technology…" Martin Layton[25], Senior Programme Leader at Woodbrooke Quaker Study Centre, is currently experimenting with online Meetings and suggests that "Like any worshipping community, it takes time to know and trust each other – and to some extent virtual meetings are faced with new barriers to this – but even at this early stage in our experiment, we are finding that relatively simple technologies can be more than just a superficial means of contact for isolated worshippers, and that they can offer a space where an authentic sense of presence can be sought and found."

Despite arguments that online Meetings for Worship remain authentic to the spirituality of Friends, the process dimension of an online Meeting for Worship, of course, is likely to require a different set of processes than physically-present Meetings. For example, while a Clerk may still steward proceedings, online Meetings often require strict adherence to a set of rules for joining the Meeting so that the silence is not continually disrupted by Friends joining or leaving the Meeting. Furthermore, ministry remains possible via commenting using the computer keyboard or touch-screen and sharing with participants. The risk of course, is well-argued by Barnett (2015) that:

> An essential element of local community is that we cannot evade accountability for our words and actions. In our Quaker meetings we know that what we do and say will have potentially long-lasting consequences for our relationships with each other, which may affect our lives beyond the Meeting House. Purely online relationships do not necessarily have this characteristic. Participants in an online group or discussion can instantly disappear, and may choose to be anonymous or adopt an alternative identity. It is this capacity for anonymity, combined with the increased potential for misunderstandings and lack of contextual information that encourages such widespread hostility and argumentativeness in online discussions, including in Quaker forums.

---

[25] Via personal communication

New communication technologies continue to emerge and evolve and Friends are only beginning to understand how their use may affect spiritual discipline and sense of community. Online Meetings for Worship are one step in a new technological direction, however online Meetings for Business are a further step that many Friends have yet to take. Whether physically-present or on-line, it seems reasonable to assume that decision-making the 'Quaker way' in business organisations may remain possible for 'simple' decisions, but its potential to aid complex or contentious decisions remains untested. Moreover, as the use of new communication technologies continue to proliferate in society, advocates of online QBM cannot currently point to many examples of its successful use either within or without the Religious Society of Friends. It seems apparent that further discernment (and indeed, research) is required to understand how QBM can improve decision-making in contemporary organisations, whether face-to-face or on-line. It is entirely possible that QBM remains a decision-making process of the future rather than the past.

Bibliography

Anderson, P. 1995. "The World as Influenced by Quaker Convictions." *Faculty Publications – College of Christian Studies*, Paper 128, http://digitalcommons.georgefox.edu/ccs/128 accessed on 12 December 2015.

Anderson, P. 2006. "The Meeting for Worship in which Business is Conducted: Quaker Decision-Making Process as a Factor of Spiritual Discernment." *Quaker Religious Thought* 106-107, pp. 26-47.

Barnett, C. 2015. "Quaker Social Media." *Quakers in Transition Essay.* http://transitionquaker.blogspot.co.uk/2015/03/quaker-social-media.html accessed on 31 January 2016.

Beeson, I. 2016. "Actions and Solutions." *The Friend.* The Friend Publication Ltd, London. UK. Pp. 12-13.

Bishop, B. 2006. "Discernment—Corporate and Individual Perspectives." *Quaker Religious Thought* 106-107, pp. 18-25.

Bradney, A. and F. Cownie. 2000. *Living without law: An Ethnography of Quaker Decision-Making, Dispute Avoidance and Dispute Resolution,* Ashgate, Aldershot, UK.

Brigham, M. and D. Kavanagh. 2015. "The Sense of the Meeting: Silent Organisation." Paper presented at European Group of Organizational Studies EGOS Annual Conference Athens, Greece. July 2015.

Cadbury, A, 2003. A talk in the 'Faith Seeking Understanding' series. http://www.leveson.org.uk/stmarys/resources/cadbury0503.htm accessed on 1 February 2016.

Cadbury, H. J. 2000. *George Fox's 'Book of Miracles*. Quaker Uniting in Publication (QUIP). Philadelphia, PA.

Cranmer, F. 2003. "Regulation Within the Religious Society of Friends." *Ecclesiastical Law Journal* 7, pp. 176-194.

Cresson, O. 2009. "On Quaker Unity." *Friends Journal* 55/7, p. 5.

Dandelion, P. 2002. "Those who Leave and Those who Feel Left: The Complexity of Quaker Disaffiliation." *Journal of Contemporary Religion* 172, pp. 213-228.

Gentry, M. 1982. "Consensus as a Form of Decision Making." *Journal of Sociology and Social Welfare* 9, pp. 233–244.

Grace, E. 2000. *An Introduction to Quaker Business Practice*; paper presented at the subcommittee meeting of the Special Commission on Orthodox Participation in the World Council of Churches. Damascus, Syria, March 2000.

Grace, E. 2006. "Voting Not to Vote: Toward Consensus in the WCC." *Quaker Religious Thought* 106-107, pp. 48-54.

Grundy, M. 2002. "The individual and the meeting." *Quaker Religious Thought* 98, pp. 5-16.

Karkkainen, V-M. 2002. *An Introduction to Ecclesiology: Ecumenical, Historical & Global Perspectives*. InterVarsity Press. Downers Grove, IL.

Law, J. 1998. "After Meta-Narrative: On Knowing in Tension." in R. Chia, ed. *In the Realm of Organization: Essays for Robert Cooper*. London: Routledge.

Leadership Management Development Center, Inc. "Decision Making Styles." Leadership Management. http://www.leadershipmanagement.com/html-files/decision.htm downloaded 13 December 2015.

Lewis, M. 2009. "Doing Business the Quaker way." http://www.forbes.com/2009/10/09/quaker-business-meetings-leadership-society-friends.html accessed on 15 May 2016.

Mace, J. 2012. *God and Decision Making: A Quaker Approach*. London: Quaker Books.

Mendoza, A. 2014. "Beyond the Oatmeal Box." *Friends Journal* podcast. http://www.friendsjournal.org/beyond-oatmeal-box/ accessed on 19 March 2016.

Michaelis, L. 2010. *Transforming Impasse: The Way through Conflict with Quaker Listening*

Processes. Paper produced by the Quaker Council for European Affairs QCEA.

Molina-Markham, E. 2014. "Finding the 'Sense of the Meeting': Decision making through Silence Among Quakers." *Western Journal of Communication* 782, pp. 155-174.

Niyonzima, D. 2013. *Transcending the Cultural and Socio-Political Conditions in Friends Decision-Making Processes: Case of Burundi.* Unpublished Doctor of Ministry thesis, http://digitalcommons.georgefox.edu/dmin/56/# accessed on 13 March 2016.

Pollard, B. 1954. "Quaker Group Procedures." *Health Education Journal* 121, pp. 4-11.

"Quakers in Britain." 1994. *Quaker faith and practice: the book of Christian discipline of the Yearly Meeting of the Religious Society of Friends.* London, UK.

Quaker Life 2012. "Holding Quaker Business Meetings by Telephone Conference." *Quaker Life* Central Committee, London, UK.

Reis-Louis, M. 1994. "In the Manner of Friends: Learnings from Quaker Practice for Organizational Renewal." *Journal of Organizational Change Management* 71, pp. 42–60.

Sheeran, M. 1983. *Beyond Majority Rule.* Philadelphia Yearly Meeting of the Religious Society of Friends, Pennsylvania.

Steere, D. 1984. *George Fox, Quaker Spirituality: Selected Writings.* Paulist Press, New York.

Velayutham, S. 2013. "Governance Without Boards: The Quakers." *Corporate Governance: The International Journal of Business in Society* 133, pp. 223–235.

Vogel-Borne, J. 1990. *Friends Meeting at Cambridge Book of Current Practices.* Unpublished manuscript.

Wall, G. 2010. *Becoming Friends: Living and Learning with Quakers.* London: Quaker Books.

Willcuts, J. 1984. *Why Friends are Friends.* Barclay Press.

Index

A

B

C

S

T

U

V

W

Printed in Great Britain
by Amazon

43233324R00162